Bonn & the Bomb

Transnational Institute Series

The Transnational Institute is an independent fellowship of researchers and activists living in different parts of the world, who develop innovative analyses of world affairs.

It serves no government, political party or interest group.

Other titles available in the TNI series:

Short Changed:
Africa and World Trade
Michael Barratt Brown and Pauline Tiffen

People and Power in the Pacific:
The Struggle for the Post-Cold War Order
Walden Bello

Dark Victory:
The United States, Structural Adjustment
and Global Poverty
Walden Bello

Beyond Bretton Woods:
Alternatives to the Global Economic Order
*Edited by John Cavanagh, Daphne Wysham
and Marcos Arruda*

The Debt Boomerang:
How Third World Debt Harms Us All
Susan George

Paradigms Lost:
The Post-Cold War Era
Edited by Chester Hartman and Pedro Vilanova

Pax Americana?
Hegemony or Decline
Jochen Hippler

For information about forthcoming titles in this series contact
Pluto Press

Bonn & the Bomb

German Politics and the Nuclear Option

Matthias Küntzel

Pluto Press

with

Transnational Institute (TNI)

First published 1995 by Pluto Press
345 Archway Road, London N6 5AA
and 5500 Central Avenue
Boulder, Colorado 80301, USA
in association with
the Transnational Institute (TNI),
Paulus Potterstraat 20, 1071 DA, Amsterdam

Distributed in the Netherlands by
the Transnational Institute

British Library Cataloguing in Publication Data
A catalogue record for this book is available from the British Library

ISBN 0 7453 0910 0 (hbk)

Library of Congress Cataloging in Publication Data
Küntzel, Matthias.
        [Bonn und die Bombe. English]
        Bonn and the bomb: German politics and the nuclear option /
Matthias Kuntzel; translated by R. Range Cloyd, Jr. and Helke Heino
                p.   cm.
        English version of Bonn und die Bombe.
        "In association with the Transnational Institute."
        Includes bibliographical references and index.
        ISBN 0-7453-0910-0
        1. Nuclear weapons—Government policy—Germany (West)
        2. Treaty on the Non-proliferation of Nuclear Weapons (1968)
        I. Title.
        U264.5.G3K8613   1995   94–40247
        355.02'17'0943—dc20

98   97   96   95
4   3   2   1

Designed and produced for Pluto Press by
Chase Production Services, Chipping Norton, OX7 5QR
Typeset from author's disk by Stanford Desktop Publishing Services
Printed in the EC by TJ Press

Contents

Foreword

Nuclear proliferation after the end of the Cold War has rapidly become one of the major challenges to international peace and security. Traditional analysis tends to highlight the so-called 'threshold states' (in recent years Iraq, and currently the Democratic Peoples Republic of Korea and Iran); the recent cases of nuclear smuggling, including plutonium, have further raised the proliferation issue to new heights. This view of proliferation, selective and dangerously deceptive as it is, will unfortunately be most widespread during the debate on the future of the Treaty for the Non-Proliferation of Nuclear Weapons, or NPT, a decision on which will be made in 1995.

Fortunately, and at a most appropriate time, Matthias Küntzel has sought to redress the imbalance in the proliferation debate by focusing on the Federal Republic of Germany, a country which has both the technical and financial means to 'go nuclear', and in addition, has had a historical record on non-proliferation that at the very least is ambiguous. The book tracks the development of the nuclear programme of Germany, from the 1940s to the present. Of particular interest is the relationship between the Federal Republic and the international community during the 1960s, a time when there was considerable ambiguity over the former's intentions and efforts were being made to conclude a draft NPT.

It will be difficult for Küntzel's critics to reject the accuracy and implications of his analysis. Indeed in the past his analysis was almost formal policy as far as the major powers were concerned. As the author reminds us, the leading advocates of the NPT in the 1960s were the principal allies of the 1939–45 war: the United States, Britain and the Soviet Union. Their priority at that time was to establish a regime to deter nuclear weapons development in two of the former axis powers: the Federal Republic and Japan. Whereas today the threshold states are considered to be in the Middle East or on the Korean peninsula, it was these two states that were of primary consideration three decades ago. Küntzel details efforts by the Federal Republic to dilute the effectiveness of the NPT and internal political resistance to treaty ratification. Although the NPT became effective

vii

in 1970, only in 1975 did both the Federal Republic and Japan finally ratify the treaty.

Although the political circumstances are very different, there are clear parallels with Germany in the way in which Japan's nuclear programme evolved. For example, from the 1950s onwards, both countries committed themselves to developing the nuclear fuel cycle, including the use of large quantities of plutonium. As a result, advanced skills in plutonium reprocessing and handling have been acquired by each nation. As Küntzel stresses, these skills have both a civilian and military application. Similarly, influential political figures and ministries in both countries have over the years argued for the militarization of their peaceful nuclear programmes.

As Küntzel quite rightly concludes, the nuclear programmes of these countries have now reached such an advanced state that the technical limitations of proliferation no longer apply. Both countries by the year 2000 will have amassed a combined stockpile of over 100 tonnes of weapons usable plutonium. Nuclear safeguards are more to do with maintaining public confidence than detecting diversion of nuclear materials for military purposes. Thus only political considerations are currently preventing weaponization. It is an obvious observation, which Küntzel makes clearly: political circumstances can and do change, with little prior warning.

As the debate over the future of nuclear non-proliferation and the NPT intensifies, analysis that has lessons from the past and for the future will be of crucial importance. Although focusing on one country – the Federal Republic – *Bonn and the Bomb* exposes the true global scale of the proliferation problem, which cannot be limited to one country or geographic region. An effective non-proliferation regime, unlike the present NPT, cannot discriminate between one country's nuclear programme and another's. Further damning evidence exposing the fallacy of the peaceful atom has been provided by this book.

Shaun Burnie
Greenpeace International   September 1994

Preface

Communiqués and contracts in international relations are dry documents. They reveal little of the months or even years of fighting over their wording carried out in the back rooms of diplomacy. To discover the truth, it is not the phrases of compromise which are important but the controversies hidden behind them. How can those background disputes be brought to the public eye when the files, with their explosive dossiers, telegrams and telexes concerning atomic weapons, are kept under lock and key?

There are only two possibilities. First, you must interview the officials who worked out the basic papers, and the diplomats who were seated face to face around the same bargaining table. Second, you have to try to lay hands on as many of the documents used in those negotiations as possible: the minutes of a government's committee meetings; confidential reports written in plain language; the diaries of and notes taken by high-ranking government officials. That both of these conditions were met in the writing of this book is mainly due to luck!

Fifteen years ago, I asked myself why West Germany, as a non-nuclear-weapons state, wanted to establish a plutonium industry where the return on investment, from the financial point of view, was practically zero. Were some military interests perhaps involved? Did the Federal Republic of Germany want 'civilian plutonium' to help create the possibility of going nuclear?

Ten years ago I recognised that there was a barrage of opposition to the Non-Proliferation Treaty (NPT) from the Federal Republic – and not only from within the ranks of conservatives. This realisation was in direct contradiction to the view that the Federal Republic had renounced atomic weapons voluntarily and willingly. Why was Germany's accession to the treaty so controversial? Was there or is there an interest on the part of the German government in having nuclear weapons? I decided to try to get to the heart of these questions. Writing a book on Germany's nuclear policies seemed to be a good way to do so. Two lucky events facilitated this decision. First of all, in summer 1984, the German Green Party Fraktion in the Bundestag offered me a position as its consultant on questions of nuclear energy and nuclear weapons. Although not a member of the Greens, I worked for and with them in Bonn for four years, and thanks to my position found many doors open which otherwise would have remained closed. Second, in 1986, Professor Dr K.J. Gantzel accepted me as a Ph.D. candidate in Hamburg. His friendly letter of recommendation helped me gain access not only to both state and private archives but also to all those diplomats and government officials in the United States, the Soviet Union, Great Britain, France, Belgium, the Netherlands and the FRG who were dealing with Germany's nuclear policy and the controversy over the NPT during the past few decades. My political job had given me opportunities a Ph.D. candidate usually does not have, and the work on my dissertation opened doors that might otherwise have remained closed. A third factor arose through the 'Nuclear History Program' run by the Wissenschaft und Politik Foundation in Ebenhausen together with the Center for International Security Studies in Maryland. The aim of this programme was to bring together people from a variety of backgrounds to discuss particular episodes of nuclear history as well as to analyse their broader implications. Being a participant in this programme proved to be of benefit for this book.

My work in preparing the book, however, was not limited to interviewing retired and friendly diplomats. Archives in Germany and other countries had to be combed through; literature on the subject, memoirs, parliamentary reports and other documents had to be read; facts had to be checked and re-checked. I was allowed to go through classified material and individual files. Although much of this material could not be analysed in its overall context, it often presented a quite different picture of Germany's nuclear policies. The knowledge acquired through these sources was also of prime importance in asking the right questions of the right people. The interviews have not only produced a wealth of new insights and information, they have sometimes made possible a view behind the scenes of international nuclear diplomacy and thus have shown more than once just how international diplomacy works.

I would like to take this opportunity to thank the many people who have been so helpful and patient in sharing with me their memories and experience with regard to Germany's nuclear policy. Special thanks to Dr Jochen Hippler, Director of the Transnational Institute, who encouraged and helped me in the publication of this English edition of my book. My translators, Helke Heino and R. Range Cloyd, Jr., did a tremendously good job, and it was always very rewarding to work with and to learn from them – many thanks!

The long version of this book was accepted by the University of Hamburg in 1991 as a dissertation, with the title 'Die Bundesrepublik Deutschland zwischen Nuklearambition und Atomwaffen-Verzicht – Eine Untersuchung der Kontroverse um den Beitritt zum Atomwaffensperrvertrag'. In 1992 it was published by Campus Verlag, Frankfurt am Main, under the title *Bonn und die Bombe – Deutsche Atomwaffenpolitik von Adenauer bis Brandt*.

The English version of my book is a third shorter than the German original, as many details in the German edition would have little meaning for the English reader, but the sense of the original text has not been changed. Since the publication of the German edition some new issues have arisen concerning the question of the NPT as well as Germany's foreign policies. I have, therefore, tried to include some of these new developments in the introduction to the English edition.

Hamburg, May 1994
Matthias Küntzel

Abbreviations

AA	Auswärtige Amt (Foreign Affairs Ministry)
ABC	atomic-biological-chemical (weapons)
ABM	anti-ballistic missiles
ACD	author's collection of documents
ACDA	Arms Control And Disarmament Agency (US)
AdDL	Archiv des Deutschen Liberalismus (Gummersbach, Germany)
AdG	Archiv der Gegenwart (published annually)
AEC	Atomic Energy Commission (US)
AK	Arbeitskreis (Working Committee)
ANF	Atlantic Nuclear Force (Great Britain's counter-proposal to the MLF)
atw	*atomwirtschaft* (official nuclear energy magazine)
AZ	Notes
BK	*Bayernkurier* (Bavarian weekly newspaper)
Blätter	Blätter für deutsche und internationale Politik (monthly journal, Cologne)
BMVg	Bundesministerium für Verteidigung (Ministry of Defence)
BPA	unkorrigiertes Manuskript der Bundespressekonferenz (original, unedited minutes of the German government's press conferences)
BR	Bundersrat (Upper House of German parliament)
Bulletin	*Bulletin des Presse- und Informationsamtes der Bundesregierung* (Bulletin of the Press and Information Office of the German Government)
BVR	Bundesverteidigungsrat (German Security Council)
CDU	Christian Democratic Union (Bonn)
CSU	Christian Social Union (Bavaria's sister party to the CDU, Bonn)
DAS	Dokumentation zur Abrüstung und Sicherheit (German Documents on Disarmament and National Security)
DBT	Deutscher Bunderstag (Lower House of German parliament)

DGAP	Deutsche Gesellschaft für Auswärtige Politik (German Society for Foreign Affairs)
DoD	Documents of Disarmament (US)
DS	Drucksache des Deutschen Bundestages (printed matter of the Bundestag)
DUD	Deutschland-Union Dienst (Press Information Service of the CDU)
EA	*Europa-Archiv* (bi-weekly journal of the DGAP)
EC	European Community
EDC	European Defence Community
ENDC	Eighteen-Nations Disarmament Conference (UN, Geneva)
EP	European Parliament (Brussels/Strasbourg)
Euratom	European Atomic Energy Community
EWK	*Europäische Wehrkunde* (semi-official monthly journal on military matters, Munich)
FA	*Foreign Affairs* (US quarterly journal)
FAZ	*Frankfurter Allgemeine Zeitung* (daily newspaper, Frankfurt am Main)
fdk	Freidemokratische Korrespondenz (Press Information Service of the FDP)
FDP	Free Democratic Party (Bonn)
FNP	*Frankfurter Neue Presse* (daily newspaper, Frankfurt am Main)
FR	*Frankfurter Rundschau* (daily newspaper, Frankfurt am Main)
FRG	Federal Republic of Germany
FRUS	Foreign Relations of the United States (series of historical documents, Washington, DC)
GDR	German Democratic Republic (East Germany)
HA	*Hamburger Abendblatt* (daily newspaper, Hamburg)
HB	*Handelsblatt* (daily business newspaper, Germany)
IAEA	International Atomic Energy Agency (UN, Vienna)
IHT	*International Herald Tribune* (Paris)
INF	Intermediate Nuclear Force
INFCIRC	Information Circular (IAEA series of documents)
KFA	Kernforschungsanstalt (Nuclear Research Centre, Jülich, Germany)
KWU	Kraftwerksunion (German power-plant manufacturer)
Materialien	Gesetzesmaterialien des Deutschen Bundestages (semi-confidential collection of documents on Bundestag leglislation procedures)

MLF	Multilateral (Nuclear) Force
mw	megawatt (million watts)
NPG	Nuclear Planning Group
NPT	(Nuclear) Non-Proliferation Treaty
NYT	*New York Times*
n.z.p.U.	nur zur persönlichen Unterrichtung (confidential)
NZZ	*Neue Züricher Zeitung* (daily newspaper, Zurich)
RM	*Rheinischer Merkur* (weekly German newspaper)
SACEUR	Supreme Allied Commander Europe (highest-ranking European military officer in NATO)
SIPRI	Stockholm International Peace Research Institute
SPD	Social Democratic Party Deutschland (Bonn)
Studiengruppe	Studiengruppe für Rüstungskontrolle, Rüstungsbeschränkung und Internationale Sicherheit (Semi-official DGAP Study Group for Arms Control, Disarmament, and International Security)
SWP	Stiftung Wissenschaft und Politik (Science and Politics Foundation, Ebenhausen, Germany)
SZ	*Süddeutsche Zeitung* (daily newspaper, Munich)
TBT	Test Ban Treaty (today called the PTBT: Partial Test Ban Treaty)
UAA	Urananreicherungsanlage (uranium enrichment facility)
USAEC	United States Atomic Energy Commission (=AEC)
USS	United States Senate
VBT	*Verhandlungen des Deutschen Bundestags* (proceedings of the German Bundestag)
WEU	Western European Union
WK	*Wehrkunde* (former name of the *EWK*)
WaS	*Welt am Sonntag* (weekly newspaper, Hamburg)

Introduction

'I understand that Germany has actually stopped the sale of uranium from Czechoslovakian mines which she has taken over' – with these alarming words Albert Einstein addressed the US president, F.D. Roosevelt, in summer 1939. The warning that Hitler might be the first to possess the bomb triggered the US's 'Manhattan Project', Hiroshima, the Cold War, the 'Atoms for Peace' programme and the fight against nuclear proliferation that followed. While the nuclear powers have always tried to prevent countries like Sweden and India from obtaining atomic weapons, the 'German bomb' has been regarded in both the East and the West as a 'worst case scenario' which must be prevented at all costs. Why is this?

Probably the main reason for this is the after-effect of the horror which has always been provoked by the thought that Hitler might have been the first with 'the bomb' and thus might have conquered the world. There are other reasons too. As long as Germany was divided there was the fear that a West Germany in possession of nuclear weapons might be tempted to end this status with force. Since the beginning of the post Cold-War era, other fears have surfaced. Germany as a nuclear power would disturb the delicate balance of power in Western Europe and could become an 'adversarial rival' to the United States and a 'new global enemy', as the Pentagon has claimed (*NYT*, 17 February 1992). Such a 'redefinition of Germany's role', Henry Kissinger wrote in 1993, would be 'registered immediately as an hostile action' by the United States.

It appears that the Federal Republic accepted this difference in status. Because of its renunciation of ABC weapons, West Germany was able to become a member of NATO, the accession to the NPT in 1969 was the basis of the Ostpolitik of Willy Brandt, and the confirmation of that renunciation in 1990 made possible Germany's reunification. Since then, Germany has promised to support the extension of the NPT in 1995, and to strengthen it. Bonn has also supported in numerous committees the unlimited and unconditional extension of the NPT. The combination seems to be perfect: on the one hand, the Allies who insist on Germany's renunciation of nuclear weapons;

on the other, the German government which seems to be content to renounce this nuclear burden.

Or is this the case? The truth is a little more complicated. This book presents proof that a voluntary German renunciation of nuclear weapons never took place. On the contrary: in 1954, 1969 and 1990, many would have liked to *renounce* nuclear renunciation. Bonn's rejection of atomic weapons was never the result of a policy that turned on self-imposed moderation, but always the consequence of external conditions and power relations. This volume focuses on the NPT, against which German politicians of all parties protested fiercely between 1961 and 1974. Konrad Adenauer called it a 'Morgenthau plan raised to the power of two' and a 'death sentence' for the Federal Republic. Franz Josef Strauss considered the treaty to be a 'new Versailles of cosmic dimensions' and Helmut Schmidt regarded it as 'questionable' even if it was desirable.

These statements are less irrational than they seem. With the treaty, the United States was trying to prevent nuclear proliferation even if it meant that its German ally would be handcuffed by it. The Federal Republic wanted just the opposite. It wanted to have a maximum of military options as well as freedom of nuclear trade. The controversy over the NPT was the prototype of a conflict which was woven into the fabric of NATO right from its very beginnings up to the present time: on the one hand, the endeavours by the victorious Second World War powers to prevent an equal, i.e. nuclear, status for Germany; on the other, Germany's efforts to minimise the differences in its nuclear status with respect to France and Great Britain.

The German-American dispute over the NPT began in 1961, and from 1967 onwards it reached heights which dwarfed all other controversies between the two countries. It was a stumbling block in the talks between Kennedy and Adenauer, Johnson and Erhard, and Johnson and Kissinger; it even kept the governments of Nixon and Brandt busy. The fierce quarrel over the details of the NPT safeguards did not come to an end for the Federal Republic until 1977, under Helmut Schmidt. At the end of these long controversies, however, a compromise was reached: the treaty was accepted, but only at the price of containing major loopholes – loopholes that would allow tons of plutonium to pass through them.

This study also reveals that the renunciation of nuclear weapons is not the same as the renunciation of the nuclear option. The Federal Republic has always kept open the door that would lead to having its own nuclear weapons. This book makes clear that every German government, regardless of party, has wanted to ensure that Germany *could* become a nuclear power.

This finding is important for a realistic evaluation of the NPT, the extension of which will be decided in 1995 by a United Nations conference. The Federal Republic is not just a party to the treaty, it also has the largest stock of plutonium in the world, as far as non-nuclear-weapons states are concerned. At present, more than 2,000 kilograms of plutonium are deposited at Hanau in Hesse. There are strong indications that there is not only reactor plutonium in the Hanau depot, but also highly enriched uranium and weapons-grade plutonium in metallic form. This sector of the 'civilian' nuclear programme was classified as secret by the federal government in April 1994, and parliamentary inquiries about it were left unanswered (DS 12/7472). Another 6,600 kilograms of German plutonium are deposited in France. The total amount of plutonium which has to be reprocessed in France or Great Britain by order of German companies amounts to some 76,000 kilograms (DS 12/7472). A Nagasaki-type bomb requires less than 5 kilograms of plutonium.

Isolating plutonium is expensive. Economic or ecological arguments for this investment have lost whatever persuasive power they may have had. But the original, strategic argument is still valid: a country that has great amounts of plutonium is a nuclear-power-on-call. 'No safeguards, including the IAEA, can be effective if such sensitive materials and facilities are available in non-nuclear-weapon states', warns a US Department of Defense-sponsored Rand study released in December 1993. What is a 'civilian' plutonium stockpile today can become an arsenal for atomic weapons tomorrow. 'Civilian' stockpiles of raw materials for the bomb and atomic weapons programme in NPT member states such as Iraq illustrate the crisis in which the system of global non-proliferation finds itself today.

Bonn & the Bomb takes a close look at the beginnings of this development. It deals with Germany's atomic weapons policies and the establishment of the NPT. The first chapter describes the military character of German and European nuclear policies during the 1950s, which was camouflaged behind a civilian mask of respectability. The contract on the joint production of atomic weapons, for example, which was signed in 1958 by the defence ministers of France, Italy and the Federal Republic, was more or less unknown until the end of the 1980s. Chapter 2 examines the way in which the NPT project was sabotaged by Konrad Adenauer and Ludwig Erhard during the 1960s. A special role here was played by the MLF project, the multilateral nuclear force which was supported by Bonn.

Chapter 3 describes the threshold power programme of the Federal Republic of Germany and analyses the nuclear policies of Germany's political parties. At the beginning of 1967, it became clear that there was no way to block the NPT, but no other non-nuclear power had more influence on its wording in the following years than did the FRG. In Chapter 4, the central, thrilling part of the NPT's history is reconstructed. Chapter 5, with the aid of insider reports, recounts how the Federal Republic has openly influenced negotiations on safeguards over the last 40 years, with one aim in sight: the watering down of safeguards.

Chapter 6 measures the loopholes which the NPT and its special interpretations have retained for the Federal Republic of Germany. In Chapter 7 a balance is drawn on the nuclear-weapons policy of the old Federal Republic in order to draw conclusions about the nuclear future of the new Republic.

The German edition of *Bonn und die Bombe* was finished in the winter of 1991/2. Developments since that time confirm some of the predictions made in the book. Japan's nuclear option is evident today. 'For the first time since the bombing of Hiroshima in 1945, Japan no longer rules out the possibility of producing its own nuclear weapons', warned the *International Herald Tribune* in 1993. *The Times* reported in 1994 that, according to the British Ministry of Defence, Japan had already developed the detonator mechanisms and the carrier capacities for atomic weapons. This was denied by Tokyo, although not very convincingly. The former foreign minister of Japan, Kabun Muto, had stressed outspokenly in 1993 the advantages of Japan's dual-purpose plutonium programme:

> If North Korea develops nuclear weapons and that becomes a threat to Japan, first there is the nuclear umbrella of the United States upon which we can rely. But if it comes to the crunch, possessing the will to build nuclear weapons is important. (Takagi, 1993, p. 2)

The nuclear histories of Japan and the Federal Republic show some amazing parallels. During the 1960s, powerful political groupings in both countries demanded more nuclear participation. In both countries there were strong feelings against the NPT and its ratification. Both countries campaigned successfully for the watering down of NPT controls. Japan and the Federal Republic are the only non-nuclear-weapons states with great stockpiles of plutonium. Both countries have always fought against any internationalisation of their plutonium stocks. Both intervened successfully against the Clinton plan to ban the separation of plutonium globally and without exception. Both have demanded that the United States should not interfere with their plutonium policies in future. At present, Germany is trying to prohibit the United States from having any say within the European Union on the use of 'US-origin plutonium'. Should the US be reluctant to give up its rights to a say in this matter, threats have already been made within Euratom's internal papers of the 'negative effects' which 'could spill over into various other fora, such as the Extension Conference of the NPT (Hibbs, 1993). Thus the impression is given that Germany and Japan are today, in view of the coming NPT conference in 1995, obviously determined to defend their nuclear weapons options. But will such options be realised?

The crisis in the nuclear global order is still growing, and the disintegration of NATO continues. President Bill Clinton has not only accepted Germany as a 'partner in leadership' but has urged the Kohl government to play a more 'normal' international role. The expectation is that Germany should engage in power politics on a global level. The idea of 'normalisation' suggests that the Holocaust has been forgotten and that the last remaining arms limitations stemming from memories of the Second World War will fade away. But the international supporters of German 'normalisation' do not, as a rule, want to go that far:

> There are, of course, potential dangers associated with normalization and clear limits beyond which it must not go. ... No one wants to see Germany forget the lessons of the past, and both Germans and their friends must be vigilant in making sure that Germans remain sensitive to the consequences of their might and the meaning of their history. (Gordon, 1994, p. 239)

The vision of a 'limited normalisation' in Germany's foreign policy has several problems. The first is a lack of agreement in the non-German world about where to draw the line. The suggestion made by some US senators, for example, that Germany should 'with substantial German troops, in tanks' intervene in the former Yugoslavia presupposes that the past can be forgotten. A greater problem is related to whether, in the long run, there is any basis for 'limited normalisation' in Germany. In April 1992 SPD politician Peter Glotz wrote in *Die Zeit* that anyone who wants to teach the idea of normalisation to the Germans should be aware of the kind of questions the idea will provoke. Sooner or later a conservative politician would crop up

> who will spill the beans by speaking out openly and saying that it would be absurd that Brazilians, Indians and even Libyans will get atomic weapons, but not Germans. ... It might well be that in

the near future the proud victors of the Gulf War will long for that despised 'Genscherism' which has up to now choked off such aggressiveness in so-called 'wishy-washy' and 'sentimental' behaviour. (*Die Zeit*, 19 April 1992)

Peter Glotz has good reason for such pessimism.

This is a key dichotomy: whereas the supporters of 'limited normalisation' outside Germany praise 'the responsible German behaviour' of the past 40 years, and give as proof of this the fact 'that the FRG has proved itself as a good Western partner', within Germany those 40 years are increasingly viewed with contempt. The editor of the *Frankfurter Allgemeine Zeitung*, Frank Schirrmacher, writes: 'literally overnight an ironic farewell was given to that which yesterday was regarded as raison d'état and global common sense. The history of the Federal Republic, as Baring sums up, has taken place in a "doll's house"' (*FAZ*, 10 June 1994). Commentators who now characterise the old Federal Republic as 'an impotent dwarf' and those 40 post-war years as 'a political state of emergency' are by no means social outcasts. Support for this position comes from a group of highly influential political scientists, historians and journalists gathered around Michael Stürmer, Arnulf Baring, Rupert Scholz and Klaus-Peter Schwarz. 'This little Western state, a pocket-handkerchief between the rivers Rhine and Weser' is, according to Arnulf Baring, 'on sick leave in substantial questions of national existence' (Baring, 1991, p. 16). 'When looking back, it seems to me that the last 40 years were a respite in world history for us Germans' (Baring, 1991, p. 125). Michael Stürmer, head of Germany's most important foreign policy think-tank in Ebenhausen, has also declared that the post-war years were a 'holiday from history'. Furthermore, it has been said that the new Germany should emulate the German Reich under Bismarck rather than the tradition of the old Federal Republic: 'Germany still is, or is again, the Reich of Bismarck, but in the shape given to it by the Adenauerian republic' (Baring, 1991, p. 19).

All this suggests that for Germany the change in 1989 has not only had a quantitative dimension with regard to population, territory, and economic power, but also, and more importantly, a qualitative dimension with regard to the country's view of its own history and the ideological preconditions for a new foreign policy.

The quarrel over the interpretation of Germany's history has not been finally decided. But the protagonists of the *Historikerstreit* (historians' controversy), who normalised the Nazi past in the 1980s and are exceptionalising the FRG's past now, are gaining ground. The attitude towards a country's history influences the vision of its future.

Thus it is no surprise that the supporters of this position either state explicitly, as Arnulf Baring does, that 'we should have German nuclear weapons' (Baring, 1991, pp. 209–11), or try to fuel resentment at having been denied atomic weapons, as Michael Stürmer did in May 1994 when he wrote in the *International Herald Tribune*:

> Germany has yet to find a new vision and voice to replace nuclear angst. ... German diplomacy has not yet shed reflexes conditioned by the need to defer to its allies' particular interests: a nuclear option for Britain and France (today devalued but always denied to Germany) and a ground army holding the alliance's front line. (*IHT*, 2 May 1994)

'Limited normalisation'?

In contrast to Peter Glotz, I personally do not long for a despised 'Genscherism', because it expresses the same longing for status and power in a different guise. However, at a time when everything indicates that a storm is brewing and nuclear deterrence results in nothing more than nuclear proliferation, there is more at stake: there has to be a conscious break with the characteristics of a German foreign policy that has soaked Europe in blood twice within this century. As long as this break has not taken place, 'normalisation' and 'limitation' will not fit together. Without such a break, 'the German question' will remain a problem of global policy. The line of continuity in foreign policy will be closed as long as the option of a German atomic bomb is kept open. Only after Germany has unilaterally blocked the path that leads to nuclear weapons can the hope that it might have learned something from the past be justified. Only then could the Federal Republic bring its weight to bear in a credible way to end the use of atomic weapons as instruments of power.

1

Adenauer and the Bomb

'Hurrah for France! Since this morning she is stronger and prouder,'
announced General de Gaulle on the morning of 13 February 1960.
Minutes before, the first French atomic bomb had been detonated
in the Sahara (Kohl, 1971, p. 103).

More groundshaking than the detonation itself was the political
upheaval touched off by this explosion. For the first time in history,
a country had developed its own bomb independently – and against
the will of the superpowers – and had thereby lobbed a potential
bombshell at NATO. Would other countries follow, and if so, which
ones? Helmut Schmidt, later Germany's chancellor, wrote in 1961
that 'in Washington [people recognised] clearly that the establishment of an independent French nuclear military force ... would
with a measure of certainty induce Germany, Italy and perhaps
other NATO partners to follow in her footsteps' (Schmidt, 1961, p.
106). These fears made the French bomb the seed of a project that
was bitterly opposed in Paris at the time: the establishment of a
universal regime against the proliferation of atomic weapons by
means of a Non-Proliferation Treaty (NPT). The United Nations
General Assembly also protested against the test preparations in the
Sahara on 20 November 1959. On the same day, 'recognizing that
the danger now exists that an increase in the number of States
possessing nuclear weapons may occur', it also passed for the first
time a proposition for a global NPT. Although the protest from New
York faded like an echo in the wilderness, more and more attention
began to be paid to the NPT proposition.

On 18 February 1960, five days after the detonation in the desert,
US Secretary of State Herter declared that the proliferation of atomic
weapons was the 'chief risk' within the continuing armaments race.
Due to fears of a possible German nuclear capacity and, according
to Helmut Schmidt, 'as an answer to official claims from Bonn', the
Parliamentarian Assembly of the Western European Union (WEU)
approved a report which called for 'all possible measures aimed at
limiting the proliferation of nuclear weapons in more and more
countries' (Schmidt, 1961, p. 202). In 1960 the most probable atomic
weapons candidate – a candidate feared by both East and West – was

1

the Federal Republic of Germany. A paradox? Wasn't the Federal Republic the only NATO partner which had voluntarily and with great ceremony renounced its nuclear option? Hadn't it placed its entire military potential under NATO's command? Why then this lack of trust in the nuclear policies of West Germany?

The Involuntary Renunciation

On 3 October 1954, during Western European Union negotiations in London, Konrad Adenauer announced 'that the Federal Republic of Germany pledges that it will not produce atomic, biological, or chemical weapons anywhere within its borders'.

Although any signs of a *diktat* from the Allied forces were carefully avoided during the London negotiations, one can hardly consider this renunciation of ABC weapons on the part of the Federal Republic of Germany to be a voluntary one. From the point of view of the Second World War's victorious Western Allies, the Adenauer Declaration was the necessary prerequisite for Germany's becoming a member of NATO as well as for restoring German sovereignty – a fact which is confirmed by the debates concerning the establishment of the European Defence Community (EDC) which immediately preceded Adenauer's statement.

The call for 'equal weapons' for post-war Germany predates the founding of the Federal Republic. As early as June 1948, in a pamphlet on German rearmament, former Wehrmacht general, Hans Speidel, called for the equal treatment of a future German army with regard to both the production and the supply of weapons. Adenauer supported Speidel's position and appointed him to head the German delegation to the EDC negotiations when they began in 1951; but by early 1952 these negotiations were on the verge of breaking down completely. France feared a revival of German militarism and insisted upon a total prohibition of heavy weapons production by the Germans. Adenauer's reply was:

> short and sharp: he would never make such a declaration and called on all concerned to take note of this fact. ... No German Chancellor (could) make such a pledge – not because there was a desire to produce such weapons, but because one could not allow oneself to be discriminated against. (Baring, 1969, pp. 117–20)

The US and Great Britain supported France, and furthermore they demanded that Germany renounce all use of nuclear weapons. 'In spite of vehement resistance', Adenauer was forced to give in to the demands of the Allies at a conference of foreign ministers in February 1952. In the course of what the French foreign minister termed an embarrassing but very useful exchange of views, a list of prohibited arms was drawn up. Adenauer was willing to accept it on two conditions: first, there was to be equal treatment with respect to the equipping of the future German Bundeswehr; second, the Allies would have to accept a *voluntary* declaration on the part of the Germans, rather than imposing a formal prohibition on production (Kelleher, 1975, p. 20).

On 7 May 1952, Germany's chancellor signed the Federal Republic's first renunciation of nuclear weapons, in the form of a letter to the foreign ministers of France, Great Britain and the US. This renunciation never took effect, however, since the EDC treaty was not ratified by the French National Assembly. A comparison of the declarations of 1952 and 1954 is nonetheless quite revealing. Due to Germany's weak position, Adenauer had been forced to make more far-reaching concessions earlier on, concessions which he was able to rescind two years later. If one views these two declarations as each reflecting the state of affairs in international relations at a particular moment, then the difference between them marks the shift in the balance of power.

Adenauer's 1952 renunciation declaration dealt with the following:

1. The development, production and possession of atomic weapons.
2. The import or production of more than 500 grams of plutonium or uranium (of more than 2.1 per cent U 235 grade) per year.
3. The stockpiling of more than 18 tons of natural uranium.
4. The development, construction or possession of reactors with an energy output of more than 1.5mw, since this reactor size produced more than 500 grams of plutonium per year.
5. Military nuclear research.

The declaration of 1954 was quite different, however. The prohibitions specified in points two to five were left out and the renunciation of atomic weapons was confined to proscribing their production.

During the diplomatic turbulence which followed the failure of the EDC treaty, the pattern of earlier conflicts remained: the Federal Republic of Germany again tried to have all the former EDC limitations removed, whereas France demanded that all those prohibitions be included in the WEU treaty as well. The conference of the nine powers in London in early October 1954 was on the verge of failure because of this dissent, until Adenauer, unilaterally, conceded that

Germany would renounce weapons production. 'The crisis was ... thus overcome', he later noted in his memoirs (Adenauer, 1966, p. 347).

The basic elements of this concession, however, had been carefully prepared and decided upon in agreement with the German Foreign Ministry. As stated later by Count Johann Adolf von Kielmansegg, then an adviser to Adenauer, pains were taken during the formulation of the text to renounce merely the production of atomic weapons and *not* their possession (NHP doc. 1, p. 5).

The Adenauer Declaration did not end the conflict, however. The nine-power conference in London dispersed on 3 October and reconvened in Paris from the 20th to 23rd. In the meantime, the German renunciation of ABC weapons was made even more concrete. An American telex of 19 October 1954, for example, reports that the British had suggested a compromise which would increase the amount of fissionable material Germany was allowed to maintain to 1 kilogram instead of the 500 grams specified in the EDC treaty. The telex went on to say that Adenauer, who had German nuclear physicists, under the leadership of Heisenberg, breathing down his neck, rejected this proposal. Adenauer was no longer willing to accept a general limit on fissionable material; at the most he might agree to a specific limit for an interim period of five years (Department of State, 1983, p. 1,400). With regard to the list of weapons types to be controlled, a further telex, on 22 October 1954, reports on 'strong pleas by Adenauer, Beyen, and Spaak for keeping list to barest minimum' (Department of State, 1983, p. 1,400).

For the most part, the chancellor got his way in Paris. The 1954 compromise was a substantial success for the recently established Federal Republic of Germany. By agreeing to forgo a German atomic weapons industry, Adenauer pulled off quite a deal – he prevented the establishment of any limitations to Germany's development of atomic energy for non-military purposes. This was heavily criticised by the French Gaullists as de facto opening up a back door for Germany's nuclear option (Kelleher, 1975, p. 27). The Adenauer Declaration also allowed the acquisition and possession of atomic weapons or their production on the territory of another country. Nonetheless, the renunciation of 1954 was not considered the final word on the subject. Theo Sommer gives an account of a view which was quite prevalent, and not just in Bonn:

> The price which we had to pay for our new status was discrimination, camouflaged and mitigated by military integration. You cannot really say that this renunciation was of one's own free will. ... But since this renunciation of atomic weapons was in the final

analysis an act of discrimination against Germany by its allies, it is no wonder that those who imposed it, mindful of what had happened after Versailles, partially take for granted Germany's desire to free itself of its renunciation shackles as soon as conditions are promising, and partially fear it. (Sommer, 1967, p. 42)

That fear was a driving force behind the establishment of the NPT in the East and the West. And the rapid progress made by the Federal Republic in developing its nuclear programme fed this fear.

The 'Civil-itary' Atomic Programme

It was the French General L.M. Chassin who, in 1957, said in public what people in government circles in Bonn were only allowed to contemplate in private: 'If a country like West Germany wishes to secure both its military defence and its political options, then it must be capable of producing its own atomic explosives and employing them if need be' (Chassin, 1957, p. 466).

This problem was discussed as early as December 1956 at a confidential meeting of the German cabinet, and was put on the agenda after Defence Minister Franz Josef Strauss failed to win the support of the NATO Council on the question of atomic armaments for Germany. According to the minutes of the meeting, Chancellor Adenauer deplored the 'lack of influence of the Federal Republic in NATO'. In his view the reason for this was that Germany was not yet a 'power factor'. To end this problem, 'the Bundeswehr must be built up more rapidly, the consolidation of Europe must be stepped up, and nuclear weapons must be produced in the Federal Republic of Germany' (Greiner, 1986, p. 276).

From the technical point of view, the preconditions were promising. In 1939 Germany was the only country in the world that had a military department working on splitting the atom; in 1945, its atomic research programme was second only to that of the US. The German nuclear programme had suffered setbacks due to Allied restrictions, but these prohibitions had either been ignored to some extent, with the US silently condoning what was going on, or in some cases had even been circumvented by moving production facilities to other countries. Defence Minister Strauss referred in 1956 to a uranium enrichment process developed during the Nazi regime, and he pointed out that 'Germany has favourable prospects for becoming the leading atomic power in Western Europe' (*Rheinische Post*, 1 January 1956). This assessment was exaggerated, but it reflects the degree of self-confidence underlying an advanced nuclear research programme. The real obstacles in the way of a secret weapons programme were political in nature, the most prominent example being 'Der Göttinger Appell' (The Göttingen Appeal) of 1957.

On 19 November 1956 the group around Hahn, Heisenberg and Weizsäcker declared in a letter to Strauss that they were not prepared to take part in the development of atomic weapons. One reaction to this letter was a phone conversation during which the defence minister told Otto Hahn that this stance would be damaging to the government's NATO policy. Later, at the beginning of 1957, there was a heated discussion between the group of scientists and the defence minister.

Early in April 1957, the chairman of the Free Democratic Party (FDP), Reinhold Maier, issued a warning about the national production of atomic weapons. Maier 'was said to have received information from the circle of German physicists which indicated that there are developments towards producing an atomic weapon in West German laboratories' according to the *Neue Züricher Zeitung* in April 1957. On 12 April Germany's leading atomic scientists published their 'Göttingen Appeal'. Its key statements represent a clear break in the history of Germany's nuclear research: the FRG should 'expressly and voluntarily [renounce] the possession of any kind of atomic weapons. None of the undersigned would be prepared to take part in producing, testing or employing atomic weapons' (AdG, 1957, p. 6385).

With this refusal there was no longer a straightforward way of putting the national atomic weapons programme into practice. But a policy of 'non-decision' over the following years set the course for a civilian development programme along the lines of a military one. Clearly defined military interests were now replaced by a diffusion of civilian nuclear research programmes. The individual components of these programmes either served peaceful purposes in nuclear energy research, or they could be related to them in some way – but, taken as a whole, they represented a latent nuclear arms potential.

On the technical side, Germany was concentrating on the production and separation of plutonium (constructing a multipurpose reactor on the basis of natural uranium, beginning basic research into fast-breeder reactors as well as chemical reprocessing), the development of uranium enrichment (pushing work on the ultracentrifuge), reducing the politically uncomfortable dependency upon foreign deliverers (primacy of autarchy), and developing and testing high-altitude research rockets. It was a rare occasion when the German media called a spade a spade in connection with the generous government nuclear programme grants: 'spending for defence in the broader sense' (*Die Zeit*, 16 November 1962). But there is proof of at least temporary cooperation between the Ministry of Defence and the Ministry for Atomic Energy and Water Economy (soon to be renamed the 'Ministry for Scientific Research'), for example concerning uranium enrichment or the diverting of money from the defence budget for use by the Ministry for Atomic Energy (Radkau, 1983, pp. 189, 194, 564).

This double function of Germany's atomic energy development as both a research programme and a stand-by programme for military purposes was seldom mentioned in the political and scientific statements issued by the FRG. In 1972 Dieter Mahncke, who later held a position of responsibility in the Ministry of Defense, conceded that the extension of

a powerful civilian nuclear industry (including the resulting military alternatives) is of importance even before the actual production of atomic weapons; the ability to produce nuclear weapons will considerably whet the interest of existing nuclear-weapon states to prevent, jointly, the establishment of another independent nuclear power. Thus, there is a certain diplomatic value in the technical and economic ability to produce nuclear weapons. (Mahncke, 1972, p. 57)

In 1965 an informed politician on the Bonn scene added: 'We undoubtedly have much more to gain from being "persuaded" not to build the bomb than we would have once we actually started. ... The threat that "we just might do it yet" has proved quite a bargaining card' (Kelleher, 1975, p. 32). Indeed, the advantages of this dual-purpose nuclear programme were obvious:

- the FRG would be less open to criticism from outside;
- under certain circumstances, the possibility of exercising a national nuclear option could raise West Germany's stakes at the nuclear bargaining table;
- in the event of a crisis, the country's non-nuclear status could rapidly be changed;
- it brought prestige and could be used as a reference for nuclear cooperation on an international basis, as the Bonn–Paris axis clearly demonstrates.

The Bonn–Paris Axis

The spokesman of the Bonn government called it a 'gross slander': the president of Guinea, Sèkou Tourè, had claimed in a letter to UN

Secretary-General Hammarskjöld 'that West Germany had assisted France technically and financially in the development of the French atomic bomb' (*NYT*, 4 March 1960). Moreover, from Britain came the statement that 'principal scientific co-operation has been started between France and the Federal Republic of Germany in certain military matters regarding atomic weapons' (Beaton and Maddox, 1962, p. 737). These assertions were based on fact: two years before the explosion of the first French atomic bomb, Paris surprised its German and Italian allies with the offer to produce atomic weapons jointly. Although such cooperation never came about, because Paris withdrew its offer in the autumn of 1958, this French invitation had a long-term political and psychological impact – for a short time, a project for a 'Euro-bomb' had taken shape. How far did the nuclear flirtation of 1957/8 go? What were the motives of those involved? And why did it fail?

It all began in January 1957. Newly appointed German Defence Minister Franz Josef Strauss, accompanied by a high-ranking delegation, travelled to the then French Sahara. They intended 'to build a huge joint training area in the desert for certain military exercises' (*FAZ*, 16 January 1957). Together with French Defence Minister Bourgès-Maunoury, they visited the military centre for nuclear research in French-African Colomb-Béchar, and later signed a number of Franco-German agreements at ministerial level concerning cooperation in the production of 'modern' weapons. A standing committee of experts was established, and German participation in the French Institute for Arms Research at St Louis in Alsace was envisaged (Kohl, 1971, p. 55; Schütze, 1983, p. 5).

After the election of the Gaillard government (which was in office from 6 November 1957 to 15 April 1958), French willingness to cooperate soared to new heights. In his first official act, M. Chaban-Delmas, the new defence minister and later prime minister of France, called upon the governments of Bonn and Rome 'to activate and extend' nuclear cooperation. What this really meant was later summarised by C.L. Sulzberger as follows: 'Germany would contribute funds and technical aid towards the development of a French nuclear force ... and would receive an allotted number of [atomic] warheads stored in France' (*NYT*, 14 October 1964). German access to these weapons was guaranteed in a secret rider to the protocol, signed by Strauss and Guillaumat, the chairman of France's Atomic Energy Commission (Koch, 1985, pp. 301–3; Kelleher, 1967, pp. 325–7).

According to Strauss's memoirs, at the end of 1957 Chaban-Delmas suggested a triangular cooperation between France, Germany and Italy in a ratio of 45:45:10. A corresponding treaty was prepared by the negotiators for the three defence ministers in the preliminaries to a meeting in Rome scheduled for Easter 1958. In Rome 'the preliminary draft of the treaty was discussed down to the very finest detail. The central point was the joint development and production of atomic explosives' (Strauss, 1989, pp. 314–5). Chaban-Delmas is said to have taken this opportunity to confirm that Germany's 1954 renunciation of atomic weapons production still allowed the Germans to engage in such activities in a foreign country. Strauss states that he himself then proposed

> changing the text of the planned treaty in Paragraph 11 concerning atomic explosives. 'What wording are you proposing?,' M. Chaban-Delmas asked. My answer was: 'Joint research and the use of nuclear energy for military purposes.' ... The treaty was initialled and each of the undersigned took a copy. (Strauss, 1989, pp. 314–5)

In 1958 the European Atomic Energy Community (Euratom) had just been created, and the echos of the 'Göttingen Appeal' had not yet died away. In France, Prime Minister Gaillard ordered the detonation of a French nuclear bomb within the next 24 months, while in the FRG the argument over the atomic armament of the Bundeswehr had reached a peak. In this situation the signing of this treaty was a political issue of the first water and thus had to be achieved 'in total silence and secrecy, and be absolutely legal', as Chaban-Delmas and Strauss concluded (Schwarz, 1991, p. 398). In Bonn it was therefore agreed to disguise the need for the necessary money from the Ministry of Finance and the Bundestag as a German contribution to the 'European Institute for Missile Research' (Schwarz, 1991, p. 399). Strauss even stated on 26 February 1958 before the Bundestag that 'the federal government has no knowledge of any plans concerning the production of ABC-weapons in cooperation with other NATO states' (DS 3/441). This was an out-and-out lie: four weeks earlier the treaty with *exactly such a plan* had been discussed in Bonn (Schwarz, 1991, p. 400).

The Federal chancellor was the only person fully informed about this project from the very beginning and throughout its development. He supported it explicitly, but in public he did not want to be related to it in any way. He is said to have told Strauss: 'Do it, but should there be any trouble I know nothing at all about the entire business' (Strauss, 1989, p. 313).

What attracted the Federal Republic to nuclear cooperation with France? And why were the most outspoken French opponents of German rearmament suddenly interested in nuclear cooperation with the Germans? For one thing, both governments wanted to increase their influence with the United States. The very mention of a possible Bonn–Paris atomic axis put Washington under pressure. During a conversation with the chancellor, Maurice Faure, a special representative of the Gaillard government, let Adenauer know what was to take place during the coming NATO summit:

> the countries of continental Europe could take a firmer stand if they managed to agree beforehand about the joint organization of military research and weapons production. ... We cannot simply accept that only the United States and Great Britain have nuclear weapons and missiles with atomic warheads at their disposal. In principle, there should be no discrimination between NATO members.

Adenauer agreed. 'I assured Faure of my full support and agreement', he wrote later in his memoirs (Adenauer, 1967, p. 326).

On the other hand, this injection of German capital was just what France needed for its 'Force de Frappe', as the deployment of its troops in Algeria was becoming more and more expensive. A German disposition of French atomic weapons was never under discussion, however, and this fact cooled the interest of the Germans considerably. Although Strauss was prepared to pump a great deal of money into the 'triangle of armament' – he set aside the considerable sum of DM2 billion from the defence budget in 1958 for this purpose (Soell, 1976, p. 347) – he refused to accept a minor status for Germany. Paris remained stubborn concerning the question of any *joint* control arrangement: 'We were to pay – they were to retain full control', commented a Defence Ministry official close to Strauss (Kelleher, 1967, p. 335).

In this cautious flirtation, Paris enticed and Bonn hesitated. In 1958 the United States would have been a much more attractive partner for Bonn, especially as it was believed that closer relations between the two would lead to much better conditions concerning the transfer of atomic weapons on NATO terms. Thus, all exploratory talks with France had to be held under the prime condition of not alienating the Germans' most important ally.

On 1 June 1958 the era of Charles de Gaulle began. As a prisoner-of-war of the Germans during the First World War, and a leader of the Free French during the Second he would have been the last person to have allowed the Germans to interfere with the Force de Frappe. He nullified the Rome treaty and the secret contract between Strauss and Chaban-Delmas as early as the autumn of 1958 (Newhouse,

1970, p. 66). From now on, nuclear cooperation concentrated on the non-military sector. One exception was the Franco-German research institute located in St Louis in Alsace. This institute was a direct descendant of the Ballistisches Institut of the Nazi War Academy in Berlin and therefore had employed a number of German scientists. According to its director, Professor Schardin, the main mission of the institute – which remained the case under de Gaulle – was 'to investigate carefully the spreading of pressure and heat waves after an atomic bomb explosion ... and to calculate the effect of such forces.' At the institute, atomic explosions were simulated using conventional explosives (Neher, 1959, pp. 42–4). What part the institute played in the nuclear testing in the Sahara is still unknown, but what is certain is that the option of having a Franco-German bomb is to this very day a central aspect in the relationships of the Western Alliance. This option was raised for the first time in the preliminaries to the NATO summit in December 1957.

Equipping the Bundeswehr with Nuclear Arms

On 25 March 1958 the German Bundestag resolved by a majority vote 'to equip the army of the Federal Republic with the most modern [i.e. nuclear] weapons in order to carry out its duties within the framework of NATO'. An amazing phrase! There was no 'duty' within NATO to acquire nuclear weapons but rather a certain uncomfortable willingness to grant the Federal Republic a slice of the nuclear pie. 'I know quite a lot about these things – from the word go', said Fritz Erler, *the* military expert of the Social Democrats, to his party friend Willy Brandt. He continued:

> It is the German government which has always urged the issue of equipping the non-Anglo-Saxon parts of NATO with atomic weapons. It is the German government which has – with regard to equal treatment – rejected every idea of a certain division of labour and, as a result, different types of armaments within the Alliance. It is not always open and above board, and sometimes hides behind someone else; for example, the French. (quoted in Soell, 1976, p. 350)

One of the basic elements of Adenauer's persuasiveness was the ability to sell at home as an urgent NATO demand something which had been articulated previously, and had been accepted on international terms, as *his* own urgent desire – a clever Adenauerian move! In the Federal Republic, 64 per cent of the population rejected the idea of arming their Bundeswehr with atomic weapons, while just 17 per cent were in favour of it (Schwarz, 1991, p. 337). The subject was hotly debated abroad as well: in Norway, for instance, according to the *Neue Züricher Zeitung*, several high-ranking politicians declared that many people would to have to reassess their positive attitude towards NATO should the Germans get atomic weapons (*NZZ*, 29 April 1958). Denis Healey, the expert on security policy within the British Labour Party, warned of developments that would 'provide membership of the Alliance with more risks than security' (Brandstetter, 1989, p. 132). In the United States, the idea of Germany's having a slice of the nuclear pie unleashed a wave of protest. John F. Kennedy, then still a senator, pointed out in an article in the journal *Foreign Affairs* the dangers of a Germany with nuclear weapons at its disposal. The Federation of American Scientists predicted that there would be an expansion of the nuclear club. There were also disputes within the American government itself concerning the proliferation of nuclear weapons and atomic secrets among its NATO allies. The National Security Council issued the following warning in a circular letter:

> that in the future, help for our American allies could also mean lending support to an Armageddon. The current policy of the United States is threatening to establish a status quo in the short term, the prevention of which is one of its essential aims in the long term: namely, atomic anarchy on earth. (*Der Spiegel*, 16 April 1958)

Nevertheless, the United States and the Federal Republic of Germany signed a nuclear cooperation agreement which, inter alia, arranged for the transfer of secret information 'for the training of personnel in the use of atomic weapons ... and for further military applications of nuclear power'. Similar agreements were also finalised with France, Great Britain and the Netherlands. This was in line with the results of the NATO summit of December 1957. During this conference, probably the most momentous in the history of NATO, the US had agreed to install stockpiles of atomic warheads in all West European NATO member states if they so desired. The idea was that, in a crisis, these warheads should be at the disposal of the Allies, after clearance by the US president, to provide them with nuclear weapons carriers, including medium-range missiles, and at least to check the possibilities of joint production of atomic weapons (*EA* 8/58, p. 10,687).

Let us examine the background to this. As early as 1953, US army troops based in Germany had been equipped with tactical atomic weapons. In the same year, the United States decided to answer any conventional attacks with atomic weapons. This new doctrine was taken up by NATO in the winter of 1954 (Osgood, 1962, pp. 103–5). When it joined NATO, not only was West Germany confronted with the existence of nuclear weapons on German territory, it was also faced with an Allied strategy that was principally based on the use of atomic weapons. So it is not very surprising that this atomic weapons doctrine was soon taken up by Bonn. But it is worth mentioning that, among the non-nuclear-weapons states, the FRG very quickly became the strongest supporter of this doctrine. From mid-1956 onwards, the idea of being restricted to conventional defence was no longer considered (Richardson, 1966, p. 53).

Why did Bonn embark on this expensive atomic adventure although everyone knew that it had no control over these weapons? The answers are to be found in the government's defence policy and its worries about status. If one was to accept nuclear weapons on German territory, then at the least a differentiation in armaments held by NATO member states had to be avoided: Bonn feared that in the event of a war the enemy would first attack the country with the most poorly equipped troops. A second point was that the sharing of nuclear weapons could be used as an instrument to influence American nuclear strategy, an argument that became increasingly important. Due to the fact that neither conventional nor atomic weapons represented a real defence for the Federal Republic of Germany, Bonn concentrated on the effectiveness of a nuclear deterrent. From this point on, it was not just the presence of nuclear weapons that was important but also the credibility of the threat that they could be used at short notice. But the growing vulnerability of the US created by the intercontinental ballistic missiles of the Soviet Union made an early use of nuclear weapons increasingly unlikely. Would an American president risk the very existence of his own country for the sake of Germany and the Germans? Henry Kissinger is credited with saying: 'that the [Bonn] Defence Ministry seems to have no greater worry than that of how it could force the Americans into war in case of an emergency' (*Der Spiegel*, 15/1961), a statement that was rooted in differing German and American interests.

Third, the German government had set its sights on achieving equal ranking with France and Great Britain. There is no doubt that Adenauer and his defence minister would have followed the path of procuring atomic armaments unilaterally had they been sure that such a move would not have stirred up a hornet's nest within NATO. According to Strauss expert Bruno Bandulet, there was a great deal of evidence with regard to the NATO summit in 1957 that the German government first tried to achieve the maximum possible, namely to have atomic warheads at its disposal, but it did not do so openly so that it could always deny it later should it become clear that there was no possibility of reaching such a goal. (Bandulet, 1970, p. 46)

The advantages of the French procedure under de Gaulle were obvious to Adenauer. Politically, having one's own atomic weapons was the symbol of equal status with London and Paris; militarily, according to the 'final nuclear strategy', this would function as a trigger and provoke the use of the nuclear potential of the United States. In 1965, the publisher of the German journal *Europäische Wehrkunde* wrote that there was a need for German atomic weapons to 'have a chance to unleash the nuclear intervention of the allied superpower, the US, in the event of war' (Dalma, 1965, p. 3). In 1983, a request for 'Pershing II rockets, including warheads, in German hands' was given substance by using exactly the same argument:

A Germany in possession of atomic weapons would make it impossible for France and Great Britain to merely look on at developments for a while and avoid using their atomic weapons in the event of war. ... And because of the 'coupling effect', another consequence would be that the US, too, could not just stay on the sidelines with its nuclear potential. (Koller, 1984, p. 36)

Back to the 1957 NATO summit. Some months earlier, in September 1956, the *Frankfurter Allgemeine Zeitung* had suggested that 'the step to becoming a nuclear weapons power ... will soon force itself upon us' (*FAZ*, 4 September 1956). In the same month, Franz Josef Strauss came out with the following line of reasoning to some members of the Bundestag:

Power today is military power. Military power today is atomic power. Without atomic armaments, Germans will supply only the bakers and the kitchen-boys for the forces of the other allies. And with such a role, the future of Germany is decided. (Kelleher, 1975, p. 56)

The discontent with this inferior status was given a new impetus when in February 1957 the United States and Great Britain signed a treaty concerning the delivery of US medium-range missiles. During a press conference on 5 April 1957, Adenauer supported claims for atomic weapons for the Bundeswehr, pointing out 'that Great Britain had already declared weeks ago that it wants to become a nuclear weapons power ... This development is in full swing and we Germans cannot stop it. We have to adjust to it' (BPA Protocol, 5 April 1956). This British-American 'double-key' agreement of February 1957 served as a pattern for future bilateral atomic weapons treaties between Washington and Bonn from that time onwards. That Great Britain was not to be the last country to become a nuclear weapons power was obvious to the State Department. 'Great Britain has them, France is working on them', said US Secretary of State Dulles in July 1957; 'Italy, Germany, and the Netherlands cannot be held back forever from producing nuclear weapons when so many other countries are working on it' (Handzik, 1968, p. 26). It was likely that an untested but perhaps more effective way of stopping nuclear proliferation would have to be tried. Dulles's new proposal to establish stockpiles of weapons in Western Europe, thus ensuring West European NATO partners access to atomic weapons, was promptly and emphatically welcomed by Eisenhower with the words that this move would make national development of atomic weapons superfluous (Osgood, 1962, p. 220).

This new American tightrope walk – the 'fencing-in' of proliferation by extending the share in the nuclear potential – was also a reaction to the Bonn–Paris nuclear axis. At the end of November 1957 the United States had been officially put into the picture by Germany's foreign minister, Heinrich von Brentano, concerning the Franco-German convergence and the 'armaments triangle' (Department of State, 1986, p. 195). A few weeks later, John Foster Dulles suggested creating a NATO pool to coordinate military atomic research (Department of State, 1986, p. 215). Adenauer observed with satisfaction that this proposal 'undoubtedly had its roots in the initiative of the Gaillard government' (Adenauer, 1967, p. 344).

The United States tried to master two contradictory demands in its NATO policy of 1957. On the one hand, the US wanted to prevent the proliferation of atomic weapons; on the other, it wanted its allies to participate in the military use of atomic power. The possession of nuclear weapons by members of NATO, the training of their armies to use atomic weapons, and a pledge to transfer to them the stockpiled atomic warheads under US control in the event of war – from now on, all this was a sine qua non for the non-proliferation policy of the United States.

The nuclear armament of the Soviet Union in 1957 was a welcome spur for NATO decision-makers. Keeping in mind the Soviet Union's situation, the strengthening of the Alliance was more important to Eisenhower and Dulles than the minimising of proliferation. But it should not be forgotten that the American offers of December 1957 were principally aimed at 'persuading West Germany to renounce the independent production of such a weapon', as described in a secret draft of guidelines which had been drawn up before the NATO summit (Czempiel and Schweitzer, 1984, p. 218). The 'Sputnik shock' of 4 October 1957, together with the nuclear credibility crisis, had only added to the worries that a Western European country might be tempted to go it alone with the nuclear option – and in this respect the event did have a certain influence on NATO decisions in December 1957.

At the same time, the NATO decision of December 1957 made the non-proliferation policy more popular; thus it also helped to launch the idea of the non-proliferation treaty (NPT) which was first proposed in Ireland in the autumn of 1958. The French atomic test of 1960 confirmed the failure of the 'cooperative' non-proliferation policy of the United States and triggered the worldwide NPT debate.

The Superpowers and Non-proliferation

'Damned if you do, damned if you don't!' This exclamation by James Reston, publisher of the *New York Times*, emphasised the American dilemma. If the US tried to level out nuclear differences in NATO, it was precisely this that might whet the appetites of the Allies for their own individual strategic independence. But if the United States was not willing to make nuclear concessions, this could just as well push its Allies to the point where they would be tempted to go it alone. Whichever choice was made, the result would be disastrous. This dilemma was not a question of natural law, however, but the logical consequence of the nuclear privilege. Why should other countries renounce the purchasing of a weapon, the possession of which provides the nuclear powers not only with an increase in political prestige but also with freedom of action on the military side? What moral grounds could underlie the policy of a country that optimises its own nuclear stockpiles yet advises other countries to abstain from doing so? There were always two motives behind the great powers' rejection of nuclear proliferation: on the one hand, nuclear peace should be safeguarded; on the other, their own nuclear hegemony should be secured.

As early as the 'Quebec Agreement' of August 1943, not only had Roosevelt, Churchill and Canadian Prime Minister William M. King forbidden the transfer of nuclear know-how; in an additional clause, it was agreed that the US alone would decide on the essential elements of post-war use of this know-how (Pringle and Spigelman,

1981, p. 76). The element of power politics continued to be a constant factor in America's non-proliferation policy. William C. Foster, chairman of the Arms Control and Disarmament Agency (ACDA), wrote in 1965 that

> We should not lose sight of the fact that widespread nuclear pro-
> liferation would mean a substantial erosion in the margin of power
> which our great wealth and industrial base have long given us
> relative to much of the rest of the world. (*FA*, July 1965, p. 591)

Thus it is not surprising that the potential atomic powers did not want to allow themselves to be taken advantage of.

In the Interest of the US

Up to the time of writing, the central problem of non-proliferation is the imbalance in responsibility, which is also a cause of instability in the global order: as long as countries having nuclear weapons refuse to equalise power differences with non-nuclear-weapons states by disarming, the only way for non-nuclear-weapons states to balance out such differences in power is by heading off in the opposite direction, namely by trying to achieve atomic-power status. This inherent imbalance could not be compensated for by taking action within the framework of the existing nuclear global order. Moreover, the policy of nuclear isolation which was practised in the early years was unable to prevent Great Britain and France establishing themselves as atomic powers, and so this practice was ended in 1954 with regard to London (Handzik, 1967, pp. 46–71), and from 1969 onwards with regard to Paris (Ullman, 1989, pp. 3–33), by adopting a policy aimed at maintaining America's influence over these two countries through the technological support Washington would give them. The tension created by isolation on the one hand and cooperation on the other had to result in a policy of creeping proliferation. When a non-nuclear-weapons state attempted to change its status, at a certain point it became advisable for the US to abandon its resistance to proliferation, and instead to aim at gaining as much influence as possible over the nuclear strategies of that country. This inherent contradiction in America's non-proliferation policy explains its differing positions regarding the NPT. For example, the US secretary of state, John Foster Dulles, was an outspoken opponent of the NPT. In a statement to the Congressional Committee on Atomic Energy in 1958, he maintained that:

There is today an understandable resistance on the part of other free world countries to an international agreement which would have the effect of ... perpetuating for all time their present nuclear weapons inferiority. [To prohibit the sharing of nuclear technology and knowledge] would in effect make the United States a partner with the Soviet Union in imposing on our NATO allies such an incapacity ... that Soviet dominance over Western Europe would be largely achieved. (Clausen, 1973, p. 11)

It is significant for the change in priorities that began under Kennedy, that ten years later the United States ignored the 'understandable resistance' of its partners by signing the NPT as 'a partner with the Soviet Union'. In 1963, John F. Kennedy stated:

If nuclear arms were acquired by other nations, large and small, stable and unstable, responsible and irresponsible, there would be no rest for anyone. No stability, no real security and no effective disarmament: there would only be increased chance of accidental war and an increased necessity for the great powers to involve themselves in what, otherwise, would be local conflicts. (*NYT*, 9 September 1966)

No other nation in the world, not even friendly ones, should be able to enlarge the circle of nuclear powers. On the contrary: this blanket statement to the entire world by the American president was really aimed at Western Europe, including West Germany, as they were the most important nuclear power candidates on the scene at that time.

Whereas President Eisenhower wanted to preserve a nuclear monopoly without surrendering the option to make necessary changes according to any new situations that might arise, his successor wanted to consolidate this monopoly by pursuing an active non-proliferation policy even towards his allies, and to make it watertight. Because of this approach, the coordinates in the system of international relations were redefined: over and above the old East–West antagonism there was now a new division of nations into a few 'haves' and a great many 'have-nots'. Why was the non-proliferation problem so important to Kennedy? Why did he want a revaluation of international relations? There were two basic reasons for this: the nuclear stalemate, and the strategic lines of reasoning which resulted from this stalemate.

Because of the Cold War with its 'balance of fear', it seemed to make sense to opt for a policy of strategic stability towards Moscow rather than for a policy of the unilateral strengthening of Western Europe.

A new authority, the Arms Control and Disarmament Agency (ACDA), was established in Washington to look for possible bilateral agreements in certain sectors of arms control. Within that strategy of stability, the NPT achieved a significance far beyond what was intended with political arms controls: neither the horrors of Vietnam, nor the invasion of Czechoslovakia, nor the 1967 war in the Middle East had damaged the NPT project as a refuge for common interests and as a stabiliser for relations between the superpowers.

The direct interest in the NPT was a result of the new US strategy of 'flexible response'. This strategy called for a concept to be developed between the NATO partners that envisaged a 'limited' preliminary use of atomic weapons. Thus, 'the importance of unity in planning, concentration of executive power, and central leadership' was increased (McNamara, 1962, p. D368). It was of prime importance to prevent the US from being forced into an atomic war just because one of its allies had used its nuclear weapons prematurely.

The nuclear coupling of the US with other countries was never automatic but always related to the degree of Washington's responsiblities within the Alliance. The more non-committal the pledge to NATO, the greater the chance of an overall reduction of commitment and the less the danger of a 'catalytic war'. The more binding the American pledge to NATO, the greater the danger of involuntary coupling. It is a paradox of the nuclear era that one's closest ally can put one at the greatest risk (Clausen, 1973, p. 136).

Following the Chinese atomic tests in 1964, the American non-proliferation policy took on a global dimension which, up till then, had been more or less just good publicity. Nevertheless, the prospect of German atomic power remained a special nightmare. Not only might this lead to the collapse of NATO, it might also precipitate a considerable destabilisation in world policy. A statement by Adrian S. Fisher, the American head of NPT diplomacy, makes this clear. According to Fisher, not only West Germany but also such countries as Canada, Japan, Israel, Pakistan and even Sweden had all the conditions in place to develop into atomic powers. What would happen if some of these countries should reach out for the 'bomb'? Adrian Fisher told the Notre Dame American Assembly:

> If that happens, then can the political inhibitions which now exist continue to prevent the Federal Republic of Germany from seeking its own national nuclear defenses against the rather large number of nuclear weapons aimed at it? ... If the decision to develop their own nuclear weapons were to be made, we would probably have an international crisis which would make the ten

days preceding October 27, 1962 [the Cuban crisis] look like ten relaxed days indeed. This is the thing we are trying to prevent. This is the reason, we – all of us, and I say this on both sides, both the Warsaw Pact powers and the NATO powers – want earnestly to develop a non-proliferation agreement. (Fisher, 1967, pp. 40–1)

In the Interest of the Soviet Union

The leaders in the Kremlin were also well aware of the risks of 'nuclear coupling'. The problems surrounding the Formosa Straits Quemoy Crisis (involving Taiwan and the People's Republic of China) came close to forcing the USSR into war with the United States in 1958, a war which would have been caused by the independent action of an allied country.

The Russian launching of *Sputnik I* gave rise to feelings that the Soviet Union had nuclear superiority over the United States. With this in mind, in August 1958, China began to bombard the nearby island of Quemoy, which was occupied by Taiwan. It was the express aim of Peking to occupy Quemoy and annex Nationalist China. The United States mobilised its troops and threatened to defend its ally, Taiwan, with atomic weapons if necessary. A great deal of evidence suggests that China had reckoned on the support of the Soviet Union, backed up by its entire nuclear potential, during this crisis (Thomas, 1962, pp. 38–40). But the Russian government refused to go along with this strategy. Peking was forced to terminate its bombing attacks without having achieved any of its aims. In the aftermath, Mao Tse-tung sharpened his criticism of the stability-oriented policy of the Kremlin, whereas Khrushchev blamed the Chinese government for its 'irresponsibility', and stated that it was he who had maintained peace in the world, thanks to his reticence and moderation. The Soviet Union's control over the course of events would have been much more difficult if China had already possessed its own atomic weapons in 1958. Quemoy not only marked a turning point in relations between China and the Soviet Union, it was also the trigger for Soviet opposition to nuclear proliferation (Lambeth, 1970, p. 310).

The specific motive underlying Soviet interest in the NPT was the fear that West Germany might gain possession of the atomic bomb. 'We primarily designed the whole treaty to close all doors and windows on the possibility of the Federal Republic of Germany having nuclear weapons', recalled Oleg Grinewski, a former member of the Soviet NPT negotiation delegation (author's interview with Oleg Grinewski, 25 February 1988).

For Moscow, the potential nuclear armament of West Germany was different in quality to that of any other country. The penetration of Germany's Wehrmacht into Russia was still fresh in their memories, and it was a hard and cold fact that Wehrmacht officers continued to serve in senior positions in West Germany's Bundeswehr. More important than all this, however, was the fact that the Federal Republic of Germany had acknowledged neither the western borders of Poland nor the sovereign status of East Germany; and, moreover, the FRG was openly working for territorial changes in Central Europe, albeit by peaceful means. For the Soviet Union, Germany's renunciation of the purchasing and possessing of atomic weapons was a basic condition for the European detente based on the acknowledgement of the territorial status quo.

It was obvious that the FRG, even as a nuclear-weapons state, would not constitute a real security problem for the Soviet Union. For Moscow, the military danger was much less that of an isolated German potential than the coupling of German and American capacities. For Washington, nuclear cooperation with the Bundeswehr would always mean that the US was in control. From Moscow's point of view, however, the chances of escalation increased in direct proportion to the degree of American-German nuclear integration. And the Kremlin did not completely rule out the possiblity that the German government, perhaps misled by false interpretations of a particular situation, and exploiting their nuclear coupling with the US, might embark on a hazardous military venture to achieve its territorial claims by force. The Soviet balking at making any compromise on the question of common nuclear solutions was based on such fears. In the Soviet's worst-case scenario, the share of the nuclear pie controlled by Bonn was interpreted as being a German finger on the American trigger – something to be feared and fought against.

The common denominator of American and Soviet non-proliferation policies was clearly evident in the Irish resolution which was adopted unanimously by the United Nations General Assembly on 4 December 1961. In this resolution all nations, but most especially the nuclear powers, were asked:

to do their utmost to reach an agreement in an international treaty in which nations possessing nuclear weapons undertake not to transfer their disposal over nuclear weapons to those nations not yet in possession of such weapons, and not to transfer to such nations the information needed to produce nuclear weapons, whereby the non-nuclear weapons nations undertake not to produce nuclear weapons and not to try to obtain them in any other way. (DoD II, p. 155)

The FRG was not compelled to take part in the vote on this resolution, as it was not yet a member of the United Nations. Adenauer's course was just the opposite of that of the UN. In New York, the French atomic bomb test had been a catalyst for the NPT, but in the Federal Republic, France's achievements had only increased Germany's desire to get a bigger slice of the nuclear pie. Adenauer and his defence minister were aware that it would not be feasible for Bonn to follow the same route de Gaulle had taken. The historical burden was too heavy, the dependence on the Western Allies too great. The nuclear dilemma confronting the German government was how to reconcile the special German conditions with the desire for an equality of status with France.

In September 1960, a possible solution to this problem began to emerge. At Adenauer's holiday resort of Cadenabbia on Lake Como, NATO's Commander-in-Chief Norstad, NATO's Secretary-General Spaak and the NATO ambassadors from the Netherlands, Belgium and West Germany met together with Adenauer. Here a plan was worked out that would transform NATO into a fourth nuclear power. This project seemed capable of satisfying every demand, regardless of the direction it came from: on the one hand, West Germany would have equal access to atomic weapons; on the other, the use of such weapons would be controlled by a kind of NATO council (Mahncke, 1972, p. 76). While the Irish resolution was accepted unanimously in New York, the contradictory project of NATO becoming a nuclear power was number one on Chancellor Adenauer's list of nuclear priorities (Lider, 1986, pp. 331–3). Thus the United States came up against fierce and unyielding resistance when it tried to have the Irish resolution accepted in West Germany.

2

Germany's Battle against the NPT

On 13 August 1961 the Berlin Wall began to go up. Berlin was divided into two. Just six weeks later, John F. Kennedy presented an extensive disarmament plan to the United Nations, for the first time demanding a Non-Proliferation Treaty. These two events are inextricably linked. The Berlin crisis of 1961 had accelerated a transformation of priorities in US foreign policy and had inspired a new round of talks between Washington and Moscow, during which, inter alia, the nuclear status of the Federal Republic of Germany was discussed.

The deepening of the German-American nuclear controversy can be traced thus: whereas Bonn was striving for more equality within the Alliance by becoming a NATO nuclear-weapons power, Washington preferred to negotiate with Moscow on a new German renunciation of nuclear weapons.

At that time, the transatlantic quarrel over the NPT was for the most part conducted behind closed doors. Even now, it is almost always overlooked in writings on contemporary history. But not only did this quarrel cause a delay in concluding the NPT, it also significantly influenced discussions concerning the Nuclear Test Ban Treaty and the nuclear Multilateral Force (MLF).

1961/2: The Berlin Crisis and the NPT

The building of the Berlin Wall was followed by a German-American controversy which, according to Ambassador Wilhelm Grewe, was 'to all intents and purposes, the prologue for the subsequent conflict over the NPT' (Grewe, 1979, p. 565). How was it possible that the first seeds of the NPT began to sprout in the shadow of the Berlin Wall? Why did those dramatic Berlin days prove to be a further catalyst for detente?

The First Probings
In 1948, the 'Realpolitik' approach of America's policies on Germany had won the day. In contrast to the group around Roosevelt and Morgenthau, the authors of this approach did not want to destroy

the military potential of the Germans but to use it for their own ends. Adenauer was more than happy with this development. For him, the Potsdam Agreement was a symbol of Germany's defeat, and thus the anti-Soviet strategy of containment provided a chance to overcome this defeat in two different ways. On the one hand, Adenauer was convinced that a strategy of power would in the long run overcome the division of Germany; on the other, with every step along the road to rearmament a little more West German sovereignty was restored. The Cold War and the subsequent linking of national emancipation and military integration lay at the heart of the special relationship between Germany and America which promised to provide the Federal Republic with military and political security.

At the beginning of the 1960s, however, circumstances had changed. With the termination of America's invulnerability, the strategy of power had lost a great deal of impetus – the new American government tried to adapt to the new situation. Adenauer did not have much sympathy for these changes: Kennedy's new foreign policy threatened the special relationship between Washington and Bonn. It was the newly awakened interest in negotiations with the Soviet Union which, alone, gave rise to mistrust: was there still any interest at all in Washington in the reunification of the two Germanys?

After Kennedy took office in January 1961, Bonn saw its fears confirmed. The new strategy of flexible response seemed to threaten the effectiveness of nuclear deterrence and at the same time to endanger the 'joint venture of risk' between the Federal Republic and the United States. The German longing for an effective influence on America's nuclear policy increased, but Washington was less interested in this than ever before. According to the Pentagon, the NATO allies ought to concentrate on conventional armaments and leave nuclear matters to the number-one power. From the political point of view, too, Germany's wishes were inopportune: Kennedy did not want to endanger negotiations with the Soviet Union by any measures in NATO that he thought unnecessary and that could be interpreted by the Soviets as an adverse act. The stability of world policy took first priority, and Germany's desire for nuclear equality and reunification had to be subordinate to this priority.

With some surprise, the German government had to accept the fact that after the division of Berlin, relations between the two super-powers not only did not deteriorate, they even improved. What seemed so paradoxical was not very surprising, however: setting aside all its grandiloquent language to the contrary, the United States had long before accepted the government of East Germany as well as the status quo in Central Europe. The Berlin Wall was criticised, but at the same time accepted as a stabilising factor: 'While its human consequences were appalling, the officials in Western capitals were privately relieved' (Newhouse, 1970, p. 140). In compliance with the new American doctrine, West Berlin could only survive in an atmosphere of confidence between the two superpowers.

Walter Lippman and James Reston, both from the *New York Times*, were the first to identify the framework for future Berlin negotiations resulting from this doctrine. Reston, for example, wrote in the *New York Times* on 15 September 1961:

> On these three questions – Will the West accept the Oder–Neisse line as the permanent Polish-German border? Will it agree to some de facto form of recognition of the East German regime? And will it agree to strict limitations on West German armaments? – lie the possibility of a compromise on Berlin.

Shortly after this article was published, bilateral disarmament talks between the former high commissioner for Germany, John J. McCloy, and his Soviet colleague, Valerin Zorin, resulted in a 'Joint Statement of Agreed Principle' that included, among other matters, the non-proliferation of atomic weapons (McCloy, 1962, p. 349).

On 8 October 1961, in the course of discussions within the Washington Steering Committee for Ambassadors, the German government was informed of the likely extent of the pending Berlin negotiations. The Germans were 'alarmed' not only by the list of topics presented, but especially by 'the calmness with which this was accepted by the Americans and the British', as the German member of this committee, Ambassador Grewe, later wrote (Grewe, 1979, p. 501). On the same day, Bonn used its veto on the East–West negotiations with regard to non-proliferation. The list of the points which – according to Ambassador Grewe – 'most certainly cannot be deliberated on' included all those topics which jeopardised the equal status of the Germans in NATO (*Bulletin*, 12 October 1961). An exchange of letters between Kennedy and Adenauer, pouring oil on the fire, followed (Grewe, 1979, p. 511). In his letters, the chancellor agreed to continue the talks but only on condition 'that we will agree upon aims and limits of these talks beforehand'. The security of the Federal Republic, for example, could not permit any renunciation of the agreement that 'in the event of war, the Bundeswehr will have at its disposal the nuclear warheads which are under American control during peace time' (Grewe, 1979, p. 509).

The quickness and ferocity with which the German government presented its point of view against an NPT is proven by the Grewe dossier which was written when preparing for the German-American summit in November 1961 and which listed all the main points of difference between the Allies. In Point 6, Grewe noted on 14 November 1961:

> Concerning the question of 'freezing' nuclear armaments: this question, too, because it has nothing to do with the subject of Berlin, should be dismissed. It touches a vital nerve in the interests of the security of the Federal Republic of Germany and of the Alliance as a whole. Should the Soviet Union have a voice in the nuclear arrangements of NATO? As instructed, I have quite clearly stood up in opposition to this in the Group of Ambassadors. And we should not deviate from this course of action. (Grewe, 1979, p. 515)

Soon after that, Adenauer rushed to Washington, carrying the Grewe dossier with him, to try to talk Kennedy out of the 'disarmament and control measures which concerned West Germany alone' (AdG, 1961, p. 9454). The visit 'was not without stormy moments', wrote John Newhouse about this meeting, 'which included burning by mutual consent the minutes of one Adenauer-Kennedy conversation' (Newhouse, 1970, p. 142). During the talks, Kennedy agreed to limit the Berlin talks to 'Berlin' alone (Stützle, 1973, p. 176). Adenauer's 'success', however, was extremely short-lived and barely masked the conceptional contradictions. Although one consequence of the Adenauer–Kennedy conversation was that the NPT was removed from the list of topics for the superpower summit meeting, it was not taken off the United Nations agenda: just a few days after Adenauer's departure, the Irish resolution was adopted unanimously by the UN.

The drama of these weeks gave a foretaste of the altercation over the NPT in the years to follow. It also shows what a great deal of influence American foreign policy was prepared to let its West German ally have. What was the reason for this special position of the Germans? 'De Gaulle was a silent partner to all this,' wrote Grewe on the Adenauer talks in the White House (Grewe, 1979, p. 520) and gives us an important hint why. The disagreement on nuclear matters between Washington and Paris, together with the greatly feared (in the US, at least) option of a Franco-German bomb, lent weight to Bonn, a weight that it would not have had without these factors. The worry that Adenauer might be driven into the arms of de Gaulle compelled US diplomats to act with the utmost caution, and at the same time it tempted West German diplomats to make a show of strength.

An final point should be added. An editorial in the *New York Times* commented on Adenauer's arrival in Washington, saying that 'it would be intolerable for the Germans to sit back and say later (as Hitler once did) that a "Diktat" was forced upon them' (*NYT*, 17 November 1961). This statement shows the administration's concern that a former enemy should never again be given a pretext to act along the lines set by the Treaty (*Diktat*) of Versailles. The question of Germany's nuclear option was still unsettled; it seemed more prudent to take German feelings and wishes into consideration than to adopt an uncompromising attitude.

A Barrage against the NPT

Adenauer's demand that the Berlin problem sould be considered in isolation made it unlikely that negotations would be successful – East–West talks were deadlocked. In March 1962 Kennedy and his secretary of state, Dean Rusk, agreed to include other items on the agenda, including a proposal for an agreement with respect to the Irish resolution. As agreed beforehand with the NATO allies supporting this resolution, Secretary Rusk put before his Soviet colleague Gromyko the proposal for a declaration that those nations possessing nuclear weapons promised not to place atomic weapons at the disposal of the non-nuclear states, and also promised not to deliver to them any information which could be used for the production of the same (Bunn, 1989, p. 17). On 9 April 1962, in a paper bearing the title 'Draft Principles, Procedures and Interim Steps', the German government was informed about all this and was asked for an opinion on these new American proposals (Grewe, 1979, pp. 549–64).

This paper created shockwaves in Bonn. The first of its five points was concerned with the desire for a Soviet–American agreement on the non-proliferation of atomic weapons. The arduous hours of discussion during the Adenauer–Kennedy meetings were wiped out in one fell swoop. Further points in the American paper dealt with the exchange of non-aggression declarations as well as the establishment of an international authority, to include East Germans, which would supervise the access roads to West Berlin (AdG, 1962, p. 9831).

After a hurriedly scheduled emergency meeting with the leaders of all the German political parties – including Adenauer, von Brentano, Krone, Schröder, Carstens, Ollenhauer and Mende – Ambassador Grewe was given the order to report the anxieties of the German government to the US government (Grewe, 1979, p. 550). At the same time Bonn launched a sort of 'guerrilla campaign' (Smith, 1963, p. 334): the American secret paper was leaked to the press and its contents were published on the front page of the *New York Times* two days before the Soviet-American talks began.

Washington was furious about this indiscretion. The State Department announced that 'efforts to sabotage East–West negotiations on the Berlin issue' were being made (*NYT*, 15 April 1962) and declared that a 'severe violation of diplomatic conventions between allies ... which had caused irreparable damage to German-American relations' had occurred (AdG, 1962, p. 9831). Even Germany's Free Democratic Party (FDP), which at the time had been a member of the governing coalition for some months, was angered 'that in the FRG certain leading persons apparently were interested in wrecking the constructive contribution of the West towards a "Deutschland-politik" by this premature publication' (AdG, 1962, p. 9832).

For the majority of the members of the German government, however, the American proposals were far from being 'constructive' because they threatened to do away with two basic supports of Bonn's foreign policy: namely, 'non-recognition of the German Democratic Republic, and the freedom to re-arm the country with nuclear weapons as well as with conventional ones' (*Der Spiegel*, 25 April 1962). In the West German press, the nuclear controversy was not discussed at length because of a warning from Defence Minister Strauss: in the realm of military atomic policy 'every public discussion would make the calm treatment of this question more difficult and would thus put the hackles up among the negative criticisers as well as among the know-it-alls' (*Bulletin*, 1 December 1961). Nevertheless, at the meeting at Adenauer's holiday resort in Cadenabbia in April 1962, this topic was number one on the agenda. 'I will not permit badly armed German troops to face a better-armed enemy', Adenauer told his guests, who included Schröder, Krone, Globke and Carstens (Osterheld, 1986, p. 110). In the same month, a prominent commentator on the *New York Times*, C.L. Sulzberger, described the NPT plans as being a 'cardinal point' in the Berlin negotiations (*NYT*, 18 April 1962) and the chief reason for Bonn's rejection of the American proposals. The American analysts had earlier hit the nail on the head with their prediction that the NPT 'ultimately might prove a more important cause of differences among the Western powers than the approach over Berlin' (*NYT*, 15 April 1962). But the Kennedy government was not disconcerted by these fierce German protests. On 18 April 1962, within the framework of a draft agreement on universal and total disarmament, the United States presented to the 18-nation UN Committee on Disarmament a rough outline for the Non-Proliferation Treaty (DoD, 1962, p. 359).

Three weeks later, German-American discord reached a new pitch thanks to a provocative statement by the German chancellor. When Adenauer declared that he did not have 'even the slightest hope that anything would ever result from the East–West negotiations', he not only questioned the chances for success of the US exploratory talks, following the line taken by de Gaulle, but also made it clear that he did not even want them to succeed (*Die Welt*, 5 May 1962). Ambassador Grewe said that this statement was 'the sharpest public dissociation from American policy ... that has ever been heard from the lips of a German head of state and that there has been no comparable example after that time either' (Grewe, 1979, p. 555). The degree of American annoyance was even greater than it had been over the leaking of the secret negotiation proposals. Kennedy threatened 'in words that were sharper than any ever before used with Bonn ... that the United States would continue along diplomatic lines in order to find a solution to the Berlin crisis, even in the face of a veto by Adenauer' (*Die Welt*, 10 May 1962).

Now it was a matter for the Federal Republic to try to limit the damage. Following a request from Washington, the Auswärtige Amt began to work out a German proposal for the American negotiations. The wording of what was probably the first official statement by the German government on the subject of the 'Non-Proliferation Treaty' remained unpublished, but its contents did not. On 23 May 1962 an anonymous correspondent wrote in the *FAZ* that as far as security policy was concerned, the memorandum was focused on the question of nuclear armaments. The article went on to say:

> Bonn has gone so far as to oppose the 'freezing' of the current nuclear global situation as proposed by President Kennedy. Although the German government is not striving to obtain any right of control in nuclear matters, it declines to be restricted to the nuclear status quo by any agreement whatsoever, arguing that such a 'freeze' might mean that in the future the Bundeswehr could be excluded from any modern military rearmament.

All the other aspects of America's Berlin proposal were dealt with in quite a conciliatory manner in this memorandum, but as far as the question of the NPT was concerned, Bonn remained firm. Not even the brief visit to Bonn by the American secretary of state in June 1962 did anything to change this position. Once again, Secretary Rusk underlined to Adenauer and Schröder America's interest in agreements on the non-proliferation of atomic weapons which were to be discussed during the disarmament conference in Geneva. But, as a participant at this meeting noted, Adenauer replied that

> he did not want to go beyond the renunciation of 1954. And Schröder made it clear that we were not prepared to accept something which, for the most part, concerned German troops only. Rusk conceded that the Soviets were mainly interested in binding us down. The Chancellor and Herr Schröder also insisted upon maintaining the possibility of having a NATO nuclear force. Rusk agreed. (Osterheld, 1986, p. 129)

This talk brought the first round of the German-American NPT controversy to an end. Germany did not succeed in having the NPT completely removed from the catalogue of American negotiating targets: the redrafting of America's Berlin proposals on 30 May 1962 mentioned the German desire to strike out the sentence on the NPT, but the sentence was included in parenthesis (Grewe, 1979, p. 565). German opposition was successful, however, insofar as in the summer of 1962 the first attempts of the United States to achieve an NPT failed along with its Berlin plan. Kennedy did not try to hide his disappointment. 'Difficulties and frustrations are great', he remarked when opening the disarmament conference in Geneva in July 1962 (DoD, 1962, p. 657). In contrast to the situation a month earlier, the NPT no longer played a part in American contributions to the conference (DoD, 1962, pp. 666–72). The German government also had little reason to be satisfied. A matter of utmost importance to them – Germany's nuclear share as an atomic power within NATO – had not made the slightest headway. The Soviet-American tête-à-tête on Berlin, however, set the alarm bells ringing in Bonn. The more German-American interests diverged, the more urgent became the demand to exercise greater influence on the nuclear policies of NATO.

The Resignation of Franz Josef Strauss

How did the German government try to obtain this greater influence on NATO's nuclear policies? In September Adenauer stated that the Alliance should be able to use its own nuclear weapons without waiting for a decision by the American president (*NYT*, 17 November 1961). This idea ran straight into Kennedy's flat refusal. It was then followed by what was termed the 'Strauss Plan' according to which member states of NATO that might come under attack would have the right to decide together with the United States on the use of nuclear weapons (*Die Welt*, 30 November 1961). Personal notes taken by the

SPD's military expert, Fritz Erler, during a meeting of the NATO Council on 3 March 1962 give an outline of this plan. The fact that a leading Social Democrat politician was allowed into one of the most sensitive areas of NATO policymaking, something which could only happen with the express permission of Strauss himself, clearly shows that within the West German nuclear community there was no party politicking. In his report, Erler conceded that at this meeting

> there might be some arguments against the Strauss Plan in its current form; but we think it right to permit the country under attack, and perhaps the responsible military commander (SACEUR) as well, to be included in the triggering system for nuclear weapons. The wording [of the German proposal] should perhaps be extended to state that a 'country under attack' would also include a 'directly threatened country'. (Erler's unpublished papers, cassette 135)

Erler specifically named Germany and Turkey as being especially threatened countries. But the Strauss Plan, also, met with fierce opposition in the US.

It seems that the very option of becoming a 'national nuclear-weapons power' was discussed during these months, although only within exclusive circles in Germany. Defence Minister Strauss had a 'War Scenario' (*Kriegsbildbericht*) drawn up which implicitly included the demand for a German nuclear capacity. On this report, David Schoenbaum writes:

> The unspoken line of reasoning buried in this report was that the Bundeswehr was to be armed in such a way that it would be able to trigger any nuclear retaliation made by the Allies in case of an attack, and even to undertake a preemptive strike, independently if need be. (Schoenbaum, 1968, p. 57)

C.M. Kelleher, an expert on the Strauss policy, summarises this report thus: 'Securing a direct national firing trigger that would induce nearly simultaneous American action had become imperative' (Kelleher, 1975, p. 170). Apart from Adenauer and Strauss, only a few high-ranking German officials and military officers are said to have known about the contents of this report. Even the Western Allies knew nothing about it (Schoenbaum, 1968, p. 56).

Both projects, the NATO nuclear force and the approach to a national nuclear option, were doomed. As early as the summer of 1962, the German government had to face up to the fact that its room for manoeuvre was limited: in July 1962 Kennedy arranged for the dismissal of NATO's commander-in-chief, Lauris Norstad, West Germany's most important ally in the nuclear option question. This destroyed all Bonn's hopes of becoming a fourth NATO nuclear weapons power.

On 10 October 1962 *Der Spiegel* published a secret memorandum revealing information on a preemptive strike and thus touched off what was called the 'Spiegel Affair', as a result of which Franz Josef Strauss was forced to announce his resignation. A number of facts support the assumption that the United States was not just an innocent bystander in this affair or in the resulting downfall of Germany's defence minister (Brandstetter, 1989, pp. 300–3). It can be taken for granted that in 1962 it was not only the publisher of *Der Spiegel* but the White House too that was interested in eliminating this minister politically. The downfall of Strauss and the subsequent resignation of Adenauer in 1963 took the edge off the German desire for nuclear equality.

After the turbulence of 1962, the US began in 1963 to force through the Multilateral Force (MLF), a compromise project which was intended to satisfy the Germans and at the same time protect American interests and make the NPT project acceptable. It was also aimed at burying the hatchet on what in 1962 appeared to be irreconcilable differences: the NPT project and a German share in a nuclear weapons force.

1963/4: The Test Ban Treaty and the MLF

In Moscow the 'Treaty on the banning of nuclear weapon testing in the atmosphere, in outer space, and under water' was signed on 5 August 1963. The governments of Moscow, Washington and London were determined to follow up this treaty as soon as possible with a global NPT. For Bonn, it was this point which triggered certain reservations against signing the Test Ban Treaty (TBT): on close examination, German-American negotiations on Germany's signature to the TBT reveal themselves as part of the bilateral controversy about an NPT.

At the same time, the US offered its NATO partners, particularly West Germany, a share in the nuclear fleet of the MLF. The purpose of this step was to reduce the temptation for the German government to move towards Franco-German cooperation and to prevent it following the course taken by de Gaulle. Both approaches, the MLF and the TBT negotiations, were followed simultaneously. On the day after the appointment of diplomat Livingston T. Merchant as chief negotiator for the MLF, Kennedy stepped up negotiations on the TBT, reasoning that a breakthrough in this matter would also considerably increase the chances for non-proliferation (*NYT*, 1 January 1963).

After the signing of the Test Ban Treaty, the MLF and the NPT began to develop into complementary elements within America's overall non-proliferation policy. Germany's accession to the NPT was intended to establish the limited character of the nuclear fleet and to smooth the diplomatic path of the MLF project vis-à-vis Moscow. The promised share in the nuclear force was meant to make the FRG's accession to the NPT easier for Bonn. 'The US realized in 1961/2 that it was going to have a hard time if it came here and demanded our accession to the NPT. The United States viewed the MLF as a move to make the NPT more acceptable', a former official of the Auswärtige Amt explained later (author's interview with Dr Lothar Lahn, 26 January 1989). Thus the intention of the nuclear fleet was to bridge contradictory concepts in the German–American relationship. The MLF had no meaning beyond this, either in terms of NATO, or in terms of the NPT.

The Quarrel over Signing the TBT

In May 1963 British Foreign Minister Alec Douglas-Home suggested the linking of TBT and NPT diplomacy (Barnes, 1976, p. 178). During the closing phase of the Moscow TBT talks, US negotiator Averell Harriman presented a draft of a non-proliferation treaty (Schlesinger, 1965, p. 774), but this initiative did not succeed. Nevertheless, when signing the TBT, the secretary of state of the US, and the foreign ministers of the Soviet Union and Great Britain had already reached an agreement on the realisation of further disarmament control projects, including the NPT. It was the effect of setting a precedent that worried the German government. The doubts about accession to the TBT were not aimed at 'the TBT itself, but rather at possible further steps in the field of the restriction of armaments' (Haftendorn, 1974, p. 132).

For the Federal Republic, the ABC renunciation of 1954 was consolidated and extended through accession to the TBT. The treaty prohibited, in general, any carrying out of or support for nuclear tests in the atmosphere, a condition that affected the possibility of any kind of participation in the Force de Frappe.

During the TBT debates, a more US-oriented and French-oriented grouping began to develop within Germany's Christian Democratic Union/Christian Social Union (CDU/CSU). One of the supporters of accession to the treaty was Gerhard Schröder, who issued a warning about the impact of isolationism within the Western Alliance. Strauss, on the other hand, compared the Test Ban Treaty to the Munich Agreement of 1938 (Bandulet, 1970, p. 214), while Heinrich Krone repeatedly noted in his diary the keyword 'Versailles' (Krone, 1974, p. 177). According to Adenauer, the Kremlin wanted 'to tie the Federal Republic down to the Soviet Union, the Americans, and the British in such a way that another obstacle would be erected between us in order to prevent any possible use of atomic weapons on our part' (Osterheld, 1986, p. 242).

The focus of public criticism was the fact that the TBT also needed the signature of East Germany, thus threatening to consolidate the status quo of a divided Germany. This criticism, however, did not hold much water: on the one hand, it was absurd to want to absolve 'the Soviet Zone' from a disarmament pledge; on the other, there was no dearth of statements in the West declaring that East Germany's accession to the treaty would not implicitly mean an acknowledgement of the German Democratic Republic. Eventually, it was possible to get around the problem by creating three depositary governments: West Germany signed the treaty in London, Washington and Moscow, but East Germany signed the treaty only in Moscow, because the Western governments refused to recognise the German Democratic Republic.

The Federal German government was especially concerned about the way discussions had been carried out by the two other Western powers in Moscow: Bonn had not been consulted during the final stages of the three-power negotiations in Moscow, and thus found itself confronted with a fait accompli after the treaty had been signed. And if the Federal Republic of Germany had remained aloof from a signed and sealed disarmament treaty, it would have had to do so at the price of becoming totally isolated politically. The only way that Bonn could hope for any success was to try discreetly to influence the negotiation process. That this had not been possible was tolerable as far the TBT was concerned, but it was intolerable with respect to projects that had been announced which threatened to restrict Germany's field of action to a much greater extent. In return for its signature to the TBT, the German government demanded the creation of a German-American consulting mechanism that would ensure a sort of veto right for the FRG during all the debates on arms controls to follow.

This was in accord with the compromise that Germany's cabinet finally agreed on 8 August 1963 after fierce debates. The prime conditions of Germany's accession would be the Western allies' binding promise to consult with the Germans when negotiating any further East–West agreements, and the ruling out of any formal recognition of the GDR (*NYT*, 9 August 1963). These conditions formed the main topic of discussions during a seven-hour session two days later between Adenauer and the US secretary of state, Dean Rusk, 'which were in fact negotiations on the Bonn Republic's accession to the treaty'. The outcome of all this was that Dean Rusk gave his assurance that he would do his utmost to prevent any upgrading of the GDR's position, and he promised 'to consult with West Germany on any future negotiations with the Soviet Union' (*NYT*, 11 August 1963). This also meant that from now on all Western detente proposals had to be presented to the NATO Council and discussed and put to the vote among the Allied powers (*NYT*, 19 August 1963). On 16 August 1963 West Germany's Bundeskabinett agreed to accede to the treaty. In June 1964, against the opposition of the chairman of the Christian Social Union, Franz Josef Strauss, the treaty was ratified by the German Bundestag.

The new diplomatic weight that the Federal Republic had gained during the negotiations for the TBT was soon put to the test. In October 1963 the US secretary of state and the foreign ministers of the Soviet Union and Great Britain met in New York to utilise the dynamics created by the TBT in order to achieve further controls on armaments. The main topic was the question of non-proliferation (AdG, 1963, p. 10,834). With Chinese-Soviet tension raising its ugly head in the background, Andrei Gromyko in particular was pressing for the NPT, but he also stressed the point that an MLF fleet was contrary to the idea of non-proliferation (*FAZ*, 3 October 1963). The ministers' deliberations came to nothing, but that was not surprising. In the previous week, at the very same place, London's foreign minister and Washington's secretary of state had come together with Gerhard Schröder to establish a course of action for further negotiations with Moscow (AdG, 1963, p. 10824). This meeting was commented on in the *Neue Züricher Zeitung* on 29 September 1963, which stated that the task of Germany's foreign minister in New York 'was certainly not to present active and constructive assistance in the creation of a new East–West policy', whereas his partners in this discussion were especially concerned 'that the German government would neither hamper nor otherwise interfere with this policy right from the start'. After the talks between the three Western nations were concluded, it became clear to Lord Home and Dean Rusk 'just how far they could go with regard to German interests; Schröder also thought he knew the extent to which his wishes were going to be taken into consideration' (*NZZ*, 29 September 1963).

The balance of interests referred to here was typical in terms of negotiations on arms control after the TBT. The major powers stopped making attacks on each other, with Moscow concentrating on firing its rhetoric at the 'troublemakers' in Bonn and Washington trying to defend the interests of those same 'troublemakers' vis-a-vis Moscow.

The MLF and the NPT

Much has been written about the Multilateral Force. Here, for the most part it is its role with reference to the NPT controversy which is of interest. First of all, however, we need to set out some important basis facts. What was the MLF, who was interested in it, and why?

The nuclear fleet, manned by a mixture of sailors from different nations, was to be composed of 25 ships armed with 200 medium-range Polaris missiles (with a range of 2,500 miles). In September 1963 during a lecture given by Robert Bowie, the American 'inventor' of the MLF, to a group of experts from Bonn, the question 'Which nations are interested in an MLF?' was answered as follows:

> The only open supporter of the MLF is the Federal Republic of Germany. It is very likely that Italy would join in as well if a certain amount of pressure is put on it. ... The fear 'of missing the bus' might cause Great Britain to agree to accession. Belgium, the Netherlands and Luxembourg are not interested, and the negative attitude of France is common knowledge. (*Studiengruppe*, 18 September 1963, p. 6)

The financial side of the picture was worked out in line with this imbalance. In March 1963 Bonn and Washington came to an agreement 'with unexpected ease' over who was to pay what (*NYT*, 9 March 1963). The Federal Republic was prepared to assume 40 per cent of the total outlay for a period of ten years; the United States would pay between 35 and 40 per cent; the rest of the NATO partners involved would share the remaining 20–25 per cent. This meant that participation in the MLF from the point of view of both personnel and operations would be allocated in proportion to the costs involved. In other words, some 3,000 of the 7,500 crew members were to come from the Bundeswehr, and up to ten atomic vessels were to be put under German command (*NYT*, 9 March 1963).

Nevertheless, the German-American negotiations were fairly complicated, because Washington and Bonn were following different lines as far as the nuclear fleet was concerned. For the Federal Republic of Germany, after America's offers in December 1957 and the Norstad Plan of 1960, the MLF was a third attempt at securing influence over a medium-range nuclear potential and to realise at least some of the basic elements of the Norstad Plan, which had provided for a complete division of control over medium-range US missiles. Thus Germany's MLF policy concentrated on the question of decentralising control of nuclear clearance procedures in order to loosen America's hold on a nuclear monopoly by introducing alternatives, such as a majority vote or a European option.

For the American government, the MLF project was, for the most part, chiefly an element of Washington's non-proliferation policy. It was the intention that this scheme would satisfy the nuclear demands of the Federal Republic and provide safeguards against the supposed danger of either an independent or a Franco-German nuclear power. In a memo to Dean Rusk, the director of ACDA, Adrian Fisher, wrote:

> It is our understanding that the decision to move forward with the MLF was not a decision at variance with our non-proliferation policy but rather was intended to supplement our non-proliferation policy in the light of the growing nuclear ambitions of the Federal Republic of Germany. (Brandstetter, 1986, p. 221)

Around these basic principles, groups with different and competitive views once more began to form in both capitals, and their various differing influences had a considerable impact on the course of the discussions on the MLF and the NPT. This turned the atomic project into a 'most complex issue of tactics and timing' (Seaborg and Loeb, 1987, p. 95). Within the American government, in 1963/4 rivalry had developed between the 'European Group' in the State Department and the 'Atlantic Group' in the Defence Department (Clausen, 1973, pp. 64–6). The representatives of the 'European' wing (George Ball, Walt W. Rostow, Roy Kohler, Robert Schaetzel, Robert Bowie, Gerald Smith, Livingston Merchant and others) formed the true core of the 'MLF lobby'. Their philosophy was oriented towards the concepts of Jean Monnet: they saw in the integration of Europe the real solution to the German problem, and so they pleaded for an equal-rights partnership between a united Western Europe and the US. For them, the MLF was the starting point for achieving a realisation of the European idea. In their eyes the US nuclear veto was merely an interim solution.

The opposite point of view was taken by the group gathered around the American secretary of defense, Robert McNamara. Its members wanted to avoid the appearance of a second strategic centre within NATO and so they tried to maintain America's nuclear hegemony at almost all costs. For them, the guarantee of an American veto took priority over all other Alliance considerations.

The MLF estimations in Bonn varied according to this wide range of American opinions. Those who were critical of the MLF came chiefly from the Gaullist wing of the CDU and CSU. Adelbert Weinstein, an intimate of Strauss and a news analyst for the *FAZ*, believed that the MLF was 'unnecessary' and 'unfit' from the military point of view to ease tensions between West Germany and the US. The MLF would strengthen the American monopoly and would only mislead people into believing in a 'fiction concerning the participation of other Atlantic states' (*FAZ*, 6 May 1963). From 1963 onwards, there was in addition a fear within Germany's Auswärtige Amt – later expressed openly in public – that the NPT would be part and parcel of the MLF. Franz Josef Strauss declared on 30 November 1965 that 'the greatest of care must be taken with the MLF ... because the acceptance of a physical solution should not be combined with the agreement to place a German signature on the Non-Proliferation Treaty' (*VBT*, 30 November 1965, p. 208).

Last but not least, the German critics of the MLF – following the line of de Gaulle – saw the force as 'an element for splitting up Europe because it is an obstruction to nuclear cooperation within Europe' (Huyn, 1966, p. 229). And it is true that the sheer cost of the MLF had already rendered Bonn's parallel subsidising of the Force de Frappe almost impossible.

In Bonn, the advocates of the nuclear fleet (especially Schröder, von Hassel and Carstens, but also including Erhard) had more confidence in their friends in the State Department. In their opinion, the MLF was only the beginning of a development that promised to increase not only the status but also the security of the Federal Republic. The FRG's share of the nuclear pie was viewed as a pledge that the country would have more influence in nuclear decisions. Moreover, through closer links with the US, it was hoped that the credibility of nuclear deterrence would be restored (Mahncke, 1972, pp. 157–9). The specific deterrent factor of the MLF was based on an assumption that was mentioned only behind closed doors, even within the ministries in Bonn: it was taken for granted that the great share West Germany had in the MLF would be interpreted by Moscow as posing a special risk to them because the Soviet Union thought that the Germans were capable of almost anything. This psychological factor of uncertainty, the worries that, in the event of a crisis, the Germans might ignore American scruples or hindrances, would in practice increase the effect of nuclear deterrence (author's interview with Franz Krapf, 20 April 1989). In Moscow such calculations were indeed being made; that was one reason for the fierce Soviet resistance to this issue.

The active phase of the German-American MLF negotiations began early in 1963 and saw a change in priorities in Washington and Bonn in the autumn of the same year. At first, the US had pretty well pushed the German government into supporting the nuclear fleet. Later, the drive came from the other side. One important factor that influenced the intensification of the American MLF policy was the relationship between Bonn and Paris. In January 1963 de Gaulle had offered the Germans the opportunity to decide what sort of weapons they wanted to control (*EA* 4/63, p. D94). Some days later the Franco-German Friendship Treaty was signed in Paris, and as far as the question of nuclear cooperation was concerned, it 'obviously was quite deliberate in giving a great deal of leeway for interpretation' (*FAZ*, 24 January 1963). The MLF concept was not simply recommended to West Germany, it was prescribed to them as an American cure-all for all kinds of French illnesses.

In May 1963 the Franco-German treaty was modified by the addition of the German preamble which gave priority to the transatlantic partnership over and above that of the French and the Germans. After that, the danger that France and West Germany would slowly drift away from Washington seemed to have passed, and so America's interest in the MLF lessened. In the course of the discussions concerning the Test Ban Treaty, diplomatic probings with respect to the NPT began to intensify. From the American point of view, the MLF increasingly took on the function of a placebo 'undertaken to reconcile Germany to the existence of a Soviet-American dialogue', according to Alastair Buchan (Buchan, 1964, p. 14), 'thus paving the way for broader non-dissemination agreements', as Timothy Stanley added (Stanley, 1965, p. 238).

The MLF/NPT package deal was accepted in principle by Bonn, but soon the tide turned in favour of the MLF – no NPT without the MLF. The new German government's treatment of the NPT was demonstrated by an episode that took place in December 1963. On the evening before the NATO conference in Paris, during the traditional meeting of 'the Four', a sharp controversy developed between the German foreign minister, his American counterpart Dean Rusk, and the French and British foreign ministers de Murville and Butler. Gerhard Schröder explained to his colleagues 'quite emphatically that we would not sign any treaty on the non-proliferation of atomic weapons if our participation in a Western powers nuclear weapons system was not guaranteed beforehand' (*Der Spiegel*, 41/1965). When Ludwig Erhard visited the US shortly afterwards, the talks there were also about Germany's interest in the MLF, 'and its realisation before any negotiations with the East concerning agreements on the non-proliferation of nuclear weapons take place' (*FAZ*, 30 December 1963).

What had been at first little more than polite interest in the MLF had blossomed over the years into a fully fledged demand on the part of the troika of Erhard, Schröder and von Hassel. There were two main reasons for this development. First of all, it was becoming increasingly clear that the MLF was the maximum Washington would be prepared to offer with regard to the stabilising of East–West relations. Second, the MLF had become an instrument of German NPT diplomacy because Moscow had made the establishment of a non-proliferation agreement conditional on the renunciation of the nuclear fleet. Theo Sommer noted that the German government saw that 'the only possibility it had to influence negotiations on the NPT ... lay in tireless but tiresome persistence' on the MLF (Sommer, 1967, p. 32).

Accession to the NPT would be made much easier for the German government if, beforehand, the nuclear fleet project was confirmed, wrote Erhard in what was still quite a polite tone to President Johnson in the summer of 1964 (Schwartz, 1983, p. 117). Much blunter were the words of Germany's ambassador to the US, Knappstein, to the American secretary of state in the autumn of 1966: 'He emphasised that [the] FRG cannot consider participation in [the] NPT unless nuclear problems of alliance have found [a] satisfactory solution' (DoS IV, AdV).

From the German point of view, the MLF was meant not only to strengthen its own nuclear role but also to prevent the superpowers reaching any agreements in Geneva at the expense of the FRG. Bonn believed that it could rely on the American government because the US placed more value upon its relationship with Bonn than it did upon its agreement with Moscow.

The Nuclear Fleet Runs aground

In April 1964 President Johnson decided, in spite of advice to the contrary from his Arms Control and Disarmament Agency, to give priority to the MLF and to push it through even at the expense of the NPT (Seaborg and Loeb, 1987, p. 99). Two months later, he and Erhard agreed to sign the MLF treaty as early as December 1964, during the NATO Council conference if possible. They agreed on the precondition that, apart from the US and the FRG, at least one other NATO partner should be a party to the treaty (Seaborg and Loeb, 1987, p. 102).

The search for such a third supporting country was more difficult than expected. By the end of September, the first probings to explore a possible German-American effort to go it alone were undertaken at the request of Bonn. The treaty was to be signed by Bonn and Washington, but its ratification was made dependent upon the accession of other partners (Grewe, 1979, p. 624). At this stage, however, the West German diplomats who were urging on the entire matter made a faux pas from which the MLF project would never recover. Without waiting for the American statement on the proposals, on 6 October 1964 Erhard opened the debate on the option of a German-American MLF – and he did so publicly. 'This direct assault blew sky-high what had up to that point been merely the reticence of our allies', wrote Henry Kissinger (Kissinger, 1965, p. 160).

Already the great number of declarations from Bonn that should any commands concerning the use of nuclear weapons within the MLF be given, it would accept an American veto only as an interim solution, and that it would try to have this right to veto replaced as soon as possible by a 'majority vote', had most certainly created alarm in Western Europe. A German-American attempt to go it alone was considered a prime NATO detonator and represented an irrevocable step 'toward putting a West German finger on the atomic trigger' (*NYT*, 7 October 1964). On 8 October Germany's chancellor was given to understand in a secret and urgent dispatch from President Johnson that it should not 'be permitted' for either side to present the MLF as a German-American joint venture (Erhard Nachlass, 1st file 19/1). In the same month Norway and Denmark, which had remained neutral up to that point, embarked on a course of opposition to the MLF.

For France, the Erhard announcement was the straw that broke the camel's back and initiated a furious anti-MLF campaign. Paris began to follow the Soviet line of reasoning, which contended that the project would not satisfy the nuclear appetite of the Germans but would actually whet it. France declared that the MLF was not in accord with the Franco-German Treaty of 1963, and it threatened to withdraw from NATO should the MLF become fact (Seaborg and Loeb, 1987, pp. 103–4). In Britain, the chances for the MLF were not very rosy since the Labour Party had won the election in October 1964. The British arms control policy had been given new impetus by this change in government. For the first time in the history of Great Britain, a Minister for Disarmament, Lord Chalfont, and an 'Arms Control and Disarmament Research Unit' were set up within the country's Foreign Ministry.

British resistance to the MLF tended to be different from that raised in France. After years of quiet diplomacy, France had openly affronted the Federal Republic with its declaration that the setting up of a nuclear fleet would end Franco-German cooperation. The British government, whose opposition to the MLF was no less sharp than that of France, tried to resolve the problem in a diplomatic way by offering alternative proposals – which, however, did not have very much in common with the original MLF project. For example, in the British plan for an 'Atlantic Nuclear Force' (ANF), which was presented at the end of 1964, the nuclear fleet project was clearly subordinate to London's main interests; namely, the containment of the proliferation of nuclear weapons. This was clear in the annex to the British ANF proposal of December 1964, which was handed over to the German government in a 'top secret' German translation on 14 December 1964. In this annex, not only was there no attempt to establish an independent European atomic power without a US or British right to veto, but there appeared a solemn declaration with respect to the Irish resolution, which read very much like the later Sections I and II of the NPT.

This alarming proposal from London reached the German government the evening before the NATO Conference of Ministers in Paris was to be held, a meeting that was meant to provide the framework for the signing of the MLF treaty. But in the space of a few weeks the situation had changed considerably. Germany's ambassador to NATO, Wilhelm Grewe, later spoke of 'sharp clashes' during the NATO meeting, as well as a 'battle of words' (Grewe, 1979, pp. 626–7). The reporters covering the events at that time called the meeting a 'black day for the German delegation' (Brandstetter, 1989, pp. 390–1). In the final report of the NATO conference, the MLF was not mentioned at all, whereas the 'importance of preventing the spread of nuclear weapons' was stressed for the first time.

French and British resistance to the MLF had also caused America's interest in the MLF to wane, because it was the purpose of a nuclear fleet to strengthen NATO and not to destroy it. In December 1964

President Johnson issued an internal order in Washington that put an end to the MLF project: all the representatives of the American government were enjoined not to take any leading role in this area; not to propagate any American plans, but to follow lines of the greatest possible consensus that would create what the Allies wanted. ... This was more than enough to ensure any further activities along these lines would be to no purpose. (Grewe, 1979, p. 627)

Nevertheless, the 'continued efforts' that were being made with the MLF obstructed the great powers from reaching consensus on a non-proliferation treaty up to the autumn of 1966. 'The Germans are watching us like hawks to see whether we are letting them down on this', wrote President Johnson's security consultant, Bundy, in a letter to the president on 16 December 1964 (Seaborg and Loeb, 1987, p. 129). President Johnson wanted to see the MLF dead and buried, but he did not want to go down in history as its murderer. Now there began some double-dealing which the German government only began to see through at the end of 1965. The de facto sinking of the MLF – at the beginning of 1965 President Johnson closed the special MLF office of the State Department – was accompanied by rhetoric that disclaimed the end of the atomic fleet. As a ghost fleet, the MLF remained part of West Germany's negotiations, whose aim was to hinder the NPT wherever it could.

1965/6: The Quarrel in NATO over the NPT Draft

On 16 October 1964 the People's Republic of China detonated its first atomic bomb in Sinkiang. This event increased the international importance of the non-proliferation issue, and it changed the focal point of the US's non-proliferation policy. From now on, this policy was no longer aimed at the Western European situation alone, it was also aimed at the remaining nuclear candidates: India, Japan, Indonesia, Israel and Sweden.

John Foster, director of the ACDA, noted that the Chinese atomic bomb test resulted in a 'reassessment of priorities'. But still stronger efforts were required if these new priorities were to be realised: 'A delay of a year or so, or perhaps even of months, in the implementation of measures bearing on the nuclear proliferation problem could well mean the difference between failure and success.' The most important instrument of non-proliferation was the NPT, however (Foster, 1965, p. 600). Within the government, this opinion was supported by the Defense Department and the Atomic Energy Commission, but it was rejected by the State Department. It gained a great deal of significance during the summer of 1965, however.

Robert Kennedy, brother of the recently assassinated US president, urged 'immediate action' to be taken with regard to non-proliferation, as a matter of 'central priority' (DAS, III, pp. 232 ff.). In the internal report of the so-called Gilpatric Committee – a 'Task Force on Preventing the Spread of Nuclear Weapons' which had been created by President Johnson – it was recommended that the MLF project be dropped if this was the only way to achieve the NPT, according to the *New York Times* (*NYT*, 1 July 1965). In the summer of 1965 the MLF/NPT issue had also been the main topic during the debates of the UN Committee on Disarmament which met in New York to discuss the problem of non-proliferation. It was agreed by majority vote to continue negotiations, the chief aim being the adoption of the NPT during the Eighteen-Nations Disarmament Conference (ENDC) in Geneva (Shaker, 1976, p. 93). Against this background, the German government was greatly alarmed by this shift of opinion on the part of the United States. Its diplomatic retaliation followed immediately.

The Interview Bombshell
On 2 July 1965 the German government published for the first time the conditions under which it would be prepared to sign the NPT. In an interview, Foreign Minister Gerhard Schröder responded to a question on the subject as follows:

> I think that some form of nuclear organisation must be found which satisfies the security requirements of the non-atomically armed NATO members in the face of the more than 700 Soviet medium-range ballistic missiles aimed at Europe. If this can be achieved by the establishment of a multilateral atomic deterrence force or something similar, Germany could abstain from the acquisition of its own nuclear weapons vis-à-vis its allies. Should the Soviet Union be prepared, as we wish and hope it will be, to agree to take appreciable and irrevocable steps towards the reunification of Germany in freedom, this would make possible the accession of a unified Germany to a global agreement. (*Bulletin*, 9 July 1965)

In other words, the German government was not prepared to extend its 1954 renunciation of the production of atomic weapons to cover the renouncing of the purchase of atomic weapons if it was to receive nothing in return. Second, Germany would consider the renunciation of such purchases with NATO only if the MLF or a comparable institution had been established beforehand. Third, Bonn was prepared to renounce the purchase of atomic weapons with regard to the Soviet Union ('worldwide agreement') only if the latter made some considerable concessions with regard to German reunification.

This came as no surprise to Washington, London or Paris. Schröder had already presented these conditions to a small circle during the preliminaries to the NATO conference of December 1963. The only item which was new was that now an open, public threat was being made on the consequences of eliminating the MLF.

Exactly what consequences were implied depended on how one interpreted Schröder's speech. The anxiety about Germany's reaching out for the bomb was not relieved but reactivated. Someone who did not want to rule out the acquisition of atomic weapons could at least take this possibility into consideration. The international media reacted accordingly. 'Bonn Declares Right to Acquire Nuclear Arsenal' was the headline of the *New York Times* on 13 July 1963. 'Bonn Threatens to Buy Bomb' appeared on the first page of *The Times*. The British Prime Minister indicated that 'should there be further nuclear proliferation, more than one member state ... would have to undergo a painful re-evaluation of its own position within the Alliance'. The German press interpreted the interview as being an 'indirect threat that Germany might possibly purchase its own atomic weapons' (*FNP*, 13 July 1965; *SZ*, 14 July 1965).

Were Schröder's words to be regarded as a faux pas in terms of foreign policy, and nothing more than a top-heavy hint which was doomed to failure from the start? This is not very likely.

By mid-1965 Bonn realised that all its nuclear hopes were being wrecked. Since the victory of the Labour Party in the elections the previous year, Britain no longer concealed its preference for an NPT, and in June 1965 London presented to the NATO Council a first draft of the treaty which threatened to narrow considerably the possibility of achieving any collective nuclear solution. In the United States, such MLF opponents as Foster and Robert Kennedy were on the advance and they would obviously rather risk an erosion in NATO relations than accept the failure of the NPT. The Schröder statement was intended to stop this trend and at the same time ensure that any NPT without the MLF would be ruled out in the future too. But what weighty arguments could Bonn toss upon the scales in order to achieve this target? The driving force behind the American MLF policy had, for the most part, been the fear of a German or a Franco-German bomb. As early as 1963, high-ranking German authorities had given the American Embassy in Bonn to understand 'that if the MLF initiative failed, West Germany might be forced to seek parity with Britain and France' (quoted in Schwartz, 1983, p. 112). Even in December 1964, a State Department report had mentioned 'that without some sort of collective nuclear force West Germany would now probably go nuclear on its own' (quoted in Schwartz, 1983, p. 120). Bonn could thus be absolutely certain that the declaration on the conditions of its renunciation would be interpreted as a heavy hint: West Germany's nuclear energy programme had developed to such an extent that this bore out the underlying message of Schröder's statements.

This calculated provocation was successful. Shortly after publication of the interview, Secretary of State Dean Rusk in a meeting with Herr Knappstein, the German ambassador to the US, dissociated himself from the publicised conclusions of the Gilpatric Report (BPA, 12 July 1965). Some days later the declaration was also discussed at a top-level American government meeting which had been called for the purpose of setting policy for the coming ENDC conference. 'Remarkable at this meeting was the extent to which the MLF continued to be a sticking point in the formulation of a US negotiating stance', noted Glenn Seaborg, a participant at this meeting (Seaborg and Loeb, 1987, pp. 157–8).

The fact that the MLF attracted such attention in diplomatic circles was indeed remarkable. Even Ludwig Erhard had to concede during a press conference some weeks before the interview with Schröder that the atomic fleet 'was not dead, but at the moment not the most up-to-date of topics' (BPA, 18 June 1965). Given this background, how can one explain the importance accorded to the MLF in the Schröder interview? And why did Washington fall into line?

The American position was influenced by two considerations. On the one hand, the prospect of winning the Soviets round was not totally ruled out (Seaborg and Loeb, 1987, p. 159); on the other, the United States wanted to prevent the predictable breakdown in German-American relations should the MLF be renounced. In addition, the Americans were convinced that Bonn would not be a party to a Non-Proliferation Treaty which did not include a Multilateral Force.

In Bonn, all hope of bringing the MLF Treaty to a rapid conclusion had indeed been given up since the end of 1965. Now the German government was mainly interested in maintaining a legal option – something which had been the case for years with respect to German reunification. It was not known just when and how a nuclear fleet would be established, but nobody was prepared to surrender the underlying legal basis for this. Furthermore, the acronyms NPT and MLF had become symbols for what up to that point had become the most important conflict of priorities in America's European policy. Which should be given first priority: the interests of the ally Germany, or an agreement with Moscow? The Schröder interview had managed to give strength to the primacy of German-American relations for a certain period of time, but now a quarrel with Great Britain was in the offing.

The Debacle in Geneva

Great Britain was fighting against the MLF and against every attempt to achieve a European option. It preferred the proposal of the Nuclear

Planning Group and the rapid conclusion of the NPT (Neustadt, 1970, p. 12). The Federal Republic of Germany took the opposite point of view; the United States was looking for a compromise solution. In June 1965 British and German views collided during a meeting of the NATO Council. The United States had sided with Bonn. An exchange of diplomatic notes between London and Washington followed, which Dean Rusk characterised as being 'sharply critical': 'Rusk commented that NATO had never been confronted with so sharp a disagreement between the U.S. and the U.K.' (Seaborg and Loeb, 1987, pp. 1158–9).

On 26 July 1965, the day before the opening of the disarmament conference in Geneva, another fierce exchange occurred in the NATO Council. In the wake of the Council session, Great Britain had stressed its determination to present the British NPT draft in Geneva, if necessary in a go-it-alone attempt (*NYT*, 26 July 1965). But the British paper was criticised so heavily in Paris that London gave up its plan. The conference was now to be continued in Geneva, with the goal of reaching a joint Western NPT draft. On the day the ENDC convened, the United States, Great Britain, Canada and Italy formed a drafting committee in Geneva which, after three weeks of negotiations, was not able to arrive at a joint draft treaty: the draft preferred by the United States was not supported by the other Allies. At best it would be accepted as a basis for further negotiations (*NYT*, 14 August 1965). The American proposal was presented to the NATO Council again on 16 August 1965 and in spite of the previously mentioned resistance, it was presented in Geneva by the US on 17 August 1965. The quarrel was over the European option: the British government wanted to prevent both the possibility of turning the nuclear fleet into a European nuclear force at a later date and the subjecting of a decision on the use of nuclear weapons to a majority vote. London would be willing to support an MLF clause in a Non-Proliferation Treaty only on condition that either Great Britain or the United States would have the final say in decisions on the use of weapons. Bonn, however, was unwilling to accept this position. A nuclear force with such a structure would perpetuate the situation that had existed since the establishment of NATO and would only intensify the prohibitions on the non-nuclear-weapons states. Instead of this – following the German government's line of negotiation – 'the building up of a Multilateral Nuclear Force ... had to be given priority. Via a European proviso, the possibility should be kept open that the atomic fleet could be transformed into a "European" fleet as soon as progress in Western European integration has been made' (*FAZ*, 6 August 1965).

It was not easy for this point of view to be fleshed out in Geneva. The Federal Republic was not a member of the ENDC; it only had the role of observer in Geneva. Nevertheless, Bonn's special ambassador, Swidbert Schnippenkoetter, succeeded in part at least. 'Vigorous opposition from West Germany' had caused the United States to dismiss British worries, according to the *New York Times*: 'In a surprise feature, the proposed treaty goes beyond past concepts of a NATO force by providing for the creation of a nuclear force under exclusive European control' (*NYT*, 18 August 1965). Indeed, the United States's proposal had not ruled out the build-up of a multilaterally controlled MLF. And it had allowed a Western European federation of states to control those atomic weapons through a majority vote to which France or Great Britain would be willing to contribute at the price of giving up their nuclear sovereignty (DoD, 1965, pp. 369–71). The British delegate, Lord Chalfont, had already distanced himself from the US proposal in Geneva; the Soviet Union called it a joke, and in the *New York Times* it was characterised as 'Debacle at Geneva' (18 August 1965).

The German government did not welcome the American proposal either. Its statement stressed primarily the relationship between disarmament and the German Question and, second, the German 'advance concession' of 1954. Only in third place did it add that the NPT draft – thanks to German influence – was an 'important contribution' to the solution to this problem (DAS III, p. 274). A cooler statement could not have been made.

The internal assessment of the situation was even gloomier. A report (classified as 'secret') on 24 August 1965 from the inspector-general of the Bundeswehr, Heinz Trettner, to Defence Minister von Hassel, listed the following MLF/NPT alternatives:

[A Non-Proliferation Treaty without an MLF Treaty] 'Situation unfavourable. Danger of the isolation of Germany through non-accession, even should the FRG be prepared vis-à-vis its allies to make a declaration similar in content to that of the NPT. The Soviet Union would then have Germany's nuclear renunciation without having to give anything in return.

[An NPT and MLF Treaty] FRG increases its security and political importance. Potential nuclear-weapon states acceding to the treaty would not get nuclear weapons on a national basis. The Soviet Union would have Germany's nuclear renunciation without having to give anything in return.

[Neither an NPT nor an MLF Treaty] Some potential nuclear-weapons states will develop national atomic weapons and that would have a negative influence on the political importance of Germany. The FRG would maintain a certain amount of freedom in the nuclear field which would be more or less a theoretical point over the next few years. Soviet interest in Germany's nuclear renunciation would be maintained and might be used for purposes of reunification of the two Germanys.

[An MLF Treaty without an NPT] The FRG increases its security and political importance. There would be continued Soviet interest in Germany's nuclear renunciation. Additional nuclear-weapons states, however, would relativise Germany's political importance.

[Conclusions] Very important for the FRG that a solution to the problem be reached within the Alliance as well as that Soviet interest in Germany's nuclear renunciation be maintained. ... It seems to be of importance that, outwardly, the FRG appears not to be a troublemaker, thus lending weight to Soviet propaganda. (NHP IV)

The Trettner comment is a revealing one in various respects. First of all, it is remarkable that in August 1965 an MLF treaty was still on the agenda for the highest-ranking military officers. They tried to gain time and were of the opinion that an agreement on an NPT was 'not very likely at present' because of the attitude of the non-aligned countries and the Warsaw Pact countries in Geneva – all of which meant that there still was a chance of reviving the atomic fleet. Second, it was clear that the Germans considered the establishment of further nuclear-weapon states quite likely should the NPT fail. In spite of all this, however, they preferred the fourth alternative: an MLF without an NPT. Third, the statement of the inspector-general proved that the Federal Republic would have to pay the price of isolation if it remained aloof from an NPT that had already been accepted. The German attitude towards the NPT depended on a contradictory position: although it was in the interest of Germany that the NPT should fail, Bonn did not want to be seen as a troublemaker. Only one person was prepared to assume this risk: Konrad Adenauer.

Adenauer's Thunderbolt

While the German government was very careful in the way it expressed its unease over America's NPT policy, Adenauer, the 89-year-old chairman of the CDU, used sledge-hammer tactics. His well-timed appearance on 19 August 1965 during the election campaign proved to be a general criticism of what was happening in Geneva. That, according to Adenauer, was a tragedy for us Germans ... the American proposal is so outrageous, so horrible, that in the long run, Europe will be handed over to the Russians. ... I hope that we will never be confronted with such a government that will accede to a treaty like the one the Americans are proposing now. (DAS III, p. 277)

Such fundamental criticism could not be, and was not, ignored by the public throughout the world. The BBC commented that such utterances were 'grist to the mills of the Communists ... moreover, some people might ask about where Germany really stands, and what it really intends to do'. The American media came out with such expressions as 'anger', 'annoyance' and 'misgivings'. London's press editorials expressed 'astonishment' and 'regret' (BBC, 20 August 1965, according to the BPA–*Pressespiegel*). Commentaries in the Federal Republic did not display such conformity: those daily papers closest to Germany's political opposition said that it was a 'tragic and sad arabesque' that Adenauer was criticising the Americans just now, as they had clearly backed the German position in Geneva (*FR*, 2 September 1965). The conservative *Frankfurter Allgemeine Zeitung* followed a different line: it thought that the criticism of Adenauer was exaggerated, but described it as 'likely to be useful' and stressed the fact that a very desirable division of labour might result

between that party which ... has a wide range of action and the government whose actions are always limited by certain considerations. This range of action could be enlarged considerably if the government was at times able to point its finger indirectly at that party, thus making clear to its partners outside the necessary allowances it was having to make internally. (*FAZ*, 24 August 1965)

This interpretation was not without some logic. While he was chancellor, Konrad Adenauer had on more than one occasion used internal conflicts to achieve what he wanted in foreign policy. But it would be wrong to dismiss this outcry of Adenauer's as being nothing more than adroit tactical manoeuvring. The ex-chancellor and his friends did not want to strengthen the bargaining position of Germany's foreign minister: what they wanted was to stop the NPT. In this respect, Adenauer's statement was also proof of existing differences within the ranks of the CDU. For those German 'Gaullists', the wording of the MLF proposal as presented in Geneva was of no importance because they no longer saw any chance of achieving any adequate nuclear influence through the MLF. The members of the

'Atlantic Group' gathered around Schröder and von Hassel were also not supporters of the NPT, although they were very interested in the MLF. They speculated that Germany's nuclear renunciation could at least be used in favour of a multilateral atomic force.

After Germany's national elections on 19 September 1965, the inner-party split between the 'Gaullists' and the 'Atlantic Group' began to widen. The debate in the newly elected Bundestag demonstrated that the 'Erhard position' on the MLF – a keystone of Germany's foreign and security policies – did not have a majority in parliament. It was not just a question of the 'Gaullist' criticism as presented by Franz Josef Strauss: the FDP, a coalition partner in the government, was now clearly lining itself up alongside SPD opposition to the atomic fleet (*VBT*, 29 November 1965, p. 118).

More than ever, the most substantial support for the MLF option was to be found in Washington, where Chancellor Erhard, together with his two ministers Schröder and von Hassel, and under-secretary Carstens, paid a visit in December 1965. According to a CDU member of parliament, Kurt Birrenbach, the results of this trip were 'not entirely satisfactory'. It was mainly Defence Minister von Hassel and to a lesser extent Foreign Minister Schröder who pleaded vigorously for the 'hardware' solution to the MLF which ran up against 'resistance from the Americans' (Birrenbach, 1984, p. 213). Nevertheless, Ludwig Erhard received a personal promise from President Johnson that the hardware option would be held open within the framework of the NPT, and the possibility of German participation in a nuclear planning group would be secured (*NYT*, 23 December 1965).

By the spring of 1966 the chances of realising the NPT had dwindled considerably. At the beginning of the year, the hopes of the American government that the Germans would be satisfied by participating in a nuclear planning group had once again been shattered. Bonn and Rome had made it quite clear that they did not consider the con-sultative body to be any kind of substitute for a hardware solution (Barnes, 1976, p. 322). In March 1966 France's withdrawal from NATO poured oil on the fire of the American dilemma. On the one hand, Germany's status within NATO was enhanced by the French withdrawal, which made the other smaller NATO partners feel uncomfortable. Could a nuclear deal with Bonn be struck without causing even greater estrangement from NATO? (*NYT*, 27 April 1966). On the other hand, Washington wanted to make sure at almost any price that the Federal Republic would be on the American side in the quarrel with France. Could the Americans risk provoking the Germans on such a sensitive issue as that of atomic weapons?

Last but not least, the Soviet Union had also rejected the modified American NPT draft which was presented to the ENDC on 22 March 1966. This followed the lines of the British concept which the United States had rejected prior to August 1965. This proposed that collective atomic weapons organisations within military alliances should be permitted within an NPT on condition that the use of the nuclear weapons should be subject to the veto of one of the nuclear-weapons states concerned (DoD, 1966, pp. 159–60). Moscow remained adamant, however. According to the Soviets' chief negotiator, Roschtschin, any transformation of a nuclear-weapons state into an alliance of nuclear-weapons states would be a contribution to the proliferation of atomic weapons and thus unsuitable as a basis for the formation of an NPT (DoD, 1966, p. 177). In the spring of 1966 Germany's commissioner for disarmament, Schnippenkoetter, was not alone in being convinced that 'the prerequisites for a global arrangement along the lines of the American NPT-draft are constantly evaporating' (*Studiengruppe*, 28 February 1966). The American side too was pessimistic in assessing the prospects for a Non-Proliferation Treaty.

Ludwig Erhard's Downfall

On 24 September 1966 the German chancellor flew to Washington again, accompanied by Schröder, von Hassel and Westrick. For the last time, the question of the MLF option was broached by the Germans. The result was that it was scrapped for good. Since September 1966 Washington had persistently attempted to send out a warning to the German government. One proof of this is a 'secret' report by the Auswärtige Amt under-secretary, Karl Carstens, on his conversation with the American ambassador to Germany, George C. McGhee. Ambassador McGhee had visited Carstens on 25 August 1966 in order to make preparations for Ludwig Erhard's trip to Washington. Carstens took this opportunity to bring up the subject of the MLF, and he pointed out that in December 1965 President Johnson had described a new proposal on German participation

as being very helpful. The ambassador replied that President Johnson had tried to talk the chancellor out of this project in a preceding discussion [which is correct]. Furthermore, they had agreed that the project could be realised only if the British joined in, but the British had made it perfectly clear in Washington that they disapproved of any form of a joint nuclear force, including the ANF which they themselves had once proposed. ... On the whole, I had the impression that the ambassador was acting under orders from Washington and wanted to make it clear to me that the Americans no longer wanted to pursue a course leading to a joint nuclear force. The ambassador repeatedly pointed out the difficulties that the president was having with Congress because of this project. (NHP V)

Later, in the file with the negotiation papers which the defence minister was given to study for the trip to Washington, it was also made clear that President Johnson wanted to drop the MLF in order to facilitate the reaching of an agreement about the NPT. But then the papers followed a line that greatly overestimated German capacities. Johnson would decide against the MLF

should he become convinced that the resolution of the nuclear problem by creating a joint nuclear force no longer played an essential role in German policymaking. ... We should, therefore, commit ourselves to the fact that the establishment of a joint nuclear force still is, and will remain, an important German policy goal, even though it might not be practicable at the moment. A purely consultative solution to the nuclear question will not give us enough influence in the long run and thus will not be satisfactory. (NHP VI)

In the same undaunted manner the Germans held tight to a linking of the MLF with the NPT wherever the NPT was not totally out of the question. Two days before Erhard's trip, the Foreign Affairs Working Group of the CDU/CSU parliamentary group published a statement on non-proliferation written by four members of the Bundestag: Majonica, Birrenbach, Baron Guttenberg and Marx. This paper

1. questioned the advisability of an NPT as a matter of principle because 'the safety and the political roles of the non-nuclear-weapons states, especially in a united Europe of the future, could be affected negatively for an unforeseeable period of time'; and
2. made Germany's accession to an NPT dependent upon the 'securing' of a joint nuclear regulation as well as 'fully guaranteeing' Germany's sole right of representation within the framework of the treaty (DUD, 22 September 1966).

Foreign Minister Schröder expressed himself in similar terms before the Bundestag on the day before the trip to the United States. Accession to an NPT was to be rejected as long as this threatened 'to narrow the right of collective self-defence in the nuclear field'. It was the very 'prerequisite for Germany's willingness to make a renunciation on the part of those states which are in need of an alliance that it act optimally in the collective deterrence of the alliance' (*VBT*, 1966, p. 2,892).

In the summer of 1965 similar allusions in the 'Schröder Interview' had had an effect. By the autumn of 1966 the Johnson administration was no longer impressed by any of this. When Erhard arrived in Washington on 24 September 1966, he was welcomed by the number two man in the State Department, George Ball. The number one, Dean Rusk, was at the time talking with his Soviet colleague Gromyko about how to reach an agreement on the basic formulation of the NPT. Germany's foreign policy had long been losing ground. Its nuclear demands echoed back and forth, unheard; history had bypassed Bonn.

On 5 October 1966, after the failure of the Erhard mission, the FDP demanded that 'some basic positions in German foreign policy would have to be reconsidered' (*VBT*, 1966, p. 2,958). On 14 October 1966 the Bundeskabinett met in a special session on foreign policy (Krone, 1974, p. 190). On 28 October 1966 the governing CDU/CSU and FDP coalition fell apart after the resignation of the FDP ministers Mende, Dahlgrün, Scheel and Bucher. A month later, Germany's chancellor also handed in his resignation. Domestic problems had contributed to Erhard's downfall but, according to one observer, the final straw was

> his [Erhard's] trip to the United States in 1966. This was the final point in a crisis-laden development which had increasingly been coming to a head. Erhard had not been able to recognise that since 1960 priorities in America's foreign policy had changed and were now mainly concentrated on balancing relations with Moscow. (Horlacher, 1969, p. 129)

The German government was aware of this change in priorities in American foreign policy but had not accepted it. The resignation of the FDP ministers at the end of the month was followed just five weeks later by the final agreement on the main article of the NPT (Barnes, 1976, p. 355).

The Agreement on Articles I and II
The agreement between the United States and the Soviet Union on a joint NPT formulation took place in the backrooms of diplomacy. We can, however, reconstruct most of the course of its development with the aid of American publications, statements made by those

present at the time and declassified governmental documents. The government documents again give proof of the key role the FRG had played in shaping America's non-proliferation policy. From the point of view of world politics, in 1966 Bonn and Moscow were antipodes in a controversy which the United States tried to smooth out through a compromise solution.

The essential course was set in July 1966. During this month, President Johnson made the establishment of the NPT one of his personal interests. In so doing he was greatly influenced by Bill Moyers, the former chief press officer of the White House who, since April 1966, had risen to become the president's most important adviser on foreign policy. Because of this, Moyers had become the focal point for all those who were in favour of the NPT and who wanted to get around the State Department, which was lending its support to the MLF project. Included among these were the directors of the ACDA, Foster and Fisher; John T. McNaughton, who worked for McNamara; and the former staff director of the Gilpatric Committee, Spurgeon Keeny. Moyers allowed himself to be convinced by their views, and in July he presented a five-page memorandum to the president which summed up what from his point of view were the main arguments for an NPT initiative on the part of the president.

First of all, the memorandum listed the possible objections to the US's giving its strong support to the NPT. Points against the treaty were: the limited range of the NPT, which when put to the test could not seriously prevent a country from producing nuclear weapons; because China and France had not signed the treaty, this could lead to a continuation of proliferation; the discriminatory character of the treaty ('A Treaty would confer on powers not possessing nuclear weapons a clear inferiority status'); the diplomatic price that would have to be paid, because of the pressure that would have to be put on Bonn as well as the risk that, against all expectations, Moscow might reject a compromise wording. Moyers went on to say:

> This proposal will be opposed by those at State who keep alive the hope of hardware for Germany. And the German government is not going to jump up and down with joy. But the MLF Club at State and the German government are not the President of the United States. If you wish to move ahead on this proposal, these are two problems which can be resolved.

More important were the arguments in favour of the NPT. As far as Moyers was concerned, these comprised a mixture of facts and election considerations. Even in Bonn the heyday of the MLF was over, while the time was fast approaching when it would no longer be possible, without the aid of an NPT, to prevent countries like Japan, Israel or India from seeking their own national nuclear option. Moreover, President Johnson's commitment to the NPT would be 'a highly popular step' at home, because the NPT ranked fourth on a list of problems which the American public considered highly urgent. In order to underline this point, Moyers stressed the positive effect of the Test Ban Treaty on Kennedy's election campaign in 1964, and drew a parallel with the Congressional elections which were to be held in November 1966:

> It would demonstrate statesmanship, especially by emphasizing ... that you are not preoccupied with Vietnam at the expense of other policies. You know my opinion that the November elections will be influenced less by our defence of Vietnam than by *large and magnanimous Presidential actions that leave a real imprint on the public mood*. [original emphasis]

Therefore he suggested putting 'the whole pile' on the 'Non-Proliferation Treaty' and to circumvent the 'European Option' problem that hampered the NPT solution:

> You could announce our willingness to agree to simplified language that would bypass the question at issue between us and the Soviet Union – the so-called 'European Clause'. This would be interpreted by the Soviets as accepting their position. For our part, we would consider the question of the 'European Clause' as a matter for future interpretation or amendment to the Treaty if that ever became necessary. (DoS I).

Ludwig Erhard and Soviet Premier Kosygin were to be notified of a corresponding decision which afterwards would be made public in a 'great' speech. Moyers's suggestion was in line with the advice given by the American Senate. In June 1966, the Senate had unanimously passed the so-called Pastore Resolution, in which President Johnson was called upon to make further efforts in support of the NPT.

Backed by their leaders, America's negotiators began to lay out the limits for compromise in secret US-Soviet talks. The breakthrough came after weeks of negotiation: on 24 September 1966 Foreign Ministers Gromyko and Rusk agreed on the key points of a joint NPT formulation. Gromyko intimated that he was prepared to accept the existing nuclear arrangements of NATO and a nuclear planning group, and that he would raise no objections to a future European option on the basis of a 'Succession of States', as long as there was no transfer of nuclear weapons to any groups of states. ('Succession of States' means that an existing nuclear-weapons state, such as France, would give up its independent nuclear position, and that a future 'European State' would assume the former legal nuclear status of France.) A working group was given the task of preparing all the details, which it was able to do in September, and the draft of Articles I and II was presented to both governments (Barnes, 1976, p. 547). According to this draft, each nuclear-weapons state was forbidden to transfer nuclear weapons or any other nuclear explosive devices or control over such weapons to a non-nuclear-weapons state 'directly or indirectly, either individually or collectively with other members of a military alliance or group of States'. In an additional internal paper, the American delegation had listed the principal Soviet concessions. Moscow was no longer explicitly opposed to the right of non-nuclear-weapons states 'to *participate* in the *control or use* of nuclear weapons'. The Soviets also dropped their previous demand to modify the word 'control' by adding the words 'any' or 'participate' (DoS III; original emphases).

At the beginning of October President Johnson called a meeting at Camp David of his closest advisers – including Rusk, McNamara, Katzenbach, Eugene Rostow, Arthur Goldenberg, Foy Kohler and Walt Rostow – in order to confer on further proceedings. It is said that the secretary of state warned against proceeding too quickly without consulting the US's allies. Johnson, too, did not want to ignore the possibility of an Allied solution to the problem. Saying that this solution 'has to be preserved because it may be necessary to keep the Germans locked in, and for many other reasons', Johnson summed up the results of these deliberations and gave corresponding orders to the secretary of state (quoted in Seaborg and Loeb, 1987, p. 193). The draft of the bilateral working group was not accepted, but at the same time Gromyko was received at the White House in order to demonstrate America's willingness to negotiate. Although President Johnson was interested in concluding the NPT as quickly as possible, for domestic reasons as much as anything, the decision made at Camp David made clear that he did not want to come to an agreement at any price before the American elections had taken place in November 1966.

The September draft of the working group was examined over and over again in the following two months, in meetings that took place on the fringes of the United Nations General Assembly. An agreement was reached on 5 December 1966, four days after Ludwig Erhard's resignation. In contrast to the wording of the September draft, no explicit mention was made of a prohibition on the transfer of nuclear weapons, etc. to groups of non-nuclear-weapons states. What was now prohibited was the transfer 'to any recipient whatsoever' – a change which did not involve the contents but the wording of the treaty, as Seaborg and Loeb point out: 'It may have outlawed the MLF but it did not rub the Germans' nose in it' (Seaborg and Loeb, 1987, p. 195). A more important change had taken place in Bonn where, that same week, the newly formed Kiesinger government had taken office. A week later the foreign minister of the Grand Coalition, Willy Brandt, was handed the exact wording of the new NPT formulation.

Although the worries about their German ally formed the crux of the Americans' negotiating strategy, the United States had not informed the German government about any details of the negotiations of the great powers, let alone consulted them. It was not an American but a Soviet diplomat who, on 20 October 1966 at the United Nations, declared that no real obstacles were left in the way of the NPT (Seaborg and Loeb, 1987, p. 194). Shortly afterwards, Herr Knappstein, Germany's ambassador to the United States, asked the US under-secretary of state, Nicholas Katzenbach, for a clarification of the issue. According to an internal report of the State Department, Knappstein laid heavy emphasis on the unchanged attitude of his government:

> Ambassador said defence of Europe took priority over accommodation of USSR which should not be allowed achieve objectives without compensation in political or security field. Such accommodation of USSR could have unpredictable political and security consequences for Germany which is directly faced by USSR. This threat is now checked by solidarity of the West. (DoS IV)

In the light of seemingly contradictory information, Knappstein wanted to know 'whether old U.S. draft continued to represent U.S. position and what limits U.S. had set on concessions'. Bonn's suspicions were hardly dispelled by Katzenbach's evasive response: in talks with Moscow, it was not compromise but 'areas of agreement' that were sought. According to Katzenbach, Washington still supported the old US draft, 'but this does not preclude search for language which correctly expresses what each side means'. Katzenbach gave repeated assurances that there would not be a treaty 'without appropriate consultation with our allies'.

Bonn's ignorance of the existing NPT agreement continued. This is demonstrated in a report that Ambassador Schnippenkoetter presented to the DGAP Studiengruppe (Study Group) at its November conference. According to Schnippenkoetter, Washington and Moscow were becoming closer only on peripheral questions concerning the NPT; the substance of their positions had not changed (Studiengruppe, 7 November 1966).

At this time the United States had quite substantially dissociated itself from the NPT draft it had presented to the Geneva Disarmament Conference in March 1966. This previous draft had, with certain conditions, permitted the sharing of nuclear control and the joint possession of nuclear warheads within a group of states. In the new draft, however, any kind of joint possession of nuclear warheads or any kind of transfer of control within a group of states was prohibited. This position did not limit existing options. It was oriented towards American legislation, which the US Congress was not very likely to change. But for Bonn, the change in the American position was highly significant insofar as the opportunities it sought were now obstructed for a longer period of time, while at the same time the way was open for a universal NPT. In contrast to Katzenbach's assertions, this bilateral compromise had become possible not because of more precise wording but because of deliberately vague language: the heart of the agreement lay in the absence of precision. The basic formula of Article I, 'not to transfer to any recipient whatsoever nuclear weapons ... or control over such weapons ... directly, or indirectly', could mean either of two things: the preservation of the 'two-key system' or its prohibition; the approval of a nuclear planning group or its rejection. As Soviet diplomats later recalled, it had been chiefly this 'constructive misunderstanding', this rough and ready formula of 'agreeing to disagree', that made the compromise possible (author's interview with Oleg Grinewski, 25 February 1988). Even more important than the text was how it was interpreted: Moscow was not willing to acknowledge the European option openly, but was willing tacitly to accept such an interpretation by the United States. Washington was not prepared to exclude the possibility of a European union of states, but it accepted the Soviet demand to dispense with any explicit formulations in the text of the treaty.

The NPT clauses which from September 1966 onwards were circulating around members of the American government for comment were accompanied by an extensive catalogue of interpretations. At the beginning of December 1966 the last and thus authoritative version of this catalogue, which was signed by Dean Rusk himself included the following points:

This draft:

1. Would not disturb existing bilateral arrangements. ...
2. Would have no bearing on the decision of the NATO allies to go to war, or on the establishment of a permanent NATO committee for nuclear planning and consultation.
3. Would not preclude the assignment to NATO of additional Polaris submarines with U.S. nuclear weapons in a manner consistent with present legislation.
4. Would not rule out the establishment of a multilateral entity in which non-nuclear-weapons states participated, and to which they made financial contributions, so long as there was no transfer to this entity of an ownership interest in nuclear warheads (as opposed to delivery vehicles) and as long as the United States retained control over the nuclear warheads. It would not bar participants in such an entity from having their own veto either on the basis of prohibiting firing from their territory or as otherwise provided by agreement.
5. Would not bar succession by a federated European state to the nuclear status of one of its former components. It would bar transfer of nuclear warhead to a European defense community not involving a new federated European state. But it would permit the formation of a European collective nuclear force, with joint ownership of delivery vehicles, as long as any participating nuclear-weapon state (U.K. or France) retained control of its nuclear warheads. (DoS V)

It is not clear if and how far these interpretations as set down by Dean Rusk had been agreed upon previously with the Soviets, or even made known to them indirectly. What is certain is that a modified version was given to the Soviet ENDC delegation in April 1967 after internal consultations in NATO, and that it was received without comment. For the NATO states these interpretations were now a binding part of NPT history and thus part of the treaty itself; what is more, for the German government they formed the implicit basis of the treaty. The Soviet Union maintained a different point of view. Oleg Grinewski, a leading Soviet participant in NPT diplomacy, has intimated that these interpretations were never a topic in the discussions between the United States and the Soviet Union. According to Grinewski, the Soviet Union would have reacted very negatively should the points mentioned above have ever been raised in open discussion. 'Legally there is no clause,' declared Grinewski in February 1988, when he was deputy foreign minister of the Soviet Union. 'No special clause was ever drawn up. It seems to me it's just interpretation' (author's interview with Oleg Grinewski, 25 February 1988).

A New Look at the Nuclear Option

The establishment of a fifth nuclear-weapons power in Asia led to the United States's intensified commitment to a non-proliferation policy which threatened to narrow German options both politically and materially. From 1965 onwards, the United States revised its orientation towards the NPT question, as well as its nuclear export policy. The controls system of the International Atomic Energy Agency (IAEA) was upgraded. The discussion on the NPT grew louder in West Germany and in the meantime the necessary steps were quietly taken to strengthen the West German position in the NPT debate, which was obviously becoming more heated. These preparations took place on three levels: in the Auswärtige Amt (Foreign Affairs Ministry) institutional structures were broadened considerably; within the German government's think-tanks preparations were made to debate the controversies that were bound to come; in the field of science and research, the building of a nuclear industry which had military as well as civilian relevance as well was forging ahead.

Preparations in the Auswärtige Amt

In the summer of 1965 the Auswärtige Amt set up a 'Subdivision for Disarmament and Arms Control'. This division was assigned to the control of the foreign minister but its head, Swidbert Schnippenkoetter, was also the disarmament commissioner of the German government and thus reported directly to the chancellor. In his double function, Schnippenkoetter was both the chief negotiator in the NPT debate and the moving force behind West Germany's strategy. By career he was a conservative and ambitious diplomat; since the mid-1950s he had been personal assistant to Walter Hallstein, whom he followed to Brussels in 1958 as chief-of-cabinet. From 1960 to 1963, he was an Embassy consul in the United States under Wilhelm Grewe. In 1963 he became a member of the planning staff of the Auswärtige Amt. Schnippenkoetter's 'subdivision' was divided into three sections: 'General Disarmament and Global Arms Controls', 'European Security and Other Regional Measures' and 'Technological, Military and Economic Questions'. The latter section was renamed in 1966: 'Safeguarding the Peaceful Employment of Nuclear Energy, Security Measures, Research and Studies'.

In order to support the new subdivision, the 'Science and Politics Foundation' (Stiftung Wissenschaft und Politik, or SWP) was established in Ebenhausen, near Munich, as an independent research institute to be responsible for questions of strategy, disarmament and arms controls. The model for the SWP was the RAND Corporation in Santa Monica, California. The foundation was subject to the control of the Office of the Federal Chancellor and was also placed at the disposal of the Auswärtige Amt as well as the disarmament commissioner (Haftendorn, 1974, pp. 87–90). All of the twelve studies which were listed in the first research plan in 1966 dealt with the complex of problems surrounding the Non-Proliferation Treaty. Marked 'for personal information only', they were given to a small circle of experts in the German government and to a few MPs.

The third and most important advisory institution in the NPT controversy was the 'Study Group (Studiengruppe) for Arms Controls, Arms Limitation and International Security', set up in 1960/1 with the help of the Auswärtige Amt. As a study group of the 'German Society for Foreign Affairs', it met under the leadership of Fritz Erler about four times a year and brought under one roof the carefully chosen German nuclear political elite of the various ministries (the Office of the Federal Chancellor, Ministry of Defence, Auswärtige Amt), the Bundestag, the Bundeswehr, several research institutes and the press. The transfer of classified material to the Studiengruppe was not permitted, but the participating government officials were allowed to talk freely about what they knew. The discussions took place in discreet groups whose minutes were confidential. The Studiengruppe was an important aid to the work within the slowly grinding machinery of government. Its conclusions are said to have been at times more influential than the dossiers of the ministries. In the Auswärtige Amt the reports of the Studiengruppe were regularly presented to the under-secretaries. Uwe Nerlich, who was a member of the SWP and also responsible to the Studiengruppe for scientific questions, saw to it that there was close cooperation between the groups.

The Nerlich/Cornides Exposé
It was Uwe Nerlich who in mid-1965 opened the long overdue conceptual debate with a widely recognised essay, 'The Nuclear Dilemmas of the Federal Republic of Germany' (Nerlich, 1965, pp. 637–50). This paper marked a turning point because it stressed an element which up till then had received virtually no recognition in the West German literary scene, in contrast to that of the English-speaking world: the special status of the Federal Republic of Germany within NATO. According to Nerlich the problems in NATO were

not the result of a nuclear 'imbalance' but the result of the weak
political position of the Federal Republic ... which rules out military
equality. ... The problems of nuclear armament ... created from
the very beginning a fundamental and inevitable dilemma which
... demonstrated, as nothing else could, the restrictions on the
political freedom of action of the Federal Republic.

This assessment was the reason for Nerlich's criticism of the lack
of 'tactical flexibility' in Germany's foreign policy – for example, over
the question of the 'Deutschland Junktim'. The international reaction
to the Schröder interview had made it clear how difficult it was to
hold 'such a weak position of imbalance' as had been the case with
the MLF. The essay underlined two points:

First of all, the Federal Republic [is] interested in keeping open a
nuclear option in order to use it as an argument in the negotiations on reunification and to prevent the non-nuclear status of the
Federal Republic from becoming fixed for all time in the event that
reunification is ruled out as a realistic possibility. Second, the
Federal Republic is interested in full participation within NATO
in the planning of nuclear strategy. (Nerlich, 1965, p. 648)

The keeping open of the nuclear option mentioned in the paper was
intended to some extent to refer to the abstract MLF formulation,
and to a much greater extent to the political necessities within
industry and science which seemed to be essential for the maintenance of an independent option.

Nerlich presented his thoughts much more clearly during a meeting
of the Studiengruppe on 15 October 1965 which dealt with the topic
'Proliferation of nuclear weapons and the nuclear options of the Federal
Republic'. This discussion was based on an exposé written by Uwe
Nerlich and Wilhelm Cornides concerning the evaluation of the
German option. The paper ended with a number of proposals which
are worth quoting in full:

1. that the FRG must avoid every formalising of the difference
    between non-nuclear and small nuclear powers, especially if
    the latter would thus be privileged in the same way as the two
    superpowers (the pentarchy element in the Foster proposal,
2. that the FRG should not strive for a rigid 'composite' (*Junktim*)
    of 'The German Question' [of reunification] and a universal
    treaty but should ensure its tactical flexibility,

3. that the FRG should strive for regional or bilateral treaties instead of universal agreements since the only real dangers of proliferation lie outside a US-Soviet confrontation and thus outside Europe,

4. that the FRG should renounce the independent or joint possession of strategic nuclear weapons at least for the duration of the American presence in Europe, provided that solutions to the structural problems of NATO begin to materialise that could effectively be used for crisis management and would therefore make the possession of atomic weapons less important,

5. that the FRG should strive, in informal and bilateral German-American arrangements, to have a say in the strategic field as long as France is not prepared to agree to integrated solutions,

6. that the FRG must keep open an option in the field of nuclear combat and deterrence weapons, or at the very least not permit their use within NATO to be blocked by a non-proliferation treaty,

7. that the FRG, in line with the model followed by India, should not restrict peaceful nuclear programmes as soon as they might have some military relevance,

8. that the FRG should permit inspections and controls on a wider scale than has been the case up to now (perhaps also by the IAEA), and finally

9. that the FRG should strive to achieve more room for manouevre in the two other categories of military use of nuclear energy – nuclear propellants and the nuclear-weapons effectiveness programme. (Exposé on the discussion about the topic 'Proliferation and nuclear options of the Federal Republic', 15 October 1965, ACD)

Points one to three outlined the position that some months later became part of the German 'Peace Note': using flexible tactics, in the spring of 1966 the intention was to replace the global NPT concept with regional measures. Points four to six proposed giving up the MLF option in favour of a consultative solution, while the existing nuclear arrangements were to remain untouched. Points seven to nine divided the military use of nuclear energy into three categories:

*   the peaceful but militarily usable atomic energy programme;
*   nuclear propellants; and
*   the nuclear-weapons effectiveness programmes.

It was contended that the possible military uses of atomic energy should, within the context of an NPT, not be limited in category one, and should even be extended, if possible, in categories two and three. The debate provoked in the Studiengruppe by this paper may be found in the minutes of 15 October 1965 but only in an abridged form. According to these minutes, point eight (extension of IAEA controls) met with the opposition of the disarmament commissioner, Swidbert Schnippenkoetter: in his view, an overlapping of Euratom and IAEA controls on German territory should not be promoted. Point nine was commented on by Dr Strathmann, at that time the person in the Defence Ministry responsible for questions of nuclear arms research, who said that 'the weapons-effectiveness programmes were intended to investigate ways and means of counteracting the effects of atomic weapons. And in so doing, it was necessary to simulate the effect of such weapons, using special equipment in order to do so.' Basic doubts about point nine were not raised, as Fritz Erler pointed out at the conclusion of the minutes (Studiengruppe, 15 October 1965).

The Nerlich/Cornides critique was ahead of daily policymaking: the German government underwrote the proposals made in points one to three, but stuck fast to according priority to an MLF for another twelve months. After the basis for an MLF had been withdrawn, the German-American NPT controversy concentrated on points seven to nine. Until the end of 1966, the Germans tried to anchor the MLF option within the framework of the NPT, but from 1967 onwards they concentrated on maintaining and expanding the room to manouevre that was necessary for a nuclear stand-by programme. In a confidential study by the SWP, it was stated that the NPT proposal had 'a proliferation effect itself insofar as a number of states must face the problem of how to ensure a future option for themselves, and that will accelerate the opinion- forming process in this direction' (Botzian, 1967c, p. 3).

Securing the Plutonium Industry

China's nuclear test was followed in the United States by a critical revision of its 'Atoms for Peace' policy. Might not the export of 'peaceful' nuclear technology encourage the proliferation of atomic weapons? Was there a chance of preventing the military misuse of atomic facilities which had been established for civilian use?

In the summer of 1965, William Foster wrote that mankind had reached the point where the use of nuclear power promised to be economically advantageous, and 'as a result, we must expect that within the next few years a number of countries will each be producing enough by-product plutonium to sustain a modest weapons programme'. Thus, it was necessary to strengthen controls over nuclear exports. 'Particularly important are international agreements on uniform standards to prevent critical materials and equipment from being offered for sale with inadequate controls, in order to realise economic or political advantage' (Foster, 1965, pp. 592–3).

The American revision was not without consequences. In August 1965 the American Department of Commerce ordered that it would only allow certain nuclear products to be exported with special permission (AdG, 1965, p. 12,011). Moreover, in January 1966 America's Atomic Energy Commission withdrew their agreement for the building of a German-American fast-breeder test reactor (*atw*, 2/66, p. 51). At the same time, 'all support for Germany as far as chemical reprocessing was concerned was stopped' (Häfele, 1966, p. 19). In the Federal Republic the strengthening of US export regulations was not seen as a means to achieve nuclear non-proliferation but as a threat to the German nuclear programme. Atomic power was not yet significant in terms of Germany's energy economy, but it provided justification for the country's energy policy plans, and the programme followed by Bonn was quite ambitious. Up to the end of 1966, the German government had invested some DM4.3 billion (approximately $ 1.1 billion at that time) in atomic energy (DBT, 1966, p. 3,089) and an army of 8,000 scientists was employed at the state-owned atomic research centres (*Der Spiegel*, 20/65). Some of these research projects could also be used for military purposes – for example, the 'hot cells' which were completed at the Jülich nuclear research centre in February 1965 (*Bulletin*, 1965, p. 288) and at the 'Institute for Transuranium' of the Karlsruhe nuclear research centre which was opened two months later (*atw*, 5/66, p. 205). It is no wonder that from 1966 onwards some nuclear scientists began to take part in the discussions about the Non-Proliferation Treaty because they felt that their sphere of activity was being threatened.

An important role was played by the so-called Badenweiler Paper written by Wolf Häfele, a leading expert in research into breeder reactors, based at the nuclear research centre in Karlsruhe. This paper was soon being read in political circles as well, and was seized upon by Kurt Birrenbach, a CDU MP. The stimulus created by Häfele's paper had considerable consequences for the future of the NPT controversy. What were its main points?

First of all, Häfele proceeded from the assumption that the Federal Republic, as a non-nuclear-weapons state, had a genuine interest in the unrestricted use of atomic energy. Because the impetus that might have come from military nuclear technological work was lacking, the plutonium economy 'had to be pursued in an effort that was specific and particular to Germany'. Second, Häfele forecast the rapid advance of atomic energy and, over the medium term, the replacement of light-water reactors by fast-breeders. Third, he warned of two effects of the new American non-proliferation policy which aimed 'to maintain control over the question of plutonium technology in Germany, at least indirectly and with regard to concessions towards Moscow'. On the one hand, the new American strategy wanted to introduce IAEA controls – in opposition to that, it was essential to insist 'that the controlling authority for Germany is, and has to remain, Euratom'. On the other hand, there was an underlying move within the United States to turn its delivery monopoly of uranium into a political instrument. That was why in the negotiations on the NPT it was important to ensure that the conditions for supplying uranium 'would not violate control over plutonium technology and, more generally, the fuel cycle of the light-water reactors and fast-breeder reactors in Germany'. An NPT could be 'feasible' only as long as 'it did not interfere with German chemical reprocessing and also did not demand that the IAEA become the controlling authority, should the occasion arise' (Häfele, 1966, pp. 16–25).

Häfele's words found many eager listeners in Bonn. His arguments could be used by those who wanted to bolster their basic rejection of the NPT with a new argument, or in the event of Germany's accession to the treaty, to insist that some nuclear options at least be maintained in a kind of 'stand-by' programme. In the months that followed, many implied they had a specific interest in nuclear developments having military potential. With regard to its technological perspectives, the German government should 'not be more casual than the Indian or Israeli governments who, by the way, are a lot closer to atomic armament' advised the *FAZ* on 21 August 1965. The warning that 'soon only a state that can make decisions of a nuclear strategic nature will be regarded as being sovereign' had earlier been made by Alfons Dalma, editor-in-chief of *Wehrkunde,* the German journal on arms and armament (*WK* 8/65, p. 401). In November 1965, three months after the announcement of the Uniteds States's more restrictive export policy, the then minister for scientific research, Gerhard Stoltenberg, reached agreement with the German Atomic Energy Commission on the basis that

it is absolute necessary to ensure the financing of the projects for the High Temperature Gas Cooled Reactor (HDR), the Nuclear Power Plant in Niederaichbach (KnK), and the Reprocessing Plant for Spent Fuel (WAK) in the form of a *self-contained, uniform national crash programme* in the area of technological test facilities [as well as] to ensure a long-term supply of nuclear fuel from abroad [and] to determine the precise amounts of uranium available within the FRG by continuing the project work domestically, especially in the Black Forest. (*Bulletin*, 1965, p. 1,524; original emphasis)

Accordingly, Germany's national budget for 1966 provided for a 25 per cent increase in expenditure on atomic research; and there were good prospects for another considerable increase in 1967 (*atw*, 2/66, p. 65). Although the minister for scientific research, too, stressed that the German atomic programme 'was oriented towards peaceful purposes only' (DBT, 1966, p. 3089), it cannot be denied that the 'national crash programme' was already endowed with the qualities of a stand-by programme.

To sum up: Even before the superpowers' agreement on a joint NPT draft, the key conditions for the impending controversy over the nuclear option were already in place in the Federal Republic. The atomic energy sector was reasonably well represented in the Auswärtige Amt, the Ministry for Scientific Research's support for plutonium technology was established, the relevant scientific studies were under way and the political as well as the technological 'nuclear community' had been sensitised.

At the beginning of 1967, the second major round of the German-American controversy began. From now on, securing the peaceful use of atomic energy – with all its ramifications – was well to the fore of Bonn's interests.

3

Political Parties and the Nuclear Option

After the resignation of Ludwig Erhard, the Social Democrats and Christian Democrats agreed upon jointly forming a new government known as the Grand Coalition. Kurt Georg Kiesinger, a former head of department in the Nazi Foreign Ministry, became West Germany's chancellor. Willy Brandt, a bitter opponent of the Nazis, became foreign minister. Franz Josef Strauss, head of the CSU, who had been brought in some four years previously, became minister of finance.

The foreign policy of the Grand Coalition followed two basic aims: further detente with the East and greater freedom from the West. Kurt Georg Kiesinger tried to take both aims into consideration in his first statement of policy. Where detente was concerned, it was not reunification but the wish for peace that was proclaimed as the primary target of German foreign policy. As for emancipation from Washington, after the debacle of the MLF, the new government began to demonstrate a new self-assurance in its dealings with the US. Kiesinger's pronouncement during his first visit to the United States was typical of the new style: 'We no longer regard the United States as a big brother to whom we go running when something goes wrong' (*NYT*, 17 August 1967). In the nuclear sector, this self-assured image was supported by the progress being made in West Germany's atomic industry. The more the atomic programme could be separated from its dependency upon America, the more confidently the Germans could act in their negotiations.

These two basic targets – international detente, and national freedom of manoeuvre – clashed in the debate over the NPT, creating antagonism. It was imperative at least to limit the downgrading of Germany into a secondary power as a consequence of the NPT. A simple 'Yes' to the NPT was out of the question. But an unequivocal 'No' was just as inadvisable, as this would have run counter to the very heart of the new concept of the FRG's Eastern European policy.

What were the positions of the conservative parties (CDU and CSU) and the Social Democrats (SPD)? What role did the opposition play? Under what conditions was the atomic programme being modernised?

Atomic Energy for Military Purposes

Since the foundation of the Federal Republic of Germany research
into nuclear armaments had been conducted, although it had not
been made public. To maintain and expand such research was one
goal of Germany's NPT diplomacy, but this was talked about only
behind closed doors. For instance, the Stiftung Wissenschaft und
Politik (Science and Politics Foundation) made just one remark on
this topic, in November 1967, under the title 'Comments on the
military use of controlled nuclear reaction with relation to the NPT'
(Botzian, 1967f).

Legally, nuclear research for military purposes was granted legitimacy
by the fact that in the atomic law of the FRG ('Law on the peaceful
uses of nuclear energy'), 'the use of nuclear energy for peaceful
purposes only is regulated and ... it is not applicable to the military
use of nuclear energy' (Peil, 1965, p. 21). The NPT also does not prohibit
research for military use in general, as long as no nuclear warheads
are built. In Paragraph 14 of the agreement concerning the verification of the NPT ('Non-application of safeguards for nuclear material
to be used in non-peaceful activities') this fact was explicitly stated.
But such regulations were out of the question in 1966/7. On the
contrary, the Defence ministry feared that certain areas of nuclear
defence research work might be endangered by the strengthening
of NPT controls. Germany's experience with the United States seemed
to confirm these fears.

In April 1964 the Erhard government asked the United States to
deliver a Triga Mark F reactor 'to simulate the radiation released in
a nuclear explosion'. With the aid of this reactor it was intended to
develop a method to protect armour-plate against the initial radiation
stemming from nuclear explosions. The reactor could also be used
to calculate the configuration of atomic bombs, as its fast-burst
structure becomes hyper-critical for a brief period of time (NHP VI,
ACD). Because of this, the United States was not willing to deliver a
Triga reactor to the Federal Republic (Botzian, 1967f, p. 3).

The Triga reactor came under the category of research into the effectiveness of nuclear weapons, a field of research which by 1966 had
grown enormously in Munster, Lower Saxony, and at Stohl near Kiel
in Schleswig Holstein. This required that materials and equipment
be provided to simulate the radiation created by an atomic explosion
so that its effect on armour-plate ('materials test') or on living beings
('ABC protection research') could be tested. Within the Bundeswehr,
a 'Staff for Studies and Manoeuvres' and an 'Operations Research'

group were looking into nuclear-weapons-effectiveness research as well. The German companies MBB and Dornier had similar working groups.

There is no clear dividing line between *research* into the effect of atomic weapons and the *development* of atomic weapons. Every activity in the field of nuclear defence requires 'personal judgement based upon scientific and technical research in the nuclear weapons field'. According to a member of Germany's Fraunhofer Institute, nuclear defence research in the FRG created these prerequisites 'by order of the BMVg [Defence Ministry] Referat Rüfo 2, in cooperation with different agencies within the defence sector. This was backed up by individual research programme commissioned by the BMVg and given to universities and industrial enterprises in Germany' (Leuthäuser, 1975, p. 2).

One example of the close association between the simulation of nuclear weapons and their production is given by Botzian in his reference to the fast-burst reactor:

It works with a rapidly expanding avalanche-like nuclear fission reaction which, like a bomb, is induced by unmoderated ('fast') neutrons ... and it would only be necessary to contain this reaction ('tamper') and thus prevent radioactive decay before the chain reaction is complete, thus creating one single super-critical state instead of many little brief bursts – and the result would be a bomb, although a primitive one. (Botzian, 1967f, p. 3)

Another branch of the weapons-effectiveness research programme included an order by the Defence Ministry during the 1960s for the production of tritium targets at the Hanau NUKEM factory (*FR*, 13 June 1984). It was possible to simulate the radiation of a neutron bomb by firing deuterium at these targets. The order to NUKEM was given by an influential member of Hardthöhe, Dr Strathmann, who had not only coordinated the weapons-effectiveness research programme during these years but had also been to a great extent responsible for establishing it. As a member of both an inter-ministerial NPT committee and the Studiengruppe, Dr Strathmann was directly involved in the formulation of Germany's NPT strategy.

The Federal Republic was certainly not the only non-nuclear-weapons state in NATO where atomic energy played a definite role in the military sector. What is remarkable is that Bonn commissioned to carry out the experimental and theoretical work in this field that very nuclear physicist who, more than any other person, embodied the continuity of Nazi Germany's atomic research programme:

Professor Erich Bagge from Kiel. Because of his particular association with the non-peaceful use of atomic energy, he was looked upon as an outsider by the nuclear community in the Federal Republic of Germany (Arbeitskreis Atomwaffenverzicht ins Grundgesetz, 1989, pp. 7-9).

An institute dedicated to weapons-effectiveness research was established in Stohl near Kiel which Bagge headed from 1966 to 1972. This institute was financed by the Defence Ministry, and in 1972 it employed some 50 scientists (both theoretical and experimental physicists). The plan was to install the Triga reactor there (Bagge, 1972, p. 172). In 1972, the Institute for Radiation Protection became the Institute for Trend Analyses in Natural Science and Technology as part of the Fraunhofer Institute. At the beginning of the 1980s this institute was moved to Euskirchen near Bonn; at present it is, together with the Bundeswehr's Wehrwissenschaftliche Dienststelle für ABC-Schutz (Defence Research Department for ABC Protection) in Munster, the centre for nuclear-weapons-effectiveness research in the Federal Republic of Germany.

Within the scope of such nuclear-weapons-effectiveness research there has, without doubt, always lain the possibility of utilising the results of experiments and the basic data gathered to calculate atomic bomb configurations. The source material available, however, is not sufficient to allow us to judge if this has actually happened – many of the Fraunhofer Institute's publications are classified documents. And at the moment there is no other evidence available which would clearly support such a theory. But what must be questioned is the relationship between the prospects of protection against the effects of atomic weapons and the possibilities of giving support to the development of such weapons through the research that is carried out in relation to this. Surely there are many 'civil' arguments for such research. This is clearly proven when considering the case of Sweden: there, the physicists and technicians who were secretly at work on the development of atomic weapons were given orders always to begin their written reports with a reference to their (permitted) weapons-effectiveness research work (Küntzel, 1988, p. 5).

In the Nerlich/Cornides exposé presented to the Studiengruppe in 1965, it was said that the Federal Republic should 'try to achieve more room to manoeuvre' in the field of nuclear-weapons-effectiveness programmes and that the NPT would not be permitted to hinder this. In the working paper of the SWP, therefore, the preferred proposal was to exclude this entire sector from NPT controls, as well as to cover individual cases through bilateral agreements with the United States 'in relation to the principles applied to nuclear warheads' (Botzian,

1967f, p. 5). Up to the present time, the facilities in Munster, Stohl and Euskirchen remain outside IAEA control. Thus the NPT had no effect on activities within civil–military nuclear 'grey zones'.

The Programme of a Threshold Power

In 1967 public spending on West Germany's atomic industry nearly doubled, and that was much in line with the trends of the time (Pretsch, 1968, p. 19). What was remarkable was the orientation of the programme: it was aimed chiefly at reducing dependence upon the United States as well as the further development of the plutonium industry.

At the end of 1966 a fast-breeder pilot facility in Karlsruhe came into operation. At the beginning of 1967 construction began in Karlsruhe of a reprocessing plant with an annual capacity of 30 tons of nuclear material. In 1972 the decision to build a reprocessing plant with a capacity of 800 tons per year was imminent (Pretsch, 1968, p. 21). At the suggestion of the then minister for scientific research (later the defence minister), Gerhard Stoltenberg, efforts were increased to ensure that 50 per cent of Germany's uranium requirements were met from national sources. At the same time, Helmut Schmidt raised the explosive question of 'how, and in what manner, the Federal Republic could prepare, if necessary, a sort of pilot plant, a first precursor of a German facility for the separation of isotopes' (*VBT*, 27 April 1967, p. 4,953). Stoltenberg had called this atomic programme an 'investment for peace', but it served a less peaceful purpose too. In 1967 the American scientist Catherine M. Kelleher noted after interviewing Germany's nuclear policy elite that there was definitely

> some support for a 'just-under-the-threshold' nuclear development programme similar to that presently being attempted by India and, to a lesser degree, by Japan. This would foresee an acceleration and expansion of the present efforts, to the point where a shift-over to extensive plutonium production for military purposes was possible within a period perhaps as short as a month or even a week. (Kelleher, 1967, pp. 655–6)

Kelleher wrote that the supporters of this approach were not just interested in securing political status; they also wanted to collect data and to utilise whatever scope they had before the NPT might reduce this. Kelleher's partners stressed three aspects of the stand-by programme:

First, it would significantly strengthen the German bargaining position in the future creation of a European force. The resulting advances in technical expertise and available resources would constitute a far more 'meaningful contribution'. Second, in the more immediate future, it would permit maximum gains in research and commercial technology before the restrictions foreseen or possible under a non-proliferation agreement enter full force.

Above and beyond this, further nuclear proliferation was more or less inevitable and could only be slowed down by the treaty:

> Yet, if only in terms of the number of states pursuing 'under-the-threshold' strategies, the threat of sudden proliferation would remain. ... It is therefore in Germany's interest to maintain similar 'insurance' even if it has no present intention of using it. (Kelleher, 1967, pp. 656–7)

But such a stand-by programme would not just be an answer to other countries, it would also be a challenge for them to match the FRG. Hinting at the impossibility of preventing nuclear proliferation is a pretext for refusing even to take the first step in this direction. Participating in the anticipated 'trend' is not merely acknowledging but also accelerating the logic which could be destabilising and therefore turn supposed security into real insecurity.

In addition to this, the stand-by programme outlined above was identical to the desires of those people who wanted nuclear progress in peace and nothing else. The ambivalent character of atomic technology was, therefore, turning the best-willed representatives of the 'Plutonium for Peace' solution into involuntary agents of the threshold-power policy and thus into the 'co-triggers' of an international chain reaction – to be on the safe side, it is better for me to establish my own sphere of nuclear power to counter the nuclear power my neighbours have 'on call'. It was precisely this basic problem of nuclear technology that was deliberately excluded from the German NPT controversy and from the public statements of the country's political parties.

Nuclear Policies

After the failure of Erhard's MLF policy, the tiny liberal FDP was the only political party to call for a turning back of West Germany's nuclear policy. The leadership of the SPD tried to present the change in foreign policy as part of a policy of continuity however. Between the parties of the Grand Coalition there were 'not such fundamental differences in the evaluation of the NPT as the fierceness of the controversy might at first imply' (Kohler, 1972, p. 124). Helmut Schmidt later reported that in the negotitations to set up the Grand Coalition between the SPD and the CDU/CSU, there had been 'an agreement about the fact that we would try to keep open the European option within the NPT' (Studiengruppe, 30 January, p. 16). Such thoughts and decisions determined the course of policy, but the ordinary members of the major parties remained in the dark, the rank and file of the SPD in particular would probably not have agreed with the policy of keeping a nuclear option open. Just how far did nuclear consensus within the Grand Coalition reach? Where and to what extent did the parties differ in their evaluation of the NPT?

The SPD – a Half-hearted Agreement with the NPT
Since the beginning of the 1960s, the SPD had stopped public criticism of the nuclear weapons policy of Adenauer and Erhard. This was partly a result of the conviction that quarrels over foreign security should be avoided, and partly because the SPD agreed in principle with the basic direction taken by the German government: the strengthening of transatlantic relations and the extension of Germany's influence on NATO's nuclear policy. Thus in 1964 SPD leaders Wehner, Erler and Brandt vehemently defended the European atomic power project against the opposition of their fellow parties in the Netherlands and Great Britain, as documented in internal correspondence (Erler Estate, cassette 19). The MLF was also supported at the Social Democrats' Party Congress in November 1964.

The attitude towards the nuclear question determined the attitude towards the NPT. 'The desirability of an NPT for the Federal Republic is questionable' as long as the nuclear powers continued to try to strengthen their positions through this treaty, explained Helmut Schmidt behind closed doors (Studiengruppe, 23 May 1966, p. 6). Herbert Wehner, for years the chairman of the parliamentary SPD in the Bundestag and minister for all-German affairs in the Grand Coalition, did not try to conceal his scepticism about this treaty which, according to him, had been created 'because of the special needs within Russia's European policy to maintain the Federal Republic of Germany as a scapegoat and bogeyman, and because of the special needs of American domestic policy' (*Bulletin*, 29 August 1968, p. 908). Whereas Austrian Social Democrat Bruno Kreisky, for example, wanted to see the NPT formulated as comprehensively as possible (*Die Welt*, 21 February 1967), the only agreement between the SPD and the CDU/CSU in the Federal Republic on this point was that the renunciation of atomic weapons should be on the most limited basis possible. It was the SPD especially which stressed the civil use of atomic energy in this connection. In his first basic statement concerning the NPT, Willy Brandt said that a federal government headed by the SPD would, 'while maintaining legitimate German security interests', support an international non-proliferation agreement and at the same time 'do its utmost to ensure that German industry should not suffer but that Germany would also do its share in contributing to the modern research and peaceful use of atomic energy' (SPD news release, 20 August 1965).

With this statement, the industrial factor had been introduced into the NPT debate for the first time (Haftendorn, 1974, p. 149). But the ambivalence of this industry raises questions: was the phrase 'modern research' also related to activities relevant for nuclear weapons? The statements made by the defence experts of the SPD, Erler and Schmidt, gave this impression. Both had rejected a nuclear status for the Federal Republic but supported the keeping open of the nuclear option along the lines of the Swedish model. According to Helmut Schmidt's basic work on atomic policy, *Verteidigung oder Vergeltung* (Defence or Retaliation), up to the winter of 1959/60 the Swedish government, under the aegis of Prime Minister Erlanger, a Social Democrat, had

> put off for half a decade the decision to provide the Swedish Army with nuclear weapons in order to support international efforts to close the 'atomic club' down. Only if after this period there was no longer any prospect of doing so and the proliferation of nuclear weapons in other states was increasing, would the Swedish government come to a definitive decision; but in the meantime, the conditions and consequences as well as the advantages and disadvantages of such a decision were to be continually observed and examined. Following such a course would be of benefit to the Federal Republic. (Schmidt, 1961, p. 202)

Such thoughts and analogies were far from having any relevance for the rank and file of the party. In spite of this, they were put up for debate, implicitly, in particular by Helmut Schmidt. In December 1967 Schmidt spoke in the Bundestag about 'the principle of the interest in national security' according to which, in the event of any further erosion of NATO, the Federal Republic of Germany would have to make certain 'of maintaining the opportunity to act in all situations'. In order to do this it would be necessary 'with everything which could be developed and produced together with the French, to arm ourselves as far as possible financially and technically – or at least to try to do so' (*VBT*, 6 December 1967, p. 7,158). On this point, the chairman of the Social Democrats' parliamentary party could rely on the agreement of the CDU/CSU. Where then did the differences lie? According to Beate Kohler, they were limited

> to the evaluation of the possibilities open to the Federal Republic to prevent the treaty and – if this proved impossible – to refuse Germany's signature. Corresponding to the different assessments of freedom of action, there were also differences about the way in which it was hoped to present Germany's doubts as impressively as possible. (Kohler, 1972, p. 124)

Political differences over the evaluation of possibilities were linked to differences over the evaluation of aims. The representatives of the old East policy viewed accession to the treaty as a one-sided concession that was advantageous to Moscow and thought this was probably the greatest negative factor of the NPT. In contrast, the representatives of the new East policy saw in a 'well-balanced' NPT a chance to build a bridge between East and West. The NPT differences within the Grand Coalition centred not on the treaty itself but on its becoming embedded in the architecture of a new policy of detente.

It is true that the SPD was determined to prevent any weakening of the cohesion and striking power of NATO and to maintain, or even push through, certain options with respect to the NPT. But equally important was its interest in securing the new foreign policy approach instead of endangering it by refusing their signature to the treaty and thus risking international isolation.

The CSU – Fundamental Opposition
The CSU, Bavaria's sister party to the CDU, rejected the NPT on principle, outright, and without any differences within the party. The nationalistic catchword of a new 'Versailles' had been thrown into the debate in 1965 by the CSU chairman in response to the first American NPT draft: according to Franz Josef Strauss, for everyone who was able to think reasonably

> it could only be a nightmare to have a Germany, which once again has had thrust upon it a kind of 'military Versailles' and which, being the third greatest economic power in the world, would then stand, discriminated against, between East and West. From past experience alone it would be easy to calculate just how long it would take for a new *Führer* to promise nuclear weapons or even worse

to a Germany which had been so treated; and what is more they would probably get them. (*Rheinischer Merkur*, 27 August 1965)

Strauss had fought all his life against limiting Germany's nuclear room to manoeuvre. He was never able to come to terms even with the renunciation of 1954. If Adenauer had remained firm at that time 'we never ... would have been forced to make this renunciation' (Strauss, 1989, p. 310). Some 35 years later he still thought it an indication of self-destructiveness that 'Germans do not consider themselves morally mature enough to have the sovereignty to possess atomic weapons' (Strauss, 1989, p. 435). The CSU and its chairman knew very well that a German army with nuclear weapons was out of the question for the time being, for historical, political and material reasons. As an alternative, the Federal Republic should 'be incorporated into a European framework of security ... which has nuclear weapons at its disposal' (*Bayernkurier*, 4 March 1967).

The strategic orientation towards the European option also determined the CSU's criticism of the NPT. For the CSU chairman, the real snag in the American NPT proposal of 17 August 1965 was a paragraph in Article II, according to which the non-nuclear-weapons powers would undertake not to assist in the production of atomic weapons. Strauss stated that he saw no way to develop a European atomic power step by step other 'than having the nuclear have-nots participate financially and scientifically in the establishment of Europe's nuclear armament and, in return, having a say in strategic matters' (*RM*, 27 August 1965).

How did the CSU proceed within the Grand Coalition? In contrast to their political partners, the CSU saw no reason to strive tactically for moderation. On the contrary, it was pointed out that the desire to 'bask in the sun of international popularity' sometimes had to be put aside; instead it might be necessary to 'put up with hostility from abroad' in order to protect the vital interests of the FRG (*BK*, 4 March 1967).

Marcel Hepp, managing editor of the CSU newspaper *Bayernkurier* and personal assistant to Franz Josef Strauss, was well known for his 'bulldozer approach' (Murphy, 1974, p. 28). He was his master's equal in florid polemics, spitting fire and brimstone at 'that submissive' (19), 'restraining' (60), and 'Europe-obstructing Treaty' (72) which is in the offing thanks to those who would like to turn 'West Germany into a land of fellahin' (64); that 'document of capitulation of the have-nots' (73) which 'is strangling us' (97), as well as at the 'totalitarianism of the Vienna [IAEA] controls' (110) under the verdict of which 'all the unpretentious Franco-German joint ventures which have come into existence up to now' (111) will breathe their last. According to Hepp, Henry Morgenthau was, at all events, 'nothing more than a mere greenhorn in comparison to the Geneva conspirators' (Hepp, 1968, pp. 19–111).

But neither Marcel Hepp nor Franz Josef Strauss was able to initiate a public wave of indignation against the NPT. That was why the CSU began to pursue a blockade strategy within the Grand Coalition. In February 1967 Strauss wrote in a letter to the chancellor that he was in no way prepared to accept a decision of the cabinet in favour of accession to the NPT (*FAZ*, 18 February 1967). In autumn 1968 he threatened to withdraw the CSU ministers from the cabinet and to establish the CSU throughout the entire Federal Republic (instead of in Bavaria alone) should Bonn accede to the treaty.

The CDU – Wavering and Torn Apart

With regard to the NPT, within the CDU 'opinions differed greatly' (Gerstenmaier, undated, p. 533). On the one hand, everybody thought the NPT to be an impertinence: without having to make a single concession concerning 'Deutschlandpolitik', the nuclear renunciation of the Federal Republic of Germany would fall into the Kremlin's lap just like a ripe apple. On the other hand, there was the desire to avoid international isolation. But was this possible without accession to the NPT? Torn apart by this dilemma, the CDU finally, with resignation, united all shades of rejection of the NPT, moving from a hard 'No' to a hesitant 'Yes, if'. In 1968, according to CSU politician Marcel Hepp, a part of this party

> has given up its opposition to 'Geneva' still, however, playing the coquette with its 'doubts' in a rearguard action. In the meantime, another group has been indoctrinated by American assurances. A third group – although at heart opposed to Germany's signature – is directed by fear and is only afraid of political blackmail by the United States should the FRG reject ratification. The fourth group is sharply conscious of the Atlantic crisis. They think that improvements in the treaty are irrelevant because the Geneva Agreement establishes a political status quo in the world and in Europe which could be agreed to by the Federal Republic only at the cost of its own existence. The CSU is almost totally unanimous in its support of this fourth group. (Hepp, 1968, p. 10)

Members of the last-mentioned CDU group included the president of the Bundestag, Eugen Gestenmaier, and ministers Bruno Heck and Gerhard Stoltenberg. 'Of the CDU leaders, Stoltenberg probably harboured the greatest suspicions of the treaty', according to an American dissertation on the NPT controversy in the FRG (Murphy, 1974, p. 34).

The FDP – Playing a Special Role

The liberal FDP declared in January 1967 that the 'Deutschland-politik' of Adenauer and Erhard had run into a blind alley. From now on, the FRG would have to

> take its place at the head of those Western nations which are aiming at closer and more trusting relationships with the principal victims of the Hitler war, thus helping to accelerate the process of democratisation and liberalisation in these countries.

A prerequisite for this, however, would be the willingness of the German government

> to come out with a clear and final renunciation of atomic weapons ... [i.e.] the abandonment of every German claim for a share in the nuclear potential of the West and ... limitation of the right to veto in the event of the employment of atomic weapons, as well as participation in special working groups for general planning and target planning. (AdDL, folder 123)

The FDP wanted the total renunciation of all atomic weapons in the Bundeswehr – this request was repeatedly made in parliamentary debates. The party also favoured the establishment of a nuclear-free zone in Central Europe.

The position of the FDP was not motivated by pacifism but was oriented towards the principle of practicality. The FDP was in favour of the conventional–nuclear 'division of labour' within NATO without questioning the NATO doctrine of nuclear deterrence. In the NPT controversy the Free Democrats acted on a 'wait and see' basis. Although they wanted the German government to play a pioneering role in limiting nuclear arms, they themselves were not able to play such a role in the controversy surrounding the NPT. Acting opportunistically, they did not make clear their opinion on NPT questions but they loudly criticised the indecisiveness of the Grand Coalition. They demanded that the chancellor come out with a 'word of command' but without saying which one it was they wanted. It was not until January 1969, at the same time as the SPD, that the relevant FDP committee finally, 'after long consideration', came to the conclusion that the German government should sign the treaty.

From March 1969 onwards this was also the official opinion of the FDP in general (Murphy, 1974, p. 50).

Extra-parliamentary Opposition

Among the general public of West Germany, the NPT played a role only at the beginning of 1967 – as an object of national indignation. Apart from that, the NPT controversy met with no response in domestic policy, in contrast to the debates concerning the new Ostpolitik (Murphy, 1974, p. 60). The nuclear question was of importance to government officials, MPs, scientists and editors but not to the general public. If the NPT ever was a topic, its real meaning – the dangers of proliferation and atomic war – was seldom mentioned.

The German government, moreover, was not very interested in informing the public about the dangers of nuclear proliferation. A 1967 United Nations report on the effects of atomic weapons which had roused worldwide attention because of its analysis of proliferation was passed on by Bonn to the relevant authorities; but in the view of the German government there was 'no need to inform the German public' – by issuing a German translation – as government spokesman Karl-Günther von Hase said (*VBT*, 11 March 1968). This lack of information could not head off those remaining in the 'Fight Atomic Death' initiative. It is true that in 1965 100,000 Germans signed a petition condemning the MLF (Otto, 1977, p. 151) and indeed, in 1967 the demand for accession to the NPT was still an issue of the Easter marches – the *New York Times* reported on exactly twelve demonstrations in favour of the NPT (26 March 1967). But in fact, 'Fight Atomic Death' had lost all importance with the general public and was in the process of merging into the broader spectrum of the APO (Ausser-Parlamentarische-Opposition, or extra-parliamentary opposition) movement. At home, this protest movement concentrated on Germany's 'state of emergency legislation' *(Notstandsgesetzgebung)*, and on foreign policy concerning the non-nuclear war in Vietnam. Under these circumstances, intervention in favour of West Germany's rapid accession to the NPT – an American wish from the very beginning – was out of the question.

The Grand Coalition's Conditions for an NPT

Up to the end of 1966 the Adenauer and Erhard governments had missed no opportunity to try to make the NPT project fail. From 1967 onwards, the Grand Coalition government tried to have drafts of the NPT worded in accordance with their wishes. It was still an open question as to whether or not Germany would accede to the NPT.

'We cannot take a decision on the question of accession to the treaty either in the current phase of information or in the coming phase of consultation', wrote Germany's new foreign minister, Willy Brandt, in a secret letter to the chancellor (AA–Doc. I). The implementation of NPT diplomacy was in the hands of Germany's Auswärtige Amt (Foreign Affairs Ministry) but it had no control over its formulation. The Federal Defence Council (Bundesverteidigungsrat, or BVR) was the higher body responsible. Under the chairmanship of the chancellor it had to develop the guidelines for NPT policy and to make decisions. The BVR prepared the NPT discussions for the cabinet, coordinated all the important government initiatives on the NPT and distributed all mandates for negotiating, including the safeguards discussions in the IAEA. Members of the BVR included the defence, foreign affairs, interior, finance and economic affairs ministers; the inspector-general of the Bundeswehr and the commissioner for disarmament. In the case of at least a non-proliferation problem, the scientists Wolf Häfele and Karl Wirtz were consulted (*BPA*, 20 February 1967).

For the fine tuning of the NPT policy, on 3 February 1967, the BVR decided to establish the Interministeriellen Arbeitsstab NV-Vertrag (Inter-ministerial Working Staff NP Treaty). Members of this group, which was chaired by Commissioner for Disarmament Schnippenkoetter, comprised officials from the Bundeskanzleramt (the Office of the Federal Chancellor), the Ministries for Foreign Affairs, Economic Affairs, Scientific Research and Defence, Director Ritter of the Science and Politics Foundation (SWP) and Professors Häfele and Wirtz from the Nuclear Research Centre in Karlsruhe (AA-Doc. XV). The protocols of the working staff were initialled regularly by ministers Brandt and Stoltenberg and were presented in discussions in the BVR or the cabinet. What direction did West Germany's NPT policy take under the Kiesinger/Brandt government?

Nuclear Defence
Bonn wanted to make sure that the NPT would hamper neither the further development of its 'nuclear share' nor the European option. The United States had already promised that under NPT conditions, in the event of an emergency, German carrier missiles could be equipped with American atomic warheads. Above and beyond that, in an internal Auswärtige Amt (AA) document a demand was made for the introduction of a 'two-key-system at least for the warheads stationed on the territory of the Federal Republic' and for participation in joint nuclear solutions in special cases such as 'the development of a missile defence system (with nuclear warheads) in Europe'.

According to the Auswärtige Amt paper, it would not be possible to realise these claims if the NPT draft was interpreted literally (Annex 2 to AA–Doc. I).

Encouragement of Nuclear Energy
The German government was in no way satisfied with a statement from the United States that the peaceful employment of atomic energy was not to be hampered in any way by the NPT. If the have-nots renounced the possession of atomic weapons, the nuclear powers should, at least, in return make available their nuclear know-how without any limitations, and also support the use of nuclear energy. 'Not to impede, but even to *foster* the peaceful application of nuclear energy' was how the Inter-ministerial Working Staff put it, in a whimsical play on the name of America's chief negotiator for the NTP, William C. Foster. This new give-and-take approach replaced the old MLF package deal. It was developed in January 1967 in the Federal Republic, brought into the international discussion by Bonn and later laid down in Article IV of the NPT. According to the protocol of a confidential meeting of the Inter-ministerial Working Staff on 17 February 1967, they were not just demanding an additional NPT section on the 'outspoken duty to encourage and support the peaceful use of nuclear energy', but also as limited a definition as possible of the term 'atomic weapon', a share in the results of the nuclear-weapons research of the atomic powers, and the abolition of all limitations on fissionable material of American origin in order to 'be able to move freely, especially with respect to nuclear fuel (for export as well)' (AA-Doc. IV, p. 4).

Abolition of Controls
During a meeting of the Inter-ministerial Committee in February 1967 Ambassador Schnippenkoetter summarised Germany's negotiation targets with regard to the safeguards question as follows:

- Abolition of the control clause.
- Should a control clause be unavoidable, it should be made acceptable worldwide by (a) binding it to the actual purpose of the treaty, (b) no discrimination between nuclear-weapons states and non-nuclear-weapon states, i.e. identical controls throughout the entire civil sector.
- A permanent safeguarding of Euratom interests.
- Concerning control procedures ... as few inspectors as possible; modern automatic control devices instead at important points

in the nuclear fuel cycle (black boxes on chimneys). (AA-Doc IV, p. 7).

Hidden behind the wording 'safeguarding of Euratom interests' was the deeply rooted antipathy to control by the responsible United Nations body, the IAEA.

It was also obvious to the German government that IAEA controls so far had not hampered civil nuclear programmes in any way. In a confidential dossier of the Science and Politics Foundation (SWP) it was stated that, up to that time, IAEA controls had been 'satisfactory for all those concerned' (Botzian, 1967b, p. 7). It could not even be 'clearly proven just how or in what way sterner controls would indeed hamper peaceful developments' (Botzian and Nerlich, 1967a, p. 9). Nevertheless, the German government had fiercely opposed the wishes of the two superpowers to set up IAEA controls on German territory. The basic outline for this policy had already been laid out in the first dossier of SWP members Botzian and Nerlich on 23 January 1967:

> IAEA controls are ... particularly unacceptable for the Federal Republic of Germany – apart from political and other reasons such as insufficient patent coverage – especially when, and as long as, there are still substantial differences between the East and the West in their interpretation of the NPT which would become a burden to it in an even more severe form.

The character of the safeguards would especially bear upon the development 'of reactors and other elements to close the "technological gap" ... which would be competetive in the export trade' (Botzian and Nerlich, 1967a, pp. 12 ff).

'Elements to close the technological gap' – was this a euphemism for projects within the grey zone of 'weapons-effectiveness research', the integration of which within a purely civil atomic programme might be a problem? Only in such an event could 'discovery' by an international body give rise to criticism. This assumption is backed by a statement made by Willy Brandt that the non-nuclear-weapons states 'should participate in the results of the military use of atomic energy by the nuclear-weapons states – including all information and inventions – *at least as far as the western part of the world is concerned*' (DBT, 27 April 1967, pp. 4,942 ff.; emphasis added). Subject to such a proviso, it really would not have made much sense to give the Eastern Bloc countries a right of control through the IAEA.

Duration of the Treaty

Washington and Moscow wanted the treaty to have an unlimited period of validity and a clearly specified withdrawal clause. But resorting to a withdrawal clause seemed to be as unrealistic, for the FRG in particular, as a refusal to sign the treaty as a matter of principle. Therefore, Bonn aimed at limiting the treaty's period of validity. In a letter to Dean Rusk in October 1967, Willy Brandt proposed a five-year period of validity for the NPT (*NZZ*, 19 October 1967). The CDU thought that it was 'necessary to limit its validity to five or ten years' (Birrenbach, 1967, p. 26). According to NATO Ambassador Wilhelm Grewe, Kiesinger wanted a ten-year limitation (Grewe, 1979, p. 657). But as the Germans believed that, in the end, the treaty would be valid for an even longer period of time, they decided to concentrate on the withdrawal clause too. In the draft presented by the superpowers, each party to the treaty was allowed to withdraw from the treaty in the event of any danger to 'the highest interests of its country'. What this meant exactly remained an open question.

Bonn was interested in fixing conditions under which it would be possible to withdraw from the treaty. The right to withdraw was to apply not only in the event of the establishment of an ABM system by the superpowers but also, and most importantly, in the event of the disintegration of NATO (*Die Welt*, 18 February 1967), as well as if a nuclear-weapons state infringed upon or threatened the interests of a non-nuclear-weapons state (Birrenbach, 1967, p. 27). Probably the most important reservation regarded the use of atomic energy. In March 1969 Willy Brandt declared that the German government should not hesitate 'to avail itself of the withdrawal clause of the treaty at the very moment someone seriously tries to hinder the Federal Republic of Germany in the peaceful application of atomic power' (*VBT*, 19 March 1969, p. 11,982).

The Diplomatic Offensive

This was a further innovation of the Grand Coalition. Whereas the Erhard government had relied upon its solidarity of interest with Washington and London, from the first the Kiesinger government wanted to take up a position at the head of the non-nuclear nations. The attempt to form a bloc of non-nuclear-weapons states went so far that CDU MP Ernst Majonica considered establishing a regular body to represent the interests of the nuclear have-nots, with its own secretary-general (Heiden, 1967, p. 229). These thoughts demonstrated Germany's desire for more autonomy in relation to the United States and, at the same time, its interest in avoiding isolation. And it was also a means of camouflaging any special NPT concerns which had originally been initiated by Bonn by embedding them in the solidarity of interests of the other non-nuclear nations.

The room for manoeuvre for this kind of policy was limited in two respects: at home by those who frightened away potential alliance partners with their strong opposition to the NPT, and abroad by the fact that the common interests of Bonn and the other threshold powers were limited. Individual emphases differed: with Japan there was agreement in the civil sector, but not on the Euratom question; the Netherlands wanted to keep Euratom but to block the European option; countries such as Sweden and India criticised the NPT too, but with the aim of tightening up certain proposals. So it was the Federal Republic's goal not to build a bloc but to establish a wide phalanx of bilateral relationships where all common interests could be accommodated and fully expressed on the international scene (through the ENDC, UN, NATO Council, EC, Euratom and IAEA). Germany's principal allies in this were the former Axis powers of Japan and Italy. 'The most striking aspect of the non-proliferation controversy ... was, indeed, the manner in which it regalvanised the old World War II lines of force – the "Grand Alliance" as well as the Axis', stressed the *Washington Post*'s European correspondent, Antole Shub, in 1967 (Shub, 1967, p. 7).

Italy

Italy had supported the NPT project until the end of 1966. From 1967 onwards it acted in a way that implied 'the Italian government is strictly aligned with the German position' (Calamo, 1967, p. 226). Correspondence was mainly related to the question of the European option and included the criticism on principle of the discriminatory character of the treaty (Calamo, 1967, p. 227).

In the NATO Council, where for months the various NPT proposals had been spelt out 'word by word and phrase by phrase' (Cleveland, 1970, p. 69), bilateral cooperation was particularly close. Germany's ambassador to NATO was the outspoken opponent of the NPT, Wilhelm Grewe. In January 1967 Grewe began to 'talk about the possibilities of joint tactics and close cooperation in these areas' with the representatives of the Italian foreign minister (Grewe, 1979, p. 699). In the NATO Council, the coordinated 'Italian and German resistance' to the NPT received additional support from the secretary-general (Grewe, 1979, p. 793) 'who thought that the treaty would damage the alliance'. In terms of Italy's domestic policy, however, the NPT was by no means unpopular, and the Italian representative on the NATO Council was often criticised as well as being given a warning 'against a possible Italian alignment with the German positions' (Calamo, 1967, p. 216). A typical example of the general mood of the public at that time was an open letter to Foreign Minister Fanfani in which 60 leading Italian physicists spoke out for the NPT and the IAEA as its only controlling body (Calogero, 1967, p. 243 f). When Italy signed the NPT in January 1969, extra-parliamentary opposition to the treaty was therefore weak (*NZZ*, 28 January 1969).

Japan
Japan had stated in a memo to the United States at the end of 1966 that it was prepared to support the NPT as long as peaceful nuclear explosions would be permitted (AA-Doc. I, Annex 5). In the autumn of 1966 German-Japanese consultations on the NPT got under way (*FAZ*, 7 January 1967). In February 1967 'Japan's Deputy Foreign Minister Shimoda echoed the current German dispute over the NPT and declared that the government in Tokyo shared Bonn's doubts' (*Die Presse*, 18 February 1967). This common interest with Bonn was chiefly concentrated on the securing of unlimited nuclear research and a toned down control regulation. Since the mid-1960s, Japan had followed a strategy of maintaining nuclear options. Little wonder that there was substantial opposition to accession to the NPT. Japan signed in February 1970, with ratification following in June 1976.

India
India, like Japan, saw itself confronted with the People's Republic of China as a nuclear power, even though India was not a member of any alliance. Not just in its role as a leader of the unaligned nations, but also as a great Asian power, India committed itself to an NPT that would equally sanction the nuclear armament of the haves and the have-nots, and exclude such projects as the MLF. Relying on a highly developed nuclear programme, India also tried to increase its own nuclear options. In 1967 German efforts to reach a diplomatic agreement with India and Japan alarmed the United States, which saw in this possible encouragement for those who supported the idea of India having its own atomic bomb (*Die Welt*, 3 February 1967). Only after massive pressure on the part of the Americans was the attempt to establish a tripartite agreement abandoned in favour of bilateral talks (Nerlich, 1973, p. 109). German-Indian correspondence on NPT questions concentrated on the resistance to discriminatory regulations in the field of peaceful atomic technology. The relevant reservations on the part of the German government were also carefully followed by India's press (SIPRI, 1972, pp. 16–18).

Brazil

Brazil was also a member of the Eighteen-Nations Disarmament Committee in Geneva and, together with India, she clearly stood out as one of the most severe critics of the NPT. Brazil wanted to avoid any limitations by or dependence on the atomic powers in the civil sector, including peaceful atomic explosions, and wanted to increase the possibilities of withdrawing from the agreement. Together with India, Brazil criticised the policy of effective guarantees in return for safeguards from the nuclear powers (SIPRI, 1972, pp. 47 ff.). In February 1967 some 'very intensive consultations' on the NPT between the FRG and Brazil took place in Bonn (*Bulletin*, 9 February 1967). From that time onwards there were spirited discussions with Brazil via the German Embassy in Rio de Janeiro, as well as at meetings in Geneva and New York.

These intimate talks with Brazil, India and Japan earned Germany the reputation of being a 'gang-leader' in the eyes of the Americans. But, first of all, these countries were too proud to accept a 'leader' – and most certainly not from Germany. Second, there was no reason to speak of a 'gang' in view of the heterogeneity in their interests; and, third, the misgivings expressed by the US were in fact matters that were of real interest to each of the governments concerned. There are some indications that the emissaries of the German government did sometimes rub their partners' noses in certain problems with the NPT and that they might have agreed on some lines of argument – but there is no proof of. It can be taken for granted that the German diplomats did not let slip any opportunity 'to take hold of all those who were talking pleasantly as far as we were concerned, and to encourage them to make their position slightly clearer the next time round' (from the author's interview notes).

As far as the European option and the maintaining of Euratom were concerned, however, the support of countries outside Europe could be discounted. The institutions which wielded influence on such questions were the NATO Council and Euratom, as well as the EC commission and the meetings of the ministers and permanent representatives of the European Community. Within these organisations both the Federal Republic and Italy found themselves confronted with the persistent opposition of a have-not: the Netherlands.

The Netherlands and Belgium

Within the foreign policy of the Netherlands, non-proliferation had held absolute priority since 1965. The country's nuclear policy was based on the credibility of American deterrence; the option of a European army equipped with atomic weapons was rejected, as this might question America's nuclear guarantee as well possibly increasing the nuclear influence of the Germans (Advisory Commission, 1966, p. 33). The Netherlands government's agreement to a worldwide uniform IAEA control system was the 'sacrosanct' basis of the country's NPT diplomacy (Van der Mey, 1989, p. 126). Because of increased integration within Europe, Euratom controls were rejected as being a 'self-inspection' (Advisory Commission, 1967, p. 18), and at best would only be accepted as subordinate to the IAEA. With the silent approval of Washington, The Hague tried repeatedly to undermine the German-Italian position (author's interview material).

Belgium's NPT policy adopted a midway position between the German-Italian and Dutch standpoints (SIPRI, 1972, p. 69). Since February 1967 the German government had been insisting that the member states of Euratom adopt a common stance. Bonn was backed chiefly by the EC and Euratom Commission in Brussels, which attempted both to look after the institutional interests of the community and to avoid at almost all costs the downgrading of the European Atomic Community (Euratom) which would occur if restrictions were imposed on its controls system.

The interests of the non-nuclear nations were as diverse as the scenes of NPT negotiations, which embaced the NATO Council and European Community headquarters in Brussels, the Disarmament Conference in Geneva, the IAEA headquarters in Vienna and the General Assembly of the United Nations in New York. In addition there were permanent discussions with Washington and innumerable bilateral talks with the Hague, Brussels, Rome, Paris, London and Stockholm; with Moscow and Bucharest; with Rio de Janeiro, New Dehli and Tokyo. The Non-Proliferation Treaty was born in a 'three-ring' diplomatic circus. This was a baptism of fire for the Federal Republic of Germany. For the first time in its history it was acting on its own and internationally. This was not unsuccessful. 'Never before had [Germany] been able to maintain and in a certain sense even achieve its objectives in an international treaty with such universal significance as was the case with the NPT' (Petri, 1970, p. 183).

4

The NPT on the Bargaining Table

The year 1967 saw the beginning of the most heated phase of the NPT controversy. This was a German-American confrontation that went well beyond all previous differences with regard to Berlin or the cost of stationing troops in Germany. The presentation of a complete draft of the NPT, as planned for February 1967 by the superpowers, was postponed for eleven months by German political activities. 'West Germany holds a key position', wrote the *NYT* at that time, 'since Western sources concede that the Soviet Union will not become a party to an agreement unless West Germany is a signatory' (*NYT*, 25 February 1967). These eleven months were marked by campaigns in the German press by treaty opponents, week-long marathon-like meetings of the German-American negotiating commission, and artful diplomatic manoeuvrings between the super-powers which often managed to prevent the NPT from foundering at the very last minute. In November 1969, the new Social Democrat/Liberal government acceded to the treaty. But they put their signature to a treaty whose basic substance had been almost totally eroded by the machinery of negotiations during 1967.

Campaign in Bonn

In practice, the new federal government had planned to replace the old atomic policy with its own fresh approach. The new image of being a force of detente and peace was to give German policymaking a new freedom of movement. But events proved otherwise. In February 1967 the Federal Republic of Germany presented 'a spectacle of hysteria to the world that is hard to conceive' (*Der Spiegel*, 10/1967). The repercussions of this struck Wilhelm Grewe, who had meanwhile been appointed ambassador to NATO and whose oft-published opinions proclaimed that the political status and the scientific and technical development of a country was related to the possession of atomic weapons (Grewe, 1967, p. 92). Finance Minister Franz Josef Strauss called the NPT a 'new Versailles, and one of cosmic dimensions, too'. Adenauer talked about a 'Morgenthau Plan raised to the power of two' and declared: 'I hope that the Federal Republic will not sign its own death warrant.' The president of the National Association of German Industries (BDI), Fritz Berg, stressed the 'deep concern of German industry' and contended that without modifications to the treaty 'it can be calculated at just what point West Germany will have reached the status of an agricultural country' (*Die Welt*, 20 February 1967). The newspaper *Bild*, with its massive circulation, poured nationalistic oil on the flames with such headlines as: '*Diktat* of the Atomic Giants'; 'Bonn no longer the *Voice of America*'; 'We Don't Want To Become a Nation of Beggars'; 'Bonn Must Remain Outside'; 'Have the British Taken Bonn for a Ride?'; 'German Industry in Chains'; 'That's How To Clobber the *Little Leaguers*'.

Typical of the tenor of these publications was a statement by *Bild Zeitung* about the reopening of the disarmament conference in Geneva. Under the headline 'They Give the Orders and We ...' it said:

This treaty is an affront. Why? The treaty permits everything for the nuclear-weapons states and nothing for the non-nuclear-weapon states. It turns the owners of atomic weapons into industrial controllers all over the world. The amount of nuclear research alloted to the *little leaguers* is decided by the *big leaguers* ... Everyone is allowed to talk but only the superpowers have a say in things. Moscow and Washington give the orders and everyone else has to obey. Do they really have to? (*Bild*, 20 February 1967)

As a vociferous journalistic outsider, Sebastian Haffner was reminded of the way

such campaigns were handled under Goebbels. First a few individual voices chime in on the central motif, then more and more instruments join in, and in the end the whole orchestra plays the same theme in unison, in a crescendo that ends in a wild hysterical furioso: 'Super-Versailles! Diktat! Morgenthau Plan! Signing one's own death warrant!' We have not seen such concerted action in Germany since 1945. Now an atmosphere has been created that makes a matter-of-fact discussion on the pros and cons of the matter almost impossible. (*Stern*, 5 March 1967)

With this concentrated anti-NPT hysteria, Germany stood alone in the world. Not even France showed the smallest degree of sympathy. This outcry articulated a deeply rooted German resentment which had been revitalised by the American-Soviet merger. Germany, feeling it was a power that was being punished and held on a short rein, was confronted again with the Potsdam syndrome. 'Potsdam, that means: let's agree with each other at the expense of Germany!', Adenauer had repeatedly declared. Bonn viewed the superpowers' agreement as proof of the betrayal of the MLF, i.e. betrayal of Bonn by its main ally. The underdog complex, the pent-up rage, that 'revenge at the grave of the MLF' (*Der Spiegel*, 10/1967) was publicly expressed for the first time at the *Wehrkunde* meeting in Munich:

> It is useless for the two American military theorists, Professors Schelling and Speier, to try and play down the [NPT] project and distract our attention from it. The five dozen participants in the meeting launched this point at the heart of the discussion again and again, and they demolished with sharp analyses – but also with scorn and protest – what was left of its reputation up to that point. ... For the first time, the NPT was talked about openly and honestly, and that was the result most worth mentioning, the breakthrough that this meeting achieved. ... Ambassador Schnippenkoetter condemned the endeavours of the nuclear superpowers to wrest atomic protection from those countries who thought they were most in need of it. ... Even Helmut Schmidt, chairman of the SPD ... held out the prospect of Germany's signature only on condition of a mighty 'if': it might be done if the other abstaining countries think it advisable. (*FAZ*, 31 January 1967)

The claim that Moscow wanted the treaty only 'to suppress and humiliate a free Germany' in the words of CDU MP Werner Marx (*WaS*, 5 February 1967), was well received by those who were promoting this very 'Germanocentric' campaign. The negative reactions that this point of view would certainly provoke in countries in both East and West only augmented the feeling that there was a conspiracy against Germany. But such grandiloquent rhetoric, which was intended to threaten and intimidate other governments with catchwords like 'Versailles' in order to force through German interests, was not compatible with the goal of clearing the Federal Republic of its reputation as an opponent of detente. An observer in Geneva wrote:

> The scoffing about German behaviour has a well-meaning sound to it when concerned only with the inferiority complexes, hysteria and provincialism that try to measure international proceedings by Bonn's standards. Less harmless are the feelings of scepticism which point to a lack of West Germany's preparedness to accede to the treaty when this is thought to camouflage sinister military ambitions. And some people who do not go so far shake their heads

and ask if perhaps it is not just pure defamation to portray West Germans as being the troublemakers in every detente situation. (*SZ*, 23 February 1967)

This nationalistic melodrama made an especially counterproductive impression on potential allies in the non-nuclear camp, who not only were startled into retreating from cooperation, but who, moreover, often began to combine their objections to the NPT with an aloofness from Bonn.

The German government was now chiefly interested in de-escalating the situation. Kiesinger wrote to Adenauer, asking him to be more discreet and reticent in what he said; he talked to Strauss as well. These efforts at appeasement were successful. The critics stopped their campaign in order to pursue future negotiations 'with the utmost delicacy, and to achieve what they could with as much modesty as certitude' (*FAZ*, 20 February 1967).

The least important role in this campaign was played by Germany's nuclear industry. Only after Minister Stoltenberg had expressed his 'urgent desire' did the German Atomic Forum write, on 27 February 1967, its first critical statement about the wording of the treaty. The leading editorial of the journal *atomwirtschaft* openly criticised 'the hysteria which had taken hold of the public discussion about the NPT in the Federal Republic'. The journalistic flagship of the nuclear industry went on to say that the Federal Republic should 'in principle welcome every step which prevents or impedes the further proliferation of these weapons' (*atw* 3/1967, p. 123). *The Times* was by no means mistaken when it said that the worries about the industrial future of the FRG were 'largely ... a cover'. According to *The Times* on 21 February 1967:

> The real German objective is that some Germans ... hope that by retaining the nuclear option Germany will be able to use it one day as a bargaining counter for reunification. But by putting forward this argument Germany would at once be wholly isolated. ... Herr Brandt ... has raised instead as an important objection the possibility that the non-nuclear powers, by signing the treaty, may prejudice their civil development.

Nevertheless, the campaign was useful for the German negotiating position. This is confirmed by Günter Diehl, who was then the head of the Press and Information Office of the federal government of Germany:

For tactical reasons, a certain amount of resistance was welcomed by the chancellor. The controversy had to be plausible. So he could argue to the outside, vis-à-vis the nuclear powers: 'You should be accommodating towards us because otherwise the NPT will not find a broad majority.' (author's interview with G. Diehl, 20 July 1990)

The outcry did, indeed, have two different effects. Internationally, it had pushed the Federal Republic to the very borderline of isolation; but in its relationship with the United States, the German position had been strengthened. It was no coincidence that the climax of the controversy was reached on 21 February 1967, the beginning of the disarmament conference in Geneva. On 23 March 1967 this conference had to be postponed, without having achieved any results. This marked the beginning of a phase of continuing consultations between Germany and the US.

The German-American Negotiations Marathon

After the MLF was dead and buried, Washington, Moscow and Bonn remained the key centres of the NPT controversy, but their positions had changed. The new 'pivotal point' of America's NPT policy was the agreement with Moscow, whereas Washington's relations with Bonn became more of a 'floating consideration'. It was that change of priorities in 1967 which turned the NPT into 'Negative Point No. 1' in German-American relations. 'Chancellor Kiesinger … [called] the NPT negotiations the most difficult aspect of U.S.–FRG relations', Seaborg remembers (Seaborg, 1987, p. 289).

Looking back, the real break in German-American NPT negotiations occurred in the autumn of 1966. Within the Auswärtige Amt there was already a feeling that the MLF was a thing of the past; the superpowers' consensus on the NPT was in the air. In spite of this, the United States kept silent about matters as far as the Federal Republic was concerned. Inquiries from German diplomats were answered with contradictory or misleading statements, and there were no consultations at all. The premonition was followed by a fait accompli. When the final version of the NPT, negotiated jointly by the two superpowers, was presented to Willy Brandt on 16 December 1966, Bonn found itself staring into an abyss. The deceitful calm of the previous months now suddenly became a storm. Between 16 December 1966 and 4 January 1967 Germany's diplomatic service was at work almost daily. At first everything concentrated on two questions. Were Articles I and II still reversible? If not, what exactly was meant by these vague formulations? The Americans had been caught with their fingers in the honey pot. It was not felt necessary to spare them in any respect. The US negotiators, on the other hand, tried to keep the calculated damage to a minimum. From the beginning of 1967 the bilateral negotiations were concentrated in roundtable discussions in Washington. The Auswärtige Amt sent endless telegrams with queries and directives to the German Embassy in Washington. It was up to Botschaftsrat Berndt von Staden, a longtime personal friend of Swidbert Schnippenkoetter, to present the German points of view to the Americans in meetings that took place virtually every day. The principle partners in these discussions with Herr von Staden were the head of the ACDA Foreign Department, Samuel de Palma, and his deputy, Adrian Fisher. On important occasions, the discussion was led by the director of ACDA, William C. Foster, and the German ambassador, Karl Heinrich Knappstein. Herr von Staden had no power of attorney to negotiate on his own. All American reactions and statements were telegraphed back to Bonn; the following day, the talks were resumed on the basis of new, additional orders signed by Herr Schnippenkoetter. The atmosphere of the talks was usually friendly, as Berndt von Staden reported later. Things followed a 'good and pleasant direction', just as in the first talks, telegraphed Herr Knappstein; William Foster answered all questions 'openly and in detail' (AA-Doc. I, Annex 3). Only once did Adrian Fisher show any sign of impatience, and that was when he asked for a break of a few days as the work of his entire office had already come to a standstill (author's interview with Berndt von Staden, July 1990). The German government could not complain that information was lacking. But just how far was Washington really prepared to take German concerns about the NPT into consideration?

It was chiefly to find an answer to this question that Willy Brandt visited the United States from 7 to 11 February 1967, a visit which provided new criteria for German-American relations. Not to sail in the wake of the United States but to self-confidently maintain Germany's national interests – that was the goal of the Auswärtige Amt. Not much is known about the talks with Johnson, Rusk, McNamara and Humphrey, but the results were not at all unfavourable:

- The US agreed to let the Soviet Union know details of the American interpretation to increase its legal footing.
- The US promised to include a clause on disarmament in the preamble of the treaty which would throw new light on the right of withdrawal.

- Dean Rusk promised to prevent any hindrance to the peaceful use of atomic energy. The State Department even supplied full details on this point shortly afterwards by announcing that the NPT would make it 'even easier' to export plutonium.
- It was decided to establish bilateral commissions of specialists who would discuss the remaining questions which were still open (Barnes, 1976, pp. 383–5).

Despite the success of the Brandt mission, criticism of the NPT in Bonn was not subdued – quite the reverse in fact. After the foreign minister returned, Strauss threatened to break up the Grand Coalition if the FRG acceded to the treaty (*WaS*, 19 February 1967). Disarmament Commissioner Schnippenkoetter now criticised the NPT by claiming that 'even the North Atlantic Treaty Organisation was put into question juridically and politically by the treaty' (*NYT*, 17 February 1967). The foreign minister came up with a whole range of new arguments against the way the controls in the treaty were being planned, a factor that had not even been discussed in Washington (*Bulletin*, 21 February 1967, p. 140).

German-American relations reached their nadir on 27 February 1967 when the federal chancellor publicly and 'very deliberately' criticised, as he explained to journalists much later, the undermining of NATO and the 'atomic conspiracy' between Washington and Moscow (AdG, 1 March 1967, p. 13020). Not only were American diplomats irritated by the chancellor's open criticism, 'That remark was reported to have infuriated Mr Johnson at the time and long afterward' (*NYT*, 28 April 1967). The administration hurried to issue a disclaimer of Kiesinger's criticism and tried to achieve reconciliation, but the negotiations in Geneva were interrupted at the insistence of the United States. Vice-President Humphrey was sent to Bonn to settle the German-American NPT dispute and to change the Federal Republic's evaluation of the treaty (*NYT*, 30 March 1967). But Kiesinger kept putting his visitor off. At least 30 specific points were still unclear – according to a government official – from Bonn's point of view (*NYT*, 6 April 1967).

The NPT commissions which had been set up in Washington had by this time already met 'for week-long talks on various aspects of the treaty, particularly safeguards' (ACDA, 1967, p. 11). These bilateral talks between specialists in Washington had, 'in an atmosphere of hostility' and 'in a sometimes unpleasant manner, developed rather sluggishly' – this was the unanimous opinion of participants from the FRG (Häfele, Lahusen, Ramisch) and the US (van Doren, Weiler). The Washington talks are worth examining in more detail; partly because in the course of these negotiations decisions were made and some parts of the treaty were formulated, and partly because they demonstrated once more that there was no clear connection between Germany's successes in negotiating and winning acceptance for the NPT in Bonn.

The meetings were held in the offices of the American disarmament authority, ACDA. Negotiations were intensive – it is reported that in one case discussions went on for nine days. The American delegation comprised such high-ranking personalities as Foster, Fisher and ten other officials from the State Department and the ACDA; and they were extremely well prepared. Previous statements by German diplomats on the NPT had been entered into a computer and were thus at the immediate disposal of the Americans; they were repeatedly quoted to the FRG delegation should they present divergent opinions. The German delegation was made up of five to six participants: chief negotiator Swidbert Schnippenkoetter, his colleagues Carl Lahusen and Rolf Ramisch, one or two representatives from the German Embassy, and nuclear physicists Wolf Häfele and Karl Wirtz as technical specialists.

The disputes were fought out between Foster and Schnippenkoetter. Both gave the floor to other members of their delegations. According to one German participant, some of the Americans viewed Herr Schnippenkoetter's way of leading the negotiations as slightly strange: the ambassador did not talk to Foster as if he were a junior partner but as an equal. 'Discussions were never violent but they were quite clear-cut. Voices were never raised, but pointed remarks were made' (author's interview with Rolf Ramisch, 16 August 1989). Topics ranged from debates about NATO to mini-explosions, from procedural questions to control systems. The Germans entered the negotiations with a four-page list of requests covering about 50 points that had been worked out beforehand in Bonn by a good 100 specialists (lawyers, technicians, economists, army officers). During an earlier internal working meeting of the Studiengruppe, Herr Schnippenkoetter had described what he wanted from these discussions as follows:

Three basic principles were followed: a) As little discrimination as possible; b) As much balance as possible; c) As much clarity as possible. ... The '55 Desires for Change', as they are called in the media, can be explained by the fact that the talks about disarmament and safeguards in the civil sector are very complex, and on top of that, many other areas will have to be touched upon as well. (Studiengruppe, 8 May 1967)

These negotiations were quite demanding, not only for the Americans but for the Germans as well. The Bonn delegation had been given orders to negotiate by the Bundesverteidigungsrat (Federal Council of Defence), but it had no mandate to negotiate. Therefore the German position had to be prepared and evaluated on a daily basis so that certain questions could be sent to Bonn with the request for new instructions. One participant said later that in those weeks the relevant officials in the Auswärtige Amt in Bonn had to burn the midnight oil almost every day in order to work out these new instructions.

For days, the negotiations concentrated solely on the question of control arrangements. Finally, nuclear physicist Wolf Häfele was given a mandate to formulate texts on the principle of fissionable materials controls. Parts of these texts were later included in the preamble of the treaty without any change to their wording; for example, 'safeguarding effectively the flow of source and special fissionable materials by use of instruments and other techniques and certain strategic points'. These new control arrangements which were worked out in Washington were not at all compatible with the then current regulations of the IAEA. It is said that people were thunderstruck when later in Vienna an American member of the ACDA, Ben Huberman, made the results of the German-American talks public as the new, standardised NPT regulation. The initial protests of those responsible in the IAEA were bluntly rejected by the Americans, with the observation that the purpose of the IAEA was not to serve itself but its member states (author's interview with Ben Huberman, October 1986).

The first round of negotiations with the United States lasted from 10 to 14 April 1967. What were the results? A document presented to the cabinet by the Auswärtige Amt listed the following points under the heading 'Results of the bilateral German-American negotiations':

- six 'classical' American interpretations
- shelter regulations on peaceful use in the text of the treaty
- draft of a control article conforming to Euratom
- establishment of the principle of how to safeguard the flow of fissionable materials
- prospects of further regulations on disarmament in the text of the treaty

Moreover, certain modifications in procedural regulations were guaranteed. (AA-Doc. XV)

What had happened was that Articles I and II had been interpreted; Article III (dealing with safeguards) had been reformulated, not only in favour of Euratom but also with respect to Germany's specific controls concept; Article IV, which encouraged the peaceful use of atomic energy, had been outlined; a further article on disarmament was in the offing.

When Herr Schnippenkoetter nevertheless expressed his deep dissatisfaction in Washington with the results of the negotiations, this was too much for those in the US who wanted to present a draft treaty at the reopening of the disarmament conference in Geneva. On 12 April 1967 they threatened in the NATO Council that they would hold NATO responsible for the failure of the NPT should the modified version of the treaty not be accepted by their next meeting (*NYT*, 13 April 1967). A few days later they implied that they would come to an agreement with the Soviet Union, if necessary, without taking their NATO allies into consideration (*NYT*, 20 April 1967).

On 19 April 1967 – the day Konrad Adenauer died – the German government was occupied with the results of the Washington negotiations. Willy Brandt had made clear in his report to the cabinet that, through these talks, modifications to the treaty had been reached on several points – but the cabinet itself did not make any statement on the details of the new draft NPT; it only expressed the wish that 'the bilateral and multilateral consultations with the Allies on the points that are not yet agreed have to be continued' (BPA, 19 April 1967). Relating to this, the American request to enter negotiations with the Soviet Union on the basis of the new draft NPT was not accepted but only 'taken notice of' (BPA, 19 April 1967).

The cabinet decision on 19 April 1967 served as a preparation for the NATO Council meeting on the 20th, whose results were just as meagre. After the presentation of the interpretations of Articles I and II which had been worked out in Washington, agreement was on the least common denominator. The United States received an 'amber light' to continue talks with the Soviet Union, although the modified NPT draft itself found no support because of misgivings on the part of the Germans and Italians (*NYT*, 21 April 1967).

After this not very encouraging experience, President Johnson was determined to settle the NPT dispute personally during a visit to Bonn (*NYT*, 24 April 1967). But events did not follow the expected course.

President Johnson and Chancellor Kiesinger met on 26 April, accompanied by only their interpreters, in order to talk about NPT problems. 'The atmosphere of the conversation was friendly, open and cordial', according to the official report of Bonn's government spokesman, Karl-Günther von Hase (BPA, 26 April 1967). But Kiesinger himself said that it was a 'hard discussion ... which took a very temperamental course' (Schwarz, 1985, p. 884). 'The talk was tough', agreed the *New York Times*, which went on to say:

> Mr. Kiesinger even stirred the President to anger by complaining about the nature of consultations between Washington and Bonn on vital issues. Mr. Johnson pointed out that he had sent a number of consultants to the Germans during the last three months and that Foreign Minister Willy Brandt had conferred at length with him and other senior officials in Washington. Chancellor Kiesinger persisted, saying that he was disappointed with 'the quality of the consultations.' At this, the informants said, President Johnson lost his temper. 'I have the best Secretary of State in the world,' he snapped, and was reported to have defended his other recent representatives to Bonn: Vice President Humphrey, William C. Foster, the disarmament negotiator, and John J. McCloy. (*NYT*, 27 April 1967)

With 'noticeable annoyance' and 'empty hands', Johnson returned to Washington, wrote *Die Welt*, adding, 'on none of the questions which presently stand between America and the Federal Republic did he manage to obtain a German concession (*Die Welt*, 28 April 1967). The disarmament conference in Geneva was postponed from 9 to 18 May 1967 at the initiative of the United States. It finally reopened without the presentation of a new draft NPT (*NYT*, 3 May 1967).

What was really meant when Kiesinger questioned the quality of consultations on the NPT? With no other NATO country had the United States followed the same sort of diplomacy on the NPT. At the same time that the Johnson/Kiesinger dispute was under way, Willy Brandt stressed in a conversation with Dean Rusk not only 'the spirit of cooperation and talks' but also 'the impressive result' of bilateral diplomacy on the NPT (author's interview with Dr Ulrich Sahm, March 1990). What caused trouble for the chancellor was the loss of effective co-determination in America's foreign policy as far as German interests were concerned. Under both Adenauer and Erhard, such co-determination had retained the character of a right to veto. But things had changed: Washington now approached the German government 'on all cosmetic questions ... with great charm and courtesy, but all major demands and proposals for modification were always blocked by the Americans, who pointed to the rigid and uncompromising attitude of the Soviets' (Hepp, 1968, p. 35).

Were German concerns assuaged by securing the peaceful use of nuclear energy? Not at all! The initial prophecies of doom from Bonn had created the impression that this would be so and had nourished the illusion in the United States that Bonn's worries could be overcome with a few guarantees and an Article IV. Instead, each time a series of objections was considered settled, the German government presented the Americans with a new list of requests and demands. When at the beginning of February Brandt brought home American guarantees of the civil use of atomic energy, the Euratom problem became the question of immediate interest; after the American control clause had been withdrawn, temporal limitation became the main problem. The next claim was raised by Schnippenkoetter during the negotiations in Washington: the treaty should include a clause of good behaviour in order to get Moscow to stop its allegations of and propaganda campaigns against nuclear research in the Federal Republic (*FAZ*, 14 June 1967). In June Bonn pressed for a special nuclear guarantee from the United States (*NYT*, 11 July 1967), and in August another demand arose, the so-called escape clause. If a nuclear-weapons state tried to blackmail the FRG, it should be possible to withdraw from the treaty unilaterally (*Bulletin*, 22 August 1967, p. 763).

Was Germany really interested in modifying the treaty, as it argued in its statements, or did Bonn want to hinder it, as was sometimes thought? The actions of the German government allowed both interpretations, especially as supporters of both claims were to be found within the government.

Marcel Hepp, an adviser to Strauss, stated plainly the CSU view that 'the original aim of Germany's tactics [had been] to *starve out* the treaty in a mass of discussions on details' (Hepp, 1968, p. 35; original emphasis). According to Wilfried Hertz-Eichenrode in an article *Die Welt*, there was also 'another side to the surprising success of the "Schnippenkoetter Crew". As the treaty now seems to be more acceptable, Bonn cannot go on pretending that it only wants to retouch some parts of the text' (*Die Welt*, 25 January 1968).

The group around Willy Brandt had little to offer by way of resisting such a tactic, because a strategy of conflict which always included the risk of a crisis in the government was out of the question. So the foreign minister not only had no other choice than to put his money on the willingness of the superpowers to make concessions, he actually had to press for this: a temporal limitation would make it easier for the chancellor to agree to the treaty, as Willy Brandt told his colleague Dean Rusk (author's interview with Dr Sahm, 7 March 1990).

Various strands within the NPT diplomacy were also in competition with each other in the American government. Just as in previous years, the State Department, which was more willing to make some concessions to its allies, was a counterpoint to the disarmament authority ACDA as well as to the AEC. The American president's dilemma became extremely clear on 25/6 April 1967. The Kremlin had rebuffed him on the 25th. US Secretary of State Rusk informed Willy Brand on the 26th that the Soviet Union had rejected the new draft of a safeguards regulation. The protocol of that meeting recorded: 'Soviets have not accepted Art. III ... Foster had said with regard to Article III: "Then no treaty". Roschtschin had answered: "That may well be"' (interview with Dr Sahm). On the 26th during the conversation between Johnson and Kiesinger, the next cold shower followed: the US had failed as a broker between the two fronts! However, in the White House it was clear that the treaty was not dependent only on the signature of the Soviet Union, but also upon the accession of the Federal Republic. A contradictory relationship of dependency held Washington and Bonn together: Johnson knew that he would not achieve his goal with the Soviets by going it alone. Kiesinger knew that the FRG would be able to modify the treaty, which it could not really reject, only with the support of the White House. The sharp dispute on 26 April ended in conciliation; NATO was still more important to him than the NPT, explained Johnson, and he gave his assurance that current, complete and detailed NPT consultations would be held between the two countries before any further decisions were made (*NYT*, 28 April 1967). In return, the German chancellor promised his visitor that 'major disputes' between the governments would not in future be fought in public but would be kept 'within the family' (*NYT*, 28 April 1967). Indeed, the 'atomic conspiracy' reproach remained an exception. From that time onwards, in the public portrayal of Germany's NPT policy little was said about quarrels between the two allies.

But the future of the treaty had not seemed so bleak for a long time. On 27 April 1967 Willy Brandt met with President Johnson and then with France's Foreign Minister Courve de Murville. Both were confronted with the same uneasy question: if the treaty did not materialise, would the Germans be held responsible? (interview with Dr Sahm). On the very same day the German government had, for the first time, issued a statement in the Bundestag. And the foreign minister at least hinted at the fact that some of Germany's concerns over the treaty were still unresolved with regard to temporal limitation, controls and questions of procedure. At the same time, the German government stated that it would be prepared to support an early acceptance of the treaty as long as no 'vital interests' of the FRG were prejudiced. According to Brandt, however, the treaty has to be considered in terms of four complexes of questions:

1. The unlimited use of peaceful atomic energy.
2. A clear connection to general disarmament.
3. The guarantee of safety.
4. Nothing prejudicial to Europe's striving for unity.
   (DBT, 27 April 1967, p. 4,941).

The reports on that debate give the impression that the Bundestag was filled with supporters of the NPT. Even the CSU parliamentary speaker, Friedrich Zimmermann, stated his interest 'in making the draft universally acceptable'. This obvious restraint was related to the fact that as Helmut Schmidt explained: no one wanted 'to become that person at whom a finger would be pointed as being responsible for the failure of the treaty, should it for whatever reason not come about in the end' (DBT, 27 April 1967, p. 4,953).

In August 1967 the superpowers presented, surprisingly, a joint draft of the treaty which did not include the still-controversial safeguards clause. But that by no means ended the NPT crisis. On the contrary, it worsened. It had taken the superpowers 18 months to come to an agreement on Articles I and II; agreement on Article III would take another twelve months.

The History of the Safeguards Article

To ensure compliance with the NPT, *who* would be checked, *how* and *by whom*? It was the task of Article III to answer these questions. There were three problem areas:

1. Who was to be checked? Just the non-nuclear-weapons states or the nuclear-weapons states as well? (The problem of discrimination.)
2. How were checks to be carried out? Should only fissionable materials or related facilities too be subject to safeguards? Should checks be made by inspectors or by automated processes? (The technical aspect of the safeguards.)
3. Who was to be responsible for safeguards within the EC? Inspectors of the European Atomic Energy Community, Euratom, or of the International Atomic Energy Agency, IAEA? (The institutional aspect of the safeguards.)

Articles I and II of the treaty were agreed after the MLF option was discarded and the superpowers' talks continued bilaterally. For Article III, it was vital to gain the cooperation of the West European allies. In the case of the MLF, the NPT had only confirmed its death; but where Euratom was concerned, the NPT and especially the attack on Euratom's safeguards monopoly quite unexpectedly gave new life to this institution. Whereas Western Europe was dependent on the United States in the field of defence, Euratom was a project that not only aimed at independence from the United States, it had already achieved this in certain areas. The intransigence of Bonn and the autonomy ambitions of Brussels explain why the fate of the NPT hung in the balance more than once because of Euratom. In the autumn of 1967 the NPT seemed to be doomed to failure because of Article III.

Three drafts by the United States

In a memorandum of 31 January 1967 the United States sent the Federal Republic a draft of Article III in which it was stated that every non-nuclear-weapons state had to subordinate its entire peaceful nuclear activities to IAEA controls as soon as practicable (AA-Doc. III). Euratom would be accepted as a safeguards institution only as an interim solution. For the Soviet Union, Euratom as a safeguards authority was out of the question. The Community was composed of NATO members only, argued the Kremlin. Who would rely on the effectiveness, for example, of an 'Arabatom', established by the countries of the Arab League, as a safeguards institution? For this reason, all non-nuclear-weapons states had to be treated the same, i.e. to be inspected by the IAEA. In principle, the superpowers' points of view did not differ greatly: 'There could be other groupings in other parts of the world who might wish to put together little family groups which would inspect themselves and deny outside inspections', said Secretary of State Dean Rusk. He believed in the credibility of the Euratom safeguards – 'The problem is, how do you persuade 120 other nations that that is the case?' (ACDA, 1969, p. 70).

To Euratom, the US proposal on 31 January 1967 was pure provocation. It was rejected out of hand. This stand was supported by the German government. After the first two Articles of the draft treaty had proved to be unchangeable, Bonn was very keen that in Article III, at least, its interests should be taken into consideration – the role of the atomic community should not be limited. But, among the member states of Euratom Bonn's efforts to make this stand uniform triggered 'not very positive reactions', as Willy Brandt frankly admitted (DBT, 23 February 1967, p. 4416). The Netherlands in particular was quite concerned about the negative reaction of Euratom. But the harsh reactions of Brussels and Bonn forced the United States to change its course. The Article III draft of 31 January 1967 was withdrawn. The new American draft of 3 April 1967 differed from the old one as follows. Just as in the Euratom treaty, it was now only fissionable material, but not nuclear facilities, which would be subject to inspection; Euratom was now accepted as an 'international safeguards system' and an agreement was requested for the IAEA to 'verify' the effectiveness of those controls. However, should such a verification agreement still not exist three years after the treaty had come into force, IAEA controls were to be applied.

It was this last point which, in Bonn, was immediately branded as 'taking us by the throat' and a 'guillotine' (*HB*, 11 April 1967), and was vehemently rejected, whereas the Netherlands implied that it could now accede to the NPT (*Industriekurier*, 5 April 1967). After the meeting of the Euratom ministers on 10 April 1967 this new American draft, too, was swept aside. An enthusiastic commentary in the *Frankfurter Rundschau* described the role of the German foreign minister as follows. Brandt had

> called the modified American proposal a 'step in the right direction' and thus also won over the Italians who were more than ready to sign the treaty. He also took a step in the right direction towards establishing for the first time a sort of united European front against claims to leadership by the two superpowers. ... For the first time it seems as if a German foreign minister will be able to use the Federal Republic of Germany's membership of the European Communities as a foreign policy instrument to push forward our own interests. ... Brandt's compromise formulation, accepted by Italy, Belgium, the Netherlands and Luxembourg, basically says nothing beyond the fact that the Euratom states will only permit Euratom controls and no others in their area. (*FR*, 12 April 1967)

On 25 April 1967 America's third proposal was presented. This was a direct result of 'the German-American consultations during April 1967' (AA-Doc. XV). The most important innovation was the abolition of the 'guillotine clause'. On 27 April Foreign Minister Brandt himself informed the Bundestag about this latest stage of the negotiations, saying that the IAEA should be able to convince itself of the effectiveness of other control systems. On the very same day this proposal was rejected by the Soviet delegation in Geneva (interview with Dr Sahm).

What next? According to the protocol of the Inter-ministerial Working Staff, further American plans in May 1967 were outlined in a confidential letter from Dean Rusk to Willy Brandt as follows:

First phase: advocating the language of the latest American draft;
Second phase: in the event of a lack of success in the first phase, checking of the situation in consultations with the allies with the goal of achieving a generally acceptable NPT;
Third phase: under certain circumstances presentation of the latest American proposal in Geneva. If the Soviets or other delegations claim in their own drafts IAEA controls only, *the Soviet Union should be made responsible for the non-agreement because of its refusal to allow controls on its own territory.* (AA-Doc. VII; emphasis added).

Following the 'hard' German-American NPT talks in Bonn at the end of April 1967, the United States was now introducing a scenario that included the possibility that the treaty might fail because of the safeguards article. At the same time, an assignment of blame was discussed which was very useful for the Germans with their fear of being held responsible for the failure of the NPT. The exact wording of the letter from Dean Rusk is not known and it remains an open question as to whether or not this strategy was ever seriously followed up by the American government. At any rate America's subsequent actions followed a different course: the United States changed sides. In cooperation with Moscow, Bonn had been hoodwinked.

The Foster/Roschtschin Draft
One of the secrets of NPT diplomacy, only discovered 20 years later, is described in the following episode. In the summer of 1967 a series of top-secret American-Soviet talks began, with the aim of getting the treaty going again. Bonn was not informed of this. A short time later, the negotiating group meeting in Geneva agreed on a new draft of Article III in which, for the first time, though only indirectly, Euratom was accepted by the Soviets. Firstly, all non-nuclear-weapons states were to accept controls of the pledge they made when signing the treaty 'in accordance with the Statutes of the IAEA and the Agency's safeguards system, as set forth in an agreement to be negotiated and concluded with the IAEA'. Second, such an agreement was to be negotiated either individually 'or together with other states' – the euphemism for Euratom. It is true that there was no longer a 'guillotine', but an agreement between IAEA and Euratom would have to be reached within 24 months (AA-Doc. IX).

This consensus of opinion only existed at the diplomatic level and not at that of the governments. To make it easier for the governments to approve, the negotiators in Geneva agreed on a trick: the text was presented in Washington as the new 'Soviet' proposal, and in Moscow as the new 'American' proposal. When this so-called Roschtschin Draft was conveyed to the German government on 1 September 1967, at least formally, Rusk's promise was kept that no new American draft would be drawn up without prior consultation with Bonn. 'There would have been difficulties if it had appeared to be a U.S. suggestion in view of an earlier Rusk promise to Brandt not to change the existing U.S. proposal without prior consultation', wrote Seaborg and Loeb who, in 1987, published details of this procedure for the first time, based on information provided by America's chief negotiator, George Bunn. It is said, however, that Rusk himself knew about this 'artful manoeuvre' (Seaborg and Loeb, 1987, p. 293).

The United States let the German government know that it saw a new chance for an agreement based on that 'private Soviet initiative' so that 'the NPT might be ready for signature by this coming autumn' (*SZ*, 15 September 1967). The Benelux countries also immediately declared that they were in agreement with a slightly modified American version of the 'Soviet' proposal. But it was all in vain: 'Germany, Italy and the Euratom Commission again strongly disagreed' (Van der Mey, 1989, p. 127).

The meeting of the EC Council of Ministers on 3 October 1967 was to bring this stage of the negotiations to a close. At the suggestion of the Federal Republic, the EC Commission was asked to comment on the 'Roschtschin Draft', and at the same time was given the task 'of working out a new version of the safeguards article which would be compatible with the Euratom treaty'. During the consultations of the Inter-ministerial Working Staff a week later, a German proposal for Article III was passed and then sent on as an aid to formulating policy to the EC Commission (but not to the United States). The minutes of this working staff meeting, classified as 'secret', provide just one more proof of the isolated position of the Germans and Italians. For that reason, among others, the German proposal for Article III was

urgently needed, ...
- because among the Benelux members of Euratom, there is a prevailing tendency to stick to the fundamentals of the Soviet proposal as far as the decisive point of commitment to IAEA safeguards is concerned;
- because the NATO partners are, for the most part, already following the American line of accepting the Soviet proposal. (AA-Doc. VII, p. 5)

The American government was anything but enthusiastic about the results of the meeting of the EC Council of Ministers. It had expected an agreement on Article III, but what resulted was another tabling of the problem, coupled with a waiting strategy that now seriously threatened to put an end to the NPT. 'Disarmament experts fear that this is exactly what allies like West Germany and Italy want to see happen', reported the *New York Times* on 11 October 1967. The all-time low in German-American NPT diplomacy was reached when, with reference to this situation, Willy Brandt, in a letter to Dean Rusk, criticised the dissociation of the United States from the German-American draft of April and its interest in the new 'Soviet' formulation. Moreover, his words of reproach included a few new NPT essentials put forward by the German government:

> Initially, the treaty should not be concluded for a period of more than five years. The treaty should include a revision clause which ensures that no signatory to it would be obliged to follow any changes in the treaty that it does not accept voluntarily. (*NZZ*, 19 October 1967)

Once again, Helmut Schmidt began to doubt that the treaty would ever come about, with reference to the concerns of the EC Commission which he himself shared (*FAZ*, 20 October 1967). In a meeting of the directors of the Auswärtige Amt, government spokesman Günter Diehl reported on the increasing irritation in Washington. The credibility of the chancellor was being questioned; patience had been exhausted (interview with Dr Sahm). And it was not the Federal Republic which was responsible for the change that followed, it was a Euratom dissident: the Netherlands and its foreign minister, Joseph Luns.

Agreement on Article III

It was not only the United States that was about to lose all patience. On 24 October 1967 Foreign Minister Luns threatened that his country would sign the NPT in a go-it-alone move if an agreement was not reached within a very short period of time (Van der Mey, 1989, p. 128). During the days that followed, the negotiators of the 'Five', among them Ambassador Swidbert Schnippenkoetter, agreed upon 'five principles' as a joint basis for the consultations on Article III. For the first time, these 'principles' included a role for the IAEA within the territory of Euratom. The 'five principles' and a modified American version of the 'Roschtschin Draft' were presented to the

NATO Council on 2 November 1967 as a new draft of Article III, and then it was passed on to the Soviet Union.

But now the agreement on Article III, and with it on the NPT as a whole, threatened to fall apart because of a single phrase. Roschtschin was prepared to accept all American changes as long as the United States would accept the rephrasing of one sentence in favour of a stronger emphasis on the IAEA. Although there was no real difference in the practical, political meaning, the whole treaty was once more at stake. The continued American proceedings were later described by John W. Finney in the *New York Times*:

> Rather than seek immediate agreement with the Soviet Union the Administration decided to consult once more with its European allies. The result was a long memorandum from West Germany, reviewing its reservations and reviving issues that Washington had thought were long since resolved. Within the Administration a tug-of-war was renewed between the 'European faction' of the State Department, which cautioned against taking any step that might offend the allies, and a 'disarmament faction', which saw the treaty slipping from its grasp.(*NYT*, 20 January 1968)

The diary of the chairman of the AEC, Glenn T. Seaborg, confirms this information. His notes of 20 November 1967 describe the chief negotiator of the United States as 'very disturbed by developments. According to Foster, the Germans had produced a very long list of new demands that had to be met to obtain their adherence to the NPT' (Seaborg and Loeb, 1987, p. 300).

Even though the American government gave in, when the Geneva Disarmament Conference adjourned in December 1967 there was still no sign of a final NPT draft. As in the previous year, Foreign Ministers Gromyko and Rusk now met in New York City for secret talks.

On 18 January 1968 the uncertainty was over. When the Geneva Disarmament Conference reconvened, the two co-chairman were for the first time able to present a complete NPT draft. On the controversial question of Article III, the Soviet chief negotiator agreed at the last minute to the American formulation of 2 November 1967. The German observers present in Geneva were surprised. One called 'the phrasing of safeguards Article III "a miracle" compared with previous formulations' (*FAZ*, 20 January 1968). The *FAZ* also came to the conclusion 'that the Soviets had given in. But for the moment, the reasons remained a mystery to observers of the Geneva scene' (*FAZ*, 19 January 1968).

Was it really a miracle? Had Moscow given in unilaterally? Existing evidence suggests another picture. The fact that the Soviets gave in on the question of the safeguards article was only part of a greater compromise in which the question of the time limit of the treaty also played a role.

On 2 December 1967 President Johnson complied with the wishes of the German government on a point that was very important to Bonn. The Auswärtige Amt called Johnson's consent to placing the non-military nuclear facilities of the United States under IAEA controls a 'very important step' and a 'great success'. But then, however, pressure was applied to meet Germany's demands for 'a temporal limitation of the treaty which should in no way approach unlimited validity' (AA-Doc. XV, no. 1, p. 3).

In November 1967 the Italians proposed in Geneva that the treaty should have a duration of 'X' years. For those governments that did not terminate their membership six months prior to the end of this period, the validity of the treaty would automatically be extended for an equal period. At first the United States appeared to accept this proposal. According to Vladimir Shustov, a high-ranking member of the Soviet negotiating committee at the time, the Soviet Union was prepared to agree to a temporary 25-year limitation only if the right to withdraw which was coupled with it was omitted (Bunn and van Doren, 1991, pp. 7 ff.). Washington agreed to this, but with one condition: 'We were prepared to agree to the revised duration clause, if they would accept our November 2 formulation for the safeguards article' Adrian Fisher, the chief US negotiator, later reported (Seaborg and Loeb, 1987, p. 302). Moscow agreed to this after the United States had given its binding acceptance of the so-called Guiding Principles of Article III. As a counterbalance to the 'Five Principles' of the Euratom countries, these were formulated to establish controls in such a way that all parties to the treaty could thoroughly rely upon their effectiveness. The IAEA was to make use of existing controls and data in order to prevent a duplication of work but at the same time it was the Agency's duty to guarantee that no diversions took place (DAS VI, p. 13).

All things considered, this was an artfully balanced, comprehensive package. The Germans won a limitation on the duration of the treaty in return for agreement to the 'Guiding Principles'; the Soviets achieved those guidelines and a change in the 'duration clause' in return for their agreement to Article III; the Americans, who obviously preferred the Soviet position with regard to limitation and controls, had the satisfaction of having made the essential step forward.

'Capable of Improvement'

'The intensive influence of Bonn and the other Euratom countries which was sometimes difficult and stubborn and exasperated the Anglo-Saxon allies was extremely good for the NPT', noted a satisfied *FAZ* in January 1968. But in Bonn, many saw no reason for satisfaction. The Geneva draft was 'still capable of improvement', said government spokesman Günter Diehl (AdG, 1968, p. 13,675). The initial cautious commentary was followed by a new wave of criticism, 'accompanied by a new journalistic campaign which was a reflection of the political polarisation' (Haftendorn, 1974, p. 183).

The chancellor told the Federal Defence Council that he was especially disappointed about Article III and the duration of the treaty: 'The Americans should be told that these points are not satisfactory' (interview with Dr Sahm). This directive was aimed at the foreign minister, who had once again brought up the subject of the Federal Republic's different views in a letter to Rusk (*FAZ*, 24 February 1968). The obvious sign of this was that a new campaign was initiated: Kurt Georg Kiesinger declared that the current version of the treaty was unacceptable (BPA, 24 January 1968); Karl Theodor Freiherr von und zu Guttemberg reiterated the thesis concerning the contradiction between NATO commitments and the NPT (*FAZ*, 12 February 1968); while his party colleague Friedrich Zimmermann characterised the changes in the treaty made up till then as 'negligible' (ibid.), and the former president of the EC Commission, Walter Hallstein, openly declared it was a 'compelling duty to offer resistance to the NPT in its present version' (*EA*, 6/68, p. D154).

In the previous year, the agreement on Articles I and II had provoked the campaign of February 1967. The same was now true of Article III: as long as it seemed that the treaty would miscarry because of the safeguards clause, there was no need to criticise it on principle. The fact that this difficulty had been overcome in favour of Euratom controls was a Pyrrhic victory for the treaty's opponents.

During a meeting of the Inter-ministerial Working Staff in March 1968, the Western interpretations of Articles I and II which had already been presented to the NATO Council on 20 April 1967 were again checked and 'were unanimously viewed as being incomplete and not fully sufficient'. The following points were considered to be in need of clarification:

The practicality and necessity of additional interpretations; definitions of 'manufacture', 'otherwise acquire', 'assist', 'encourage or induce' (Art. I and II); definition of 'other nuclear explosive devices' (differentiation between 'destructive purpose' and 'peaceful purpose'?); use of nuclear energy for military, but non-nuclear-weapon purposes. (AA-Doc. XIII)

Again, the 'European option' lay at the heart of the matter. According to the *FAZ*, there was a desire to insist 'in a very outspoken manner' to the United States on an interpretation 'that would allow the establishment of a European defence alliance with the inclusion of nuclear weapons before a real European Federal State was founded' (*FAZ*, 19 March 1968).

According to the *New York Times*, in April Bonn had demanded a special and new guarantee against nuclear attacks as a prerequisite to Germany's accession to the treaty (*NYT*, 23 April 1968).

In May 1968 the minister for economic affairs, Karl Schiller, spoke about making Germany's accession to the NPT dependent upon a guarantee by the four powers to keep the roads to Berlin open (*Die Zeit*, 3 May 1968), a demand that was reported as having been later taken up by the chancellor too (*NYT*, 15 June 1968).

On the international stage, Bonn was fighting for a lost cause with such demands. Even Washington reacted with a great deal of reserve to Germany's reservations in these matters. This is very clearly demonstrated by the reaction of the American government to the German government's memorandum to the ENDC in Geneva on 6 March 1968.

It was well known in German government circles that the ENDC had to present a complete report on NPT diplomacy in New York by no later than 15 March 1968. Moscow was not alone in interpreting the presentation of an entire catalogue of German changes only one week prior to this date as an attempt to obstruct the outcome of the conference. This time, the United States and Great Britain refused

> to present the document to the disarmament conference. The Italians as well were not prepared to do so. Bonn's behaviour had worsened rather than bettered the attitude towards Germany's wishes, less from a factual point of view than because of the notorious clumsiness of the German team. (*National Zeitung,* Basel, 13 March 1968)

Bonn Faced with a Difficult Decision

With the agreement on Articles I–III, the essential obstacles had been overcome. The Articles had been presented again for discussion at the Geneva Disarmament Conference only for form's sake – in fact the wording which had been agreed upon during the strenuous negotiations was sacrosanct. All other regulations of the treaty were modified after some controversial discussions in Geneva and New York. The focal point of criticism was the demand for a disarmament pledge on the part of the nuclear-weapons states and a guarantee against the danger of nuclear blackmail. Above and beyond that, hotly debated issues concerned the prohibition of the production of nuclear warheads for peaceful purposes, the safeguards clause, and the way in which a revision of the treaty might be made (*EA* 24/67, pp. D562–3). During the discussions, apart from the safeguards clause, three declarations of intent which had previously been contained in the preamble of the treaty were transformed into new provisions of the treaty: the participation of the non-nuclear states in 'any potential benefits that might result from any peaceful applications of nuclear explosions' (new Article V); the pledge to pursue negotiations in good faith 'on effective measures regarding cessation of the nuclear arms race and disarmament' (new Article VI); and the right of any group of states to establish nuclear-free zones in their respective territories (new Article VII).

After the resolution concerning the guarantees for the non-nuclear NPT signatories as presented by the United States, the Soviet Union and Great Britain had been passed by the UN Security Council, the NPT was ceremoniously signed on 1 July 1968 in Washington, Moscow and London by the participating nuclear-weapons countries, and by another 53 non-nuclear-weapons countries (DoD, 1968, p. 470). The Federal Republic saw little reason to be happy about this event or even to consider Germany's accession. On the day the treaty was signed, German embassies were given directives which justified non-accession (interview with Dr Sahm). The tenor of this justification was most likely the same as that given in the brief statement issued by the government spokesman on 1 July 1968, reproduced here in full:

> In 1954, the Federal Republic of Germany had already renounced the production and purchase of nuclear weapons and other instruments of mass extermination. The German government had already reached a sort of status in this matter long before that now aimed at in the treaty. It is self-evident that the German government approves of the aims of the NPT. It is opposed to the chaos of nuclear ownership, but the German government has reasons to examine the problems related to the NPT in more detail than other countries. One of these important problems is the fact that the Soviet Union has been putting massive political pressure on the Federal Republic

of Germany for a long time and will certainly continue to do so. (BPA, 1 July 1968)

But the general public throughout the world was not satisfied with such a statement. The British newspaper the *Guardian* claimed that Bonn's explanations were mere excuses: the treaty had been modified throughout in order to conform to the wishes of the German government (*FAZ*, 3 July 1968). Poland's *Zycie Warszawy* wrote on 2 July 1968 that each additional day of delay in Bonn's accession to the treaty 'will be an additional argument both for Poland, and the rest of Europe, to justify Polish distrust towards the real aims of the policy being followed by the Federal Republic of Germany' (BPA Ostinformationen). But the most vigorous 'finger-wagging' came from the United States: 'If there is one government on earth that cannot long refuse to sign the treaty to prevent the spread of nuclear weapons it is that of West Germany', ran the lead editorial in the *New York Times* on 8 July 1968. This prognosis was proved wrong by Bonn. Another year and a half would pass before Germany acceded to the NPT. Yet the experience of the Nuclear Planning Group was invaluable in helping Bonn to accept the NPT.

More Rights in Nuclear Planning
At the signing of the NPT, America's secretary of defense, Clark Clifford, had announced that the treaty 'would not obstruct ... the further development of the nuclear defence measures within the alliance' (DS 7/994, p. 35). During the following months this announcement proved to be absolutely right.

Within the Nuclear Planning Group (NPG), from the very beginning the German government was chiefly interested in securing more influence over planning the use of nuclear weapons stationed in the Federal Republic as well as over the provisos for their release. In October 1968 the NPG asked the British and German ministers of defence to work out tactical nuclear guidelines. This directive alone meant an increase in status for the Federal Republic. In May 1969 ministers Schröder and Healey presented to the NPG a 65-page paper containing a number of proposals which included, according to Paul Buteux, author of *The Politics of Nuclear Consultation in NATO 1965–1980*:

one, clearly reflecting German interests ... that any decision to use nuclear weapons should be taken in the last resort by those imme-diately concerned. This was understood to mean the possessors of the warhead, the possessor of the launcher and the country from which the weapon would be fired. (Buteux, 1983, p. 90)

When the NPG convened again in November 1969, the new minister of defence, Helmut Schmidt, had already taken over from his predecessor in lively style. During a meeting in Warrington, Virginia, the NATO defence ministers agreed upon a nuclear use and planning concept which was based on the Schröder/Healey (i.e. Schmidt/Healey) study. In December 1969 this concept was raised to the status of a formal NATO regulation under the heading 'Interim defence policy guideline for the defensive tactical first use of nuclear weapons by NATO' (Mahncke, 1972, p. 245). The agreement reached in Warrington also left the final decision on nuclear use to those countries who were 'directly involved' (Buteux, 1983, p. 103). However, the US monopoly on use remained untouched: the president's obligation to consult America's allies was valid only on condition that the time and situation permitted such consultation. Nevertheless, Helmut Schmidt declared in November 1969 that with these new guidelines, 'a very far-reaching agreement on co-determination for the European partners had been made. And the word "co-determination" should here be interpreted in both senses: positively as well as negatively' (quoted in Klejdzinski, 1984, p. 10). Within the Studiengruppe this was described as 'an essential step forward' in nuclear cooperation (Studiengruppe, 8 December 1969), as now bilateral elements had been brought into nuclear planning (*NYT*, 13 November 1969) and the Federal Republic had been given a special status. The concrete form that these regulations took is still unknown, as is the American interpretation of the German term *Verfügungsgewalt* ('power of disposition').

In an internal paper presented to the cabinet by Willy Brandt in June 1969, it can be seen that the Federal Republic had managed to achieve an additional American interpretation within NATO of the term *Verfügungsgewalt* with regard to the NPT controversy and as a supplement to the 'classic' interpretations of Articles I and II. This interpretation has never been made public, not even during the debate on the ratification of the treaty in the US Senate (AA-Doc. XV and *DBT*, 12 November 1969, p. 328). It is quite likely that by means of this interpretation, the question of the control over nuclear weapons to be exercised by West German troops in the event of war took on a more concrete form. From the German point of view it was necessary that if war seemed imminent, American warheads – after the approval of the American president, and armed by American officers – really would be released to the Bundeswehr and could be used by them without the permission of the US (interview material and NHP VII).

No one knows whether or not this interpretation is true, but one can be relatively certain of the fact that, after 1969, the divergent positions within NATO drew closer to each other thanks to the refinement and completion of NPG guidelines. In the words of the DGAP's research director, Professor Karl Kaiser:

> It was especially during those 16 years of Social Democrat partic-
> ipation in the German government that ... the system of Germany's
> active partnership in the planning of goals and operations in
> nuclear questions, as well as German participation in taking
> potential decisions concerning the use of nuclear weapons (whilst
> maintaining America's right of veto), was considerably extended.
> (Kaiser, 1989, p. 267)

But in the Federal Republic of 1969 even the developments in the NPG could not promote the German government's acceptance of the NPT.

The Enemy State Clause and Renunciation of the Use of Force

After the first round of signatures to the NPT, the German government was still trying to standardise certain provisos to the treaty within Euratom, but time was running out. As early as July 1968, Italy and the Benelux countries declared their willingness to accede to the treaty. Shortly before that, the EC Commission had also given the green light to accession to the treaty (DS 7/994, p. 36).

A joint proviso to the treaty concerning the European option failed because of the 'absolute no' of the French. The German foreign minister was under pressure from French Prime Minister Michel Debré to refrain from taking any initiative in that direction because it would arouse suspicion (interview with Dr Sahm). The German government was more successful with the control proviso. On 31 July 1968, the non-nuclear-weapons states in Euratom declared that they would ratify the NPT as soon as an agreement was reached in the Euratom/IAEA negotiations (DS 7/994, p. 36).

Willy Brandt wanted to present the treaty to the cabinet for agreement in October or November 1968. He wanted to make this agreement easier for the cabinet by means of a number of provisos and other limitations, but events overtook him. During the night of 20/1 August 1968, Warsaw Pact tanks rumbled across the border into Czechoslovakia and scotched Brandt's plans. Kiesinger is reported to have said later that it was almost possible to be grateful to the Russians for this invasion, because 'by doing so they have relieved us for the time being from having to make a decision about the NPT' (*Der Spiegel*, 21/1969, p. 32).

Internationally, this action on the part of the USSR had some influence on the NPT. Italy refused to sign the treaty, even though Rome had said it would do so; the US Congress tabled the ratification of the treaty, and the nicely phrased statements of the superpowers concerning further disarmament negotiations disappeared back into the drawer (Kramish, 1968, p. 900).

The events had an especially great effect on Bonn, where a decision on accession to the treaty was ruled out of the question by all parties. In his government policy statement on 26 September 1968 the chancellor announced that in principle Germany supported the idea of an international NPT, but said that at present 'there is no necessity to deal with the manifold aspects under which the German government ... will have to examine the NPT' (DBT, 25 September 1968, p. 10,054).

This point of view was supported throughout the Bundestag. Speaking for the parliamentary SPD, Helmut Schmidt stated clearly: 'In view of the current situation in Europe it seems even less suitable for us to accede to the treaty now than it did when there were still unclarified interpretations of it' (DBT, 26 September 1968, p. 10,096).

At the same time, the Soviet Union's action had created a new argument against the NPT: the 'enemy state clause' in the United Nations Charter. A CDU/CSU enquiry for the Auswärtige Amt illustrated current thinking: 'Is it possible to couple signature of the NPT with an abolition of the discriminatory rights of the victorious powers on the basis of Articles 53 and 107 of the Charter of the United Nations?' (AA-Doc. XVII, p. 37).

The 'enemy state clauses' in Articles 53 and 107 are a reminder that the United Nations was established as a result an anti-Hitler coalition. In order to prevent any new aggression by their former enemies, these Articles exempt the victorious powers of the Second World War from the obligations of UN regulations (prohibition of aggressive acts and the intervention of the UN Security Council). This means that, in certain cases, Articles 53 and 107 limit the jurisdiction of the United Nations. In contrast to the tenor of the discussions in the Federal Republic, however, they never gave the Soviet Union a right to intervention. But after August 1968 these two Articles formed one important reason for the CDU/CSU to block accession to the NPT. By means of these Articles, Moscow wanted to 'raise intervention threats against us' (according to Barzel), to institute a 'psychological campaign' (in the words of Schmidt), or to claim 'unilateral or collective intervention rights' which would make the badly balanced treaty 'even more suspect', declared the spokesman of the CSU, Richard Stücklen (DBT, 26 September 1968, p. 10,096). For the German government, these UN Articles were more a problem of status than of security, which it tried to resolve in the shadow of the Czechoslovakia crisis and in the context of the NPT: in return for Germany's accession to the treaty, the Soviet Union should make a pledge to the Federal Republic formally rejecting any use of force in accordance with Article 2 of the UN Charter. It was Moscow's turn to clarify certain NPT questions in relation to the Federal Republic before Bonn's signature could be considered, said Willy Brandt to his Soviet guest, Ambassador Semjon Zarapkin, on 10 January 1969 (AdG, 1968, p. 14,517). Kurt Georg Kiesinger also declared that Germany's signature was dependent on whether guarantees against Soviet intervention could be secured (*HB*, 23 January 1969). Some weeks later Zarapkin handed the foreign minister a letter which made it clear that the Federal Republic should be included within resolution no. 255 of the United Nations Security Council on the security of the non-nuclear signatories of the NPT (AA-Doc. XVII, p. 46).

From now on the opinions within the government camp began to diverge. Brandt did not want to obstruct the new Ostpolitik by delaying accession to the NPT any further, while from Kiesinger's point of view it was precisely this unclear relationship with Moscow which was the reason for obstructing the NPT. The foreign minister was satisfied by Zarapkin's note, and so he tried to tackle first the question of nuclear renunciation and then the question of non-aggression.

The CDU/CSU preferred to reverse this order: without an agreement on non-aggression, there should be no accession to the NPT. Directly after receiving the Zarapkin note, the chancellor stated that the 'Soviet assumption of intervention' made Germany's accession impossible. The German people must not 'remain under an extraordinary law, i.e. martial law' (DBT, 7 February 1969, p. 11,567).

In retrospect, however, the calculations of the late foreign minister and the then new federal chancellor, Willy Brandt, were proved correct: ten days after the Federal Republic's accession to the NPT, German-Soviet talks on non-aggression commenced; they were terminated with the signing of the Moscow Treaty in August 1970. Whereas Bonn acknowledged in Article III of this Moscow Treaty the inviolability of European borders, Moscow declared in Article II that in future it would let its relationship with the Federal Republic 'be led by the aims and principles stated in the Charter of the United Nations' (Auswärtige Amt, 1972, p. 762). In a verbal interpretation, Andrey Gromyko added that this passage could be seen as the renunciation of the right of intervention on the part of the victorious Allied powers (*Der Spiegel*, 34/1979). With the ratification of the Moscow Treaty in 1972 the debate on the enemy state clause came to an end. The interrelationship between the pledge not to use force, Germany's accession to the NPT and the new Ostpolitik had become very clear during this debate: accession to the treaty was the prerequisite and prelude to the new Ostpolitik. But let us now return to the closing chapter of the Grand Coalition.

The Tabling of Accession

At the beginning of 1969 the consequences of the situation in Czechoslovakia began to ease. But the German reservations on accession to the NPT remained and threatened to isolate the Federal Republic from its Western allies. As early as 1 July 1968 Bonn's non-nuclear allies Denmark, Norway, Iceland and Greece signed the treaty. Shortly afterwards Canada, the Benelux countries and neutral Sweden acceded as well, and in January 1969 Italy and Turkey followed suit. At the same time, the new American government under Nixon signalled its interest in Germany's signature (Kuan, 1973, p. 281). In 10 Downing Street, uneasiness was growing about the motives behind Germany's reticence, whereas France was virtually pushing the German government to sign: only after seeing Germany's signature on the treaty would Paris be prepared to agree to begin safeguards negotiations between Euratom and the IAEA (*NZZ*, 1 February 1969). This delay in the agreement on controls endangered the prospects for Germany's nuclear industry. It was taken for granted that after the treaty came into force, the United States would have to make its export commitments to Euratom countries dependent on the existence of an IAEA safeguards agreement (Botzian, 1969, p. 85).

Within West Germany, the nuclear industry now began to push for accession to the treaty more forcefully than anyone else. According to an editorial in Germany's principal nuclear energy magazine, *atomwirtschaft*, the decision to sign the treaty 'would have to be taken in 1969', otherwise any further postponement would 'endanger the competitiveness of German industry a great deal more than signing it would' (*atw*, January 1969, p. 17).

This situation heightened incongruities within the government camp. After Helmut Schmidt had issued a warning about the isolation of the Federal Republic (*FAZ*, 23 January 1969), at the end of January the foreign minister also began warning about a 'hasty or emotional "No", or one motivated by domestic affairs' (AdG, 1969, p. 14458).

This cautious warning from the foreign minister, however, once again mobilised the opponents of the treaty. In a harsh reply, the chairman of the CDU/CSU parliamentary party, Rainer Barzel, repeated his negative stance. Minister Stoltenberg, too, still saw 'great obstacles' to accession and demanded that 'negotiations be carried out with more emphasis than has been the case up to now' (*FAZ*, 25 January 1969). The real answer to the Brandt attempt followed at the beginning of February 1969 in Munich. During the International Defence Technology (Wehrkunde) Conference, not only did Under-Secretary Karl Theodor von Guttenberg declare his rejection of the treaty in its current version, but Ambassadors Grewe and Schnippenkoetter, who were formally under the authority of the foreign minister, did so too. All this resulted in a debate in the Bundestag on 7 February 1969 during which the chancellor stressed the continuing need to clarify the NPT with regard to both the enemy state clause and control procedures, declaring that he was 'in full agreement with the foreign minister' (DBT, 7 February 1969, p. 11576). Brandt's test flight had made a rough landing. A few days later, it was agreed to reject accession to the NPT during the current legislative period. Parliamentary party spokesman Rainer Barzel, in a confidential letter dated 11 February 1969 to the leaders of the CDU/CSU (Kiesinger, Birrenbach, Stoltenberg, Strauss and Stücklen), summed up the results of the previous day's talks as follows:

> [Agreement has been reached that] a German signature ... should not be made before the parliamentary group [Fraktion] casts a positive vote. ... The idea of signing and at the same time announcing certain provisos for ratification and then to table ratification to the next session of the Bundestag will not get my support. ... I cannot support a policy that gives away an essential part of our substance without receiving in return some progress towards the establishment of a European peace initiative. (Hanns-Seidel-Stiftung, Archive for Christian-Social Policy [ACSP]; CSU Landesgruppe: the chairman, correspondence from February 1969)

Some weeks later Willy Brandt, too, had accepted the postponement of accession to the NPT until some time after the next Bundestag elections. 'Mr Brandt explained to the Western Allies in Washington last week that his country's politics and security argued for a delay', wrote the *New York Times* in April 1969. An essential motive for this move was the attitude of the CSU: 'It was understood that the major political reason for a delay was to deprive Finance Minister Franz Josef Strauss of a potent campaign issue' (*NYT*, 16 April 1969).

Is this credible? Was there in reality a massive breeding ground for an anti-NPT campaign in the Federal Republic which had been turned upside down by the student riots of 1969? Or was it that approval fell through because of a foreign policy dilemma of the CDU/CSU, that the 'old' policy had failed and the 'new' policy was still not in sight? Even before the cabinet discussed the NPT until deep into the night of 23 April 1969, the question of when accession would take place had been swept aside. After two long speeches by Ministers Brandt and Stoltenberg (who adopted differing points of view), stating the pros and cons of the matter, it was agreed that there were still some questions open which had to be answered – 'problems of safeguarding the Federal Republic from intervention and discrimination as well as ... questions of the verification agreement'. Brandt's ministry was asked to outline a proposal for these procedures (BPA, 24 April 1969). The chancellor and vice-chancellor, moreover, were determined to keep the NPT question out of the coming election campaign. Willy Brandt said that the suspicion that Germany's renunciation of nuclear weapons was not sincere should not be reinforced for tactical reasons during the electoral campaign (*Bulletin*, 22 May 1969).

But it is precisely this point that must be questioned. Would it not be unjust to the CSU to say that it was in favour of Germany's renunciation of nuclear weapons? Even in the Auswärtige Amt there were voices which had taken up the fight against accession to the NPT. NATO Ambassador Wilhelm Grewe wrote in 1968 in a dossier for the Auswärtige Amt: 'Should the treaty fail this would be to the advantage of the Alliance, perhaps even the precondition for its future viability. NATO and the NPT are incompatible in the long run' (Grewe, 1979, p. 739). Deliberately playing down such positions was, however, just as much a part of the reasoning of the Grand Coalition as was the 'self-evident truth' that defusing the NPT and national interests all amounted to the same thing. But the signing of the NPT could not be put off for any length of time without making the Federal Republic an international outcast. The new Bundestag was elected on 28 September 1969. A CDU/CSU victory would probably have caused some problems on the NPT question. But just as at the end of 1966, it was once more a change of government that freed Germany's nuclear-weapons policy from its self-made dilemma. Only the new government under Willy Brandt could lead the way to accession to the NPT without losing credibility.

Signature

Two months after the Bundestag elections, and almost a year and a half after the official publication of the treaty, the NPT was signed by the Federal Republic of Germany in Washington, London and

Moscow on 28 November 1969. This signature was accompanied by a note on Germany's interpretation of the NPT, by a detailed explanation of this interpretation and by a statement on the government's position in answer to an important parliamentary question the CDU/CSU opposition posed on 20 October of that year (DS VI/50).

In October 1969 a Bonn delegation travelled to Washington to present the German interpretations of the NPT in advance, because Bonn did not want the US government to dissociate itself from the FRG's interpretation. But, according to Bonn, the Americans accepted the German interpretations of safeguards as well as those of nuclear energy issues 'in very general terms' only (DS VI/50 p. 4).

The statements and other supplementary material surrounding the treaty document the continuity of NPT policy from Kiesinger to Brandt. On 13 August 1969 the cabinet of the Grand Coalition had, for the last time, discussed the NPT and agreed on a catalogue of pending questions which were to be resolved (DS VI/50). At this time, the wording of the German interpretation of the treaty was fixed. As early as July 1968, the Inter-ministerial Working Staff had been concerned with suitable formulations (interview with Dr Sahm). According to Under-Secretary Gerhard Jahn, in September 1968 'the German interpretations were made public by the German delegation during the conference of the non-nuclear-weapons states in Geneva' (DS V/46943, p. 9). The new Brandt/Scheel government had taken over the old government's interpretation of the treaty without any modifications. This is a further indication of how closely the two major parties concurred in their assessment of the NPT. In his policy statement, Willy Brandt had already said that he 'would [sign] the Treaty on the Non-proliferation of Nuclear Weapons as soon as – in accordance to the decisions of the previous German government – the pending questions are clarified' (DBT, 28 October 1969, p. 33).

Within the CDU/CSU union, the intention to accede to the treaty nevertheless met with fierce opposition and rejection. The reasons for this were given in an hour-long debate in the Bundestag on 12 November 1969 by MPs Stoltenberg, Birrenbach and von Gutenberg. But the government's course could not be stopped even by a series of hectic, last-minute privileged motions made in parliament (DBT, 27 November 1969, pp. 509 ff.). Nevertheless, on essential points of the German interpretation of the treaty, the CDU/CSU position was maintained.

Security

Accession was made on condition that the security of the FRG should be guaranteed by NATO or a corresponding system of security.

Without NATO, there would be no German renunciation of nuclear weapons. The shrinking of NATO 'into a constellation endangering the security of the Federal Republic of Germany' would be considered by the Federal Republic as a reason for withdrawal. In the event of 'the jeopardising of supreme interests', the Federal Republic was permitted to claim the right to nuclear defence according to Article 51 of the United Nations' Charter ('Right to individual and collective self-defence'). With this, the German government reserved the right to withdraw from the treaty at short notice in case of emergency. Article X of the NPT stipulates that notice of withdrawal has to be given to all other parties to the treaty and to the United Nations Security Council three months in advance and that such notice must be substantiated. But a legal expert of the Göttingen Institute for International Law stated: 'To delete this [three-month period] is the essence of this point in the declaration which – as far as can be seen – has not been contradicted so that it ... must be admissible according to the general principles of international law' (Zieger, 1975, p. 167).

The European Option
Accession was agreed on condition that the treaty did not obstruct the union of European countries. But the relevant NATO interpretation is said to be 'more restrictive than necessary according to the phrasing of Articles I and II of the Treaty'.

In the preliminary draft of the German interpretation of the treaty, a reference to the nuclear components of Western European defence was dropped by the Inter-ministerial Working Staff in July 1968 (interview with Dr Sahm). But the German government did give an assurance that in the event of the development of 'defensive nuclear weapons systems' suitable for Europe it would, together with its Western allies 'sound out a possible solution within the framework of the NPT' (DS VI/50, p. 5).

Research and Development
The German government took it for granted that nuclear research and development were not to be subject to any limitations – nuclear research for military purposes not being excluded from this assumption. During the preparations for this interpretation, research in the field of small nuclear explosions had played a certain role. With regard to 'peaceful nuclear explosive devices', the German government had stated 'that the NPT must not obstruct progress in the field of the development and *application of* technology in the peaceful use of nuclear explosive devices' (emphasis added).

On the day of Germany's accession to the NPT, US Foreign Minister William P. Rogers spoke with gravity about an 'event of historical importance'. His British colleague, Michael Stewart, was unable to withhold some sarcasm. It was 'not an exaggeration', Stewart said,

> to state that the whole future of the NPT was dependent upon the position of the Federal Republic. This seems to be a paradox because of the fact that the Federal Republic had already formally renounced the production of nuclear weapons many years previously – but today's world is full of paradoxes. (quoted in Kramish, 1970, p. 118)

With Germany's accession to the NPT, probably the most complicated chapter in German-American nuclear negotiations was closed. The first tentative moves towards the Non-Proliferation Treaty which had occurred under Kennedy and Adenauer had begun in the shadow of the Berlin crisis in the autumn of 1961. In the summer of 1965, under Johnson and Erhard, the controversy surrounding the draft proposals grew. The stormy climax of the treaty was reached during the years of the Grand Coalition. And finally, under Nixon and Brandt, the final prerequisites for Germany's accession were confirmed in October 1969.

Were these really the final prerequisites? It still remained to translate Article III into safeguards obligations. The NPT controversy now began to shift from the loud political arena to a silent tug-of-war on details, the technical tenor of which barely concealed the underlying political conflicts. During the wrangling over safeguards in the years 1970–3, an American-Soviet alliance of interests was once again confronted with protests from the former Axis powers of Japan, Italy and Germany. But now the treaty had been signed by the Federal Republic. However, its ratification was still pending.

The next chapter will deal with the four years of conflict that lay between accession to and ratification of the treaty.

5

The Euratom Controversy

The NPT has contradictory aims. It wants both to support the pro-liferation of atomic technology and to prevent the proliferation of nuclear weapons. This explains the importance of the safeguards – only an effective controls system could offset this inherent contradiction in the treaty.

From the viewpoint of international law, the control regulations of the NPT were a novelty. For the first time in history, compliance with an international agreement was to be verified by foreign powers. As an executive element of the non-proliferation regime the safeguards were also a sign of the distribution of power throughout the world. The imbalance between the 'haves' and 'have-nots' was extended to and manifest in the peaceful sector of the treaty: for some, the controls are obligatory, for others, they are not. This varying degree of sovereignty explains at least in part the longing of those subject to control to minimise the extent as well as the number of those controls.

The quarrel over safeguards began in 1956 with the resistance of the later Euratom countries to IAEA controls. Nine years later, the fight over Europe's safeguards privilege was taken up again in the NPT controversy. In January 1968 this quarrel was only temporarily ended by the compromise in Article III. In order to realise the safeguards regulations for Article III, years of negotiating were required. It wasn't until 1977 that the verification agreement between the two control organisations came into effect in the Federal Republic. The German statute for implementing the verification agreement came into effect in 1980, ten years after accession to the NPT.

Primarily, the arguments in the Euratom controversy during the 1970s centred on technical and procedural details and so they were almost unnoticed by the general public. But the driving force behind these conflicts was political. It was the same old argument about independence and sovereignty in a different guise.

In this chapter, we are concerned with this political dimension of the safeguards debates. We begin by picking up the thread of the Euratom controversy at its inception, namely in the origins of the

European Atomic Energy Community and the nuclear weapons policy of the United States of America.

The Euro-Bomb and Euratom

The founding of the European Atomic Energy Community [Euratom] in 1957 was inextricably linked with France's atomic weapons project. As early as September 1954 the French General Staff had advised that an integrated European atomic force be founded:

> France ought to become a nuclear-weapons state but could not afford to do so on its own. Germany ought not to be given the status of a nuclear power but it probably would not accept such discrimination. Therefore, it was the opinion of the French General Staff that the best solution would be European nuclear integration under the leadership of France. (Soutou, 1989, pp. 607–8).

In Bonn too, Euratom was regarded as a precondition for the development of a European, or a German, bomb. In September 1956 Adenauer had declared that 'he wanted to achieve through Euratom, as quickly as possible, the chance of producing our own nuclear weapons'. The agreement on Euratom, Adenauer was quoted as saying in the minutes of a cabinet meeting on 5 October 1956, would grant the FRG, 'in the long run, the possibility of developing nuclear weapons in a normal way. All other countries, including France, have gone further in this matter than we have' (quoted in Schwarz, 1991, p. 200).

In 1957 the military dimension of the Euratom treaty also played a role in Bundestag activities. In the presence of MPs Brandt and Scheel, Karl Carstens, at that time the representative of the Auswärtige Amt, left no doubt about the dual purpose of this treaty. Its main aim was the peaceful employment of atomic capacity; but, he said, the military production of nuclear energy remained a possiblity for some countries, while military use of nuclear energy was possible for all states. Certain treaty regulations were 'so formulated that the military purposes of those countries who wanted to become active in the military sector would have to be satisfied. ... And this formulation was by no means a coincidence' (Deutscher Bundestag, 1957). This was borne out by the fact that the SPD introduced a motion to the Bundestag in 1957 to make certain 'that the use of fissionable material for military purposes which is not ruled out by the treaty does not take place; material produced or processed in Germany should never be used for military purposes.' This motion was rejected by a majority vote (DBT, 5 July 1957, p. 13,349).

It is no wonder, therefore, that France and the Federal Republic rejected US control over fissionable materials within the jurisdiction of Euratom. Up to that time, Washington and London had made the transfer of nuclear material dependent on bilateral control regulations. An attempt was made to abolish this clear dependence of the recipient country upon the supply country when Euratom was set up. This was made especially clear in an American dossier of 3 December 1956. Robert Schaetzel of the State Department stated that the Euratom countries seemed to be of one accord in their opinion

> that some special arrangement must be worked out between the U.S. and Euratom which will neither require inspection by the U.S. ... nor by the International Atomic Energy Agency. The Europeans insist that a subordinate status implicit in U.S. inspection would make the Community politically unacceptable to the participating countries. Inspection by the Agency, when neither the U.S. nor the U.K. are prepared to accept similar inspection, would be equally unacceptable. (DoS, 1986, p. 493)

European resistance to IAEA inspections fundamentally contradicted the United States's views even as early as 1956.

The Safeguards Quarrel of 1956
In 1955 the proliferation of nuclear technology for peaceful purposes got under way as a result of the Atomic Energy Conference in Geneva. The chief supplier, the United States, made delivery dependent on the granting of certain inspection opportunities. The recipient country was to submit annual reports on how the imported material had been used and, upon request, grant American inspectors access to all facilities at any time. To make it easier to accept these conditions, the Americans announced that such controls were to be assumed by an international atomic energy agency (the IAEA) as soon as possible. The IAEA's statutes were agreed upon in September 1956, and the Agency was founded a year later in Vienna as a subsidiary organisation of the United Nations. Up to the present time, its responsibilities have remained the same: it supports the development and use of nuclear energy and at the same time has to send out inspectors to make certain that no military use occurs. From its inception, the IAEA was at the heart of American non-proliferation policy, and the US made it a prime goal to win universal acceptance for the Agency. In this context, European demands for self-inspection presented a huge

challenge to the American safeguards policy: for the first time in its history, the United States was to deliver fissionable material without the opportunity of autonomously carrying out checks on the whereabouts of such material. This was the first time that Washington freed a group of states from the global safeguards principle – a move that would undermine the status and effectiveness of the Agency headquartered in Vienna even before it had been properly established.

Even in the 1950s, the conflict over priorities between the IAEA and Euratom provoked a fierce quarrel within the American government. On the one hand, there was the mighty IAEA lobby which had supporters in the Congress, in government circles and in the AEC. On the other, there were the so-called Eurocrats in the State Department. Their main worry was that 'the Germans will develop, on a nationalistic basis, their own atomic development in competition with the French unless some degree of European cooperation in this field is achieved' – the American ambassador to Bonn, James Conant, noted in a letter to John Foster Dulles in 1956 (DoS, 1986, p. 414).

It was not the perspective of a European nuclear power that worried the Dulles group. On the contrary, there were some in the State Department who definitely wanted to entrust Euratom with the production of nuclear weapons (Weilemann, 1983, p. 176). Their main worry was a possible 'go-it-alone' attempt by Germany or France. The philosophy of the Eurocrats was based on the premise that only by firmly integrating the Germans within a European context could a new 1914 or 1939 be avoided. Thus they demanded that the United States's nuclear export policy be oriented specifically towards European integration (DoS, 1986, p. 381). In a telegram sent in May 1956 Dulles said that Euratom would be supported in order

> to bind Germany to the West and to increase the strength and unity of the Atlantic Alliance, to avoid Franco-German rivalry in the nuclear question in favor of a joint field of interest, to provide the integrated organization with a safeguards autonomy, especially in that region where nuclear solo attempts would be most likely, and to support the atomic industry in Western Europe by uniting its nuclear potential. (DoS, 1986, p. 442)

The safeguards negotiations between the United States and Euratom began in February 1958. They lasted for three months and proved fairly problematic. Euratom remained firm and was finally able to obtain sole right of control even over nuclear material of American origin. In a countermove, the Europeans had to accept that the materials delivered by the United States, as well as corollary products, would be used for peaceful purposes only and would not be allowed to be sold to third parties without the agreement of the US. Moreover, the Euratom safeguards system was to 'be made suitable compatible to that of the International Atomic Energy Agency (IAEA)' and arrangements were to be made for consultations and an exchange of experience between both organisations (Euratom, 1958).

For the most part, the European Community had achieved its objectives. These had been supported by developments within NATO. President Eisenhower's hope of repressing European nuclear ambitions with an offer in December 1957 of a 'nuclear share' had been destroyed at the beginning of 1958. With the German-Italian-French atomic project which was, among other matters, to bring about a joint production of atomic warheads, the danger of a new nuclear power had become even more acute. For this reason, too, the United States felt the need to follow a policy with regard to Euratom that not only counteracted the attractiveness of Euratom's nuclear developments with generous offers, but also took into consideration political sensitivities by backing away from previous safeguards standards. Later an SWP staff member, Rudolf Botzian, wrote aptly that 'this special treatment in the question of safeguards can be regarded as a reward for a country's renunciation of the autonomous development of weapons' (Botzian, 1967b, p. 5). In other words, in 1957/8, America's tactics on the management of the civilian use of atomic energy had also a function within its atomic weapons policy; releasing NATO members from IAEA controls was also an answer to the threat that was, inter alia, part of the armament triangle.

Although Franco-German dreams of atomic weapons had been destroyed after de Gaulle took office, the atomic community continued to be of extreme importance for the Federal Republic. First of all, any work and action conducted within such a community was less exposed to international suspicions than a national atomic programme would be. Second, the United States was prepared to grant better terms and conditions to the community when delivering fissionable material than it would to any individual member country. Third, as far as the Federal Republic was concerned, Euratom offered protection – for the future too – against the IAEA. Indeed, in the years that followed all attempts failed

to induce the Federal Republic of Germany, through all kinds of pressure, to accept IAEA controls. ... Such pressure ranged from friendly attempts at persuasion from the Director-General of IAEA, via similar friendly attempts at encouragement on the part of either

Western or neutral governments, to very clear statements from Poland and Czechoslovakia during the IAEA General Conference in September 1966 that they were prepared to permit their nuclear facilities to be placed under IAEA control on condition that the Federal Republic would do the same. (Ungerer, 1975, p. 168)

Euratom and the Non-Proliferation Treaty

Looking back at the establishment of Euratom, it becomes clear that in 1967 the United States, by insisting that priority be given to the IAEA, had consciously risked creating an international crisis. At once old arguments were revived. Preference for the IAEA provoked brusque rejection from the Euratom Commission, which discovered that its control monopoly, won after a hard struggle, was being questioned. In Washington too, the old conflict flamed up again: should global non-proliferation or European integration be given first priority?

The European Desk of the State Department had rallied round Euratom; the global approach was supported by the ACDA, the AEC – and also the Soviet Union. Apart from America's interest in the IAEA, it was the Soviet refusal to compromise which gave the decisive advantage to the ACDA people. The Kremlin alternative was clear: no inspection clause at all rather than one which would upgrade Euratom. But a treaty without an inspection clause would contradict the whole orientation of the disarmament policy of the United States. Therefore, the State Department began to look for a compromise that would take Soviet interests into consideration without alienating Euratom unnecessarily.

For the Federal Republic, accession to the NPT was out of the question without making allowances for the interests of the Community: 'For domestic reasons, the entire situation was on the brink of complete failure because of Euratom – at first the United States had not understood that' (interview material). In this quarrel the principal support for the German government came from the Euratom Commission.

At all costs, the Commission wanted to prevent the duplication of inspections of atomic industries in the non-nuclear countries. To give up Euratom inspections, which would have resolved this problem, was not acceptable for several reasons. These included not just the institutional self-interest of the Eurocrats and the integration policy argument, but also the aversion to opening up facilities to IAEA inspectors from Eastern bloc nations. In March 1967 *The Economist* wrote:

It is sometimes alleged that visits by IAEA inspectors would lead to industrial espionage, and this is certainly one of the fears among European industrialists. But some of the Eurocrats and politicians are much more afraid that the discriminatory inspection provisions would rule out the creation of a political Europe which might, at some future date, have its own nuclear force.

In the Federal Republic, the bonds with Euratom were especially strong, and the rejection of IAEA controls was correspondingly very firm. The feeling was that Germany was allied to NATO and the European Community and to no one else. In contrast, the IAEA and even the United Nations were regarded as a sort of black hole: unknown, perhaps even enemy territory. This attitude might be one reason why scare reports about industrial espionage by the IAEA became so firmly established, especially in the Federal Republic.

Moreover, the preservation of the Community was thought to be the prerequisite for any future European atomic power. Bonn, which had already had to renounce the MLF option, was not prepared also to let the prerequisites for the development of an European option slip from its hands. Although no public connection was made between the maintaining of Euratom and the European option, it was most certainly present in the minds of the parties directly involved. During a session of the European Parliament, an MP from the Netherlands referred to the fact that the Euratom problem had to be viewed 'in a broader context within the development of a country's own European nuclear-weapons defence system' (*EP*, 18 October 1967, p. 64). The then president of the EC Commission, Walter Hallstein, had also, in his defence of Euratom before the European Parliament, referred to the danger to the European option as the 'main question' in the controversy over the NPT. Hallstein declared that in Europe's work on unification, discussion had always

> proceeded from the point of view that it would be the responsibility of a Europe which some day will be united, in the realm of defence too, to create its own defence policy. Is the question of nuclear defence not, by necessity, a part of all this, too? (*EP*, 16 March 1967, p. 156)

It was precisely this which was a weak point in the European line of reasoning. The more successful Euratom became as the motor of European unity, the more the safeguards would take on the character of self-inspection. There was no hint at the time that France would overcome its deep mistrust of the German nuclear option, but it is obvious that the German government did not want to rule out any possibility that in the long run this view might change. A revival of the 'armament triangle' of 1957/8 could be obstructed by the IAEA, if necessary, whereas the Euratom treaty had no effective lever against it. Another point was that the German government would have much more influence within the smaller framework of Euratom than it would in a global organisation. In 1967 only three of the 150 higher-ranking officials of the IAEA were from the Federal Republic, while Bonn supplied a third of those in Euratom, thus making the FRG its main financier (Kramer, 1976, p. 157).

The Safeguards Marathon

The early 1970s marked the beginning of the separation and industrial use of material suitable for making bombs, with the introduction of reprocessing plants and fast-breeder reactors. Although the risk of proliferation had vastly increased thanks to such technology, it was precisely this technology that was responsible for the systematic dismantling of the safeguards' effectiveness. The Federal Republic played a leading role in this respect.

As early as February 1967, agreement had been reached within the government 'to develop a revision policy with respect to the IAEA' (AA-Doc IV, pp. 5 ff.). A less important goal was the 'modernisation of Euratom inspections corresponding to the principle of instrumented control of fissionable materials at certain strategic points' (AA-Doc. XVII, p. 75). The 'revision' and 'modernisation' of the control systems were aimed at weakening them almost to the point of de facto ineffectiveness. During negotiations which lasted for many years Bonn was able to achieve many of these aims:

- In April 1970 the Board of Governors of the IAEA decided to establish a Safeguards Committee whose task it was to work out a model treaty for NPT safeguards. It took 82 sessions to reach an outline for this model treaty; this was adopted in April 1971 as Information Circular no. 153 (INFCIRC 153), also known as the *Blue Book*.
- In November 1971 negotiations began in Brussels between Euratom and the IAEA on a safeguards or verification agreement. They ended in July 1972, with the agreement signed in August 1973 by the IAEA, Euratom and Belgium, Denmark, the Federal Republic, Ireland, Italy, Luxembourg and the Netherlands.
- In May 1975 the NPT was finally ratified by the non-nuclear-weapons states in Euratom. Following that, talks began on

adapting Euratom inspections to the new NPT provisos. Only after the termination of these negotiations did the Verification Agreement between the IAEA and Euratom come into effect in February 1977. Some weeks later, IAEA inspections in the Federal Republic of Germany took place for the first time.

- In April 1979 the German government presented to the Bundestag an implementing statute for the Verification Agreement. After discussion in the Bundestag's Committee for Research and Committee for Defence, this was passed by the Bundestag in November 1979 – some ten years after Bonn had signed the NPT.

Although the results of those safeguards negotiations were very important for the future of global non-proliferation, they were handled very discreetly. The following description is based upon interviews with members of the IAEA Safeguards Committee (David Fischer of the IAEA; Myron Kratzer and Charles van Doren of the US; Vladimir Fortakov from the Soviet Union; André Petit of France; and Werner Ungerer from the FRG) and with participants at the IAEA/Euratom negotiations (David Fischer and Ben Sanders from the IAEA; Helmut Sigrist of Euratom; and Werner Ungerer and Wiegand Papsch from the FRG).

The *Blue Book* and the 'Karlsruhe Doctrine'

The IAEA Safeguards Committee went to work in June 1970. Its chairman was the then Austrian ambassador to the United Nations, Kurt Waldheim. There were delegates from more than 40 countries and they were confronted with a technical challenge: the goal was to develop a reduced and, at the same time, a more objective controls system for a totally new kind of inspection. Even greater was the European challenge: Western European nuclear threshold powers together with Japan, which had never or very reluctantly submitted to IAEA inspections, were only prepared to accept new safeguards that would not increase, but reduce, the political and technological/industrial imbalance vis-à-vis the nuclear powers. The Committee's bone of contention, overriding all technical details, was concerned with the question of the primacy of equality. This covered:

1. Equality in nuclear industrial conditions between 'haves and have-nots'; thus IAEA controls on the peaceful use of atomic energy by the nuclear powers too.

2. Equality between the threshold powers. Japan demanded that its national safeguards system receive the same preferential treatment that the Euratom countries enjoyed for their regional system.
3. Equality at the level of the lowest common denominator of what was acceptable as a control burden to all parties. This meant reducing controls for everybody.

From the point of view of non-proliferation, the first demand seems absurd. NPT inspections cannot stop a nuclear power from becoming a nuclear power. On the contrary, was it not obvious that such a waste of IAEA resources would detract from its real function? The Federal Republic in particular was prepared to submit to NPT safeguards only 'if ... the United States and Great Britain agree to submit their entire peaceful nuclear sector to the same NPT inspections' (AA–Doc. VII, p. 2, ACD). In saying this, Bonn was not thinking about non-discrimination alone. Only if the nuclear powers too submitted to inspections would they also have an interest in making this burden as light as possible. In December 1967 the United States and Great Britain finally agreed to submit their civilian nuclear sector to inspections.

Germany's demand was a controversial point not only within the IAEA Safeguards Committee, but also in Washington and London. It was, however, in the interest of the atomic powers to allow inspections in their own countries too, after they had already accepted the principle of reciprocity which stated that any country could refuse to accept inspectors from countries which did not allow such inspections. But safeguards on the 'entire' civilian nuclear industry were, however, out of the question. In 1985 only four of the approximately 250 civilian atomic facilities in the United States were inspected by the IAEA (Houck, 1985, p. 18).

The second point deal with placing Japan on an equal footing with Euratom. In 1970 the German government was interested in extending the status of the EC, as expressed to the United States in 1958, to the IAEA. Euratom controls were to be accepted without restriction, with only its methods being checked from time to time by the IAEA. No independent safeguards were to be imposed by the IAEA within the jurisdiction of Euratom. The Japanese government was prepared to accept this only if Tokyo too received such special treatment (Scheinman, 1970, p. 78). Therefore a national system of self-inspection was established in Japan, analogous to the regional safeguards organisation of the EC. From that time onwards, the Japanese representatives on the Safeguards Committee pressed for the recognition of this national safeguards system. The United States flatly rejected this claim. Nevertheless, this drive forward by Tokyo, inspired by Euratom, changed the safeguards system of the IAEA considerably. In Article 7 of the model agreement it was laid down that, in all member states of the NPT, a national safeguards system would be established – the so-called 'State System of Accountancy and Control' (SSAC) – and it would be connected to IAEA safeguards. Since that time, the primary data concerning the whereabouts of fissionable material have normally been collected by these national safeguards organisations. Although the IAEA can verify the results of these 'controls' through independent measures, since the establishment of the SSACs it has only played a secondary role. 'Thus, in many respects, IAEA safeguards are little more than a system of self-inspection', wrote a British safeguards specialist later, and 'the present system is simply a declaration by the country being examined' (Johnson, 1977, p. 183). The SSACs were established chiefly for political reasons: 'The introduction of a primary, massive international control system within intrastate areas would not have been an encouragement to countries to place themselves voluntarily under the regime of the NPT' (Zieger, 1975, p. 159). In addition, it was necessary to lighten the burden on the poorly equipped safeguards apparatus of the IAEA.

As for the demand on minimising inspection rights, according to the German government the ideal IAEA inspector would be like the official who comes to your home to check your water, gas and electricity meters without having to enter your house. In 1967 certain confidential papers of the Auswärtige Amt referred to the 'black boxes on our chimneys' (AA-Doc, IV, p. 7). This ideal concept of controls was pure fiction, particularly for those facilities involving plutonium. But in the Vienna Controls Committee, Bonn and Tokyo insisted that the assignment of inspectors, and their rights, be reduced to a minimum. Both countries played a key role in this respect: Japan had made its ratification of the NPT dependent on ratification by the Federal Republic. And the Federal Republic had made its ratification dependent not only upon the consideration of the Euratom interests but also upon the acceptance of the Karlsruhe Doctrine. In Germany's interpretation of the NPT in 1969, it is said that the government insisted 'that the safeguards ... be applied only to source materials, especially fissionable materials, and in accord with the principle of an effective securing of the flow of fissionable material at certain strategic points'.

The position of the German chief negotiator, Werner Ungerer, was supported by the implied threat to diverge from the NPT under certain circumstances. Indeed, the result of the protracted negotiations was that the inspection proviso of the IAEA statutes – 'access at all times to all places and data' – was now replaced by the systems analytical approach of the Karlsruhe Doctrine. As a rule, the IAEA inspectors were henceforth only to have access to certain strategic points within a nuclear plant. Moreover, from now on the number, intensity and lengths of the inspections were to 'be kept to the minimum' (INFCIRC 153, Art. 78).

The complete revision of IAEA controls was undoubtedly an event of global importance. IAEA analyst Lawrence Scheinman has spoken about a sharp contrast between IAEA statutes and the new controls statute (Scheinman, 1987, p. 157). Mohamed I Shaker has called it a 'dramatic shift from the older IAEA safeguards system' (Shaker, 1976, p. 655). After the agreement on the new safeguards principles, the non-nuclear nations were 'openly satisfied because they had been able to push through their demands on all important points', whereas the two superpowers were described as having acted in an 'uncommonly conciliatory' way (Simonitsch, 1970, p. 650). Bonn was satisfied too. The consultations on the model agreement had 'proceeded much quicker and more smoothly than expected. ... The safeguards system was much more relaxed in comparison with the former inspection practices of the IAEA' (*FAZ*, 22 July 1970). But the United States's disarmament experts expressed their misgivings: 'Under that system, inspectors will be limited basically to the role of auditors – a role far different from the extremely detailed one proposed by the United States in the early postwar era' (*NYT*, 28 July 1970).

How did these far-reaching agreements in the IAEA Safeguards Committee come about? What was the role of the superpowers, and of the Federal Republic of Germany? The key frontline position lay between the superpowers and the IAEA Secretariat on the one hand, and the Federal Republic of Germany and Japan on the other; Great Britain, which was awaiting a decision on its application for EC membership, was a kind of go-between. One side tried to maintain as much of the IAEA system as possible, while the industrialised threshold powers on the other hand wanted to do away with it.

The leading German negotiator, Werner Ungerer, had embarked on the talks with clear orders from the Federal Defence Council. Each meeting of the Safeguards Committee was prepared jointly by the Euratom member countries, including France. Their voices did carry some weight. All the Committee members knew very well that the pattern of the model agreement had to be such that a later agreement between Euratom and the IAEA would be possible.

At the beginning of these discussions, the USSR had still been fiercely opposed to the 'Strategic Points' philosophy. After bilateral negotiations between the German and Soviet delegations, the USSR demonstrated a quite remarkable reserve in this respect; looking back, Werner Ungerer described these bilateral negotiations as his first diplomatic masterpiece. The Soviet Union met the Federal Republic halfway, knowing that a too rigid standpoint on the safeguards question could jeopardise Germany's ratification of the NPT. At the same time this conciliation demonstrated an effort to honour the new Ostpolitik efforts of the Brandt government instead of blocking what seemed to be a less important issue.

The American delegation was led by a high-ranking member of the AEC staff, Myron Kratzer. Its work in Vienna largely consisted of ad hoc decisions: there were neither clear directives from Washington nor any consultations during the negotiations. Perhaps this freedom and the noticeable lack of interest in Washington and Moscow were the reasons for the relaxed atmosphere during the Committee's talks, which went down in the history of the United Nations as the 'Spirit of Vienna'. The leader of the British delegation, Peter Kelly, later explained what this meant. With very un-British sentimentality he remembered the musical finale to the Committee's work: when the members got together for the last time 'to sing the Safeguards' Song with its resounding chorus "We Agree!", there must have been many who, like myself, felt a tug at the heartstrings at the thought that we should no longer be working together and sharing Committee jokes' (Kelly, 1971, p. 10). Incidentally, the 'Safeguards' Song' was composed and accompanied by that enthusiastic pianist, Werner Ungerer.

Extensive consultations outside the official meetings made it possible to pave the way for mutual solutions and to prevent hostile votes within the plenary sessions. In addition, the main opponents of these negotiations were allied to each other because they all belonged to the Western camp: Myron Kratzer from the US, Imai Ryukichi from Japan and Werner Ungerer from West Germany. The negotiations between Ungerer and Kratzer took place in many different places. The two met at a swimming pool, in restaurants or in the corridors of the spacious IAEA headquarters in Vienna. Those private and confidential German-American talks were later characterised by Kratzer as 'the key to the outcome':

I think the basic compromises were between us and Germany. It wasn't just that we were trying to satisfy the Soviets. We were trying to satisfy ourselves. When we satisfied ourselves, then we felt we would be in a position to assure the Soviets that it was an acceptable outcome. (Interview with Myron Kratzer, November 1986)

Werner Ungerer had reason to be a great deal more satisfied with the results. The mandate of the Federal Defence Council was 100 per cent fulfilled. These rights of the IAEA were reduced to a rump. The safeguards rights were to be applied only to the flow of fissionable materials and no longer to the facilities themselves. The number of inspections was limited for the first time. The access of inspectors to those parts of facilities 'worth protecting' could be ruled out. The IAEA was only to verify the accounts and control systems (Randermann, 1975, p. 199). These were fine conditions to take into the beginning of negotiations with Euratom on the basis of INFCIRC 153. Nevertheless, the talks between the EC and the UN proved to be unexpectedly complicated. They began at the end of 1971 in the Egmont Palace in Brussels.

The Euratom/IAEA Negotiations

When the two delegations met for the first time on 9 November 1971, the impression was that two different worlds had crashed into each other. Just about everyone had a hangover, thanks to the welcome reception at the Belgian ambassador's the evening before. In the Euratom Centre an agreement had been made to enter negotiations 'with the gloves off'. One participant recorded that the Euratom representative from Bonn, Helmut Sigrist, made clear at the beginning of the talks, grim faced, that they were not prepared to leave NPT safeguards in the hands of the IAEA. Euratom would do the inspecting. The role of the IAEA would have to be reduced to verifying Euratom's inspection methods by auditing the books and by occasionally accompanying the inspectors on spot-checks. David Fischer, the head of the IAEA delegation, rejected these ideas in a manner that was just as sharp: it would not be Euratom but the IAEA which would carry out inspections in accordance with the NPT, and it was prepared to cooperate with Euratom for this purpose. Interests seemed to be diametrically opposed. Jurisdiction on the question of safeguards was one of the few things left to the Euratom Commission – 'For that reason we defended it like lions.' On the other hand, the mandate of the IAEA delegation was limited to model agreement INFCIRC 153, in which it was thought that the interests of Euratom had been suitably integrated. 'We would, therefore, have fought every deviation as well as we could.' Euratom was not the only issue here: both sides knew very well that a joint agreement would create a precedent on the control rights of the IAEA in other parts of the world as well. Tokyo, for example, was later determined to demand that Japan too be granted every special privilege accorded to Europe on this question. There was pressure to reach an agreement on both sides. Without an agreement with the IAEA, the Euratom countries would have put the possibility of US nuclear imports at risk. The IAEA, on the other hand, needed the agreement with Euratom to ensure the global validity of the NPT.

The final compromise complied with the conditions laid down by the German government as prerequisites for the ratification of the NPT. The essentials of the IAEA's *Blue Book* were adopted and extended in two respects: the preamble acknowledged the supranational character of the Community, while the normally vertical relationship between the IAEA and a country that had signed the NPT became a horizontal one. Euratom's safeguards system retained its independence, but now it had to be modified to fit the IAEA model agreement. The specific modes of cooperation were fixed in a 25-point appendix called the 'protocol', as well as in additional, confidential agreements. By acknowledging European safeguards as a multinational system, the number of IAEA inspections was reduced; the number of Euratom inspections was fixed with respect to the type of facility at 20–50 per cent of the maximum limits in the IAEA model agreement, and IAEA inspections were fixed at just 6–15 per cent. IAEA inspectors were allowed to accompany their colleagues for 'observation' purposes in some 20–35 per cent of Euratom's inspections. IAEA's own inspection actions were permitted only in strictly defined special cases and these were reduced to a minimum (Gijessels, 1978, p. 35). There were to be no inspections of the export of materials within the EC, including France, so the 'Common Market' was maintained in the nuclear sector.

In its firm determination to make the most of every possibility, the German government had managed, in cooperation with other threshold powers, to achieve the 'optimum possible' (Boulanger, 1972, p. 511) with respect to the defusing of the NPT system of safeguards. In a first step, the interests of Euratom effectively came into play within the framework of the IAEA, thus weakening its safeguards system. Second, Euratom was forced, by precisely those IAEA reforms, to adapt its safeguards system – against French resistance – to those weakened standards. Moreover, the introduction of the system of strategic points within Euratom territory had the perceived advantage that 'during inspections where IAEA inspectors were also present, not all parts of a facility could be entered' (Ungerer, 1973, p. 199).

Just before the conclusion of the negotiations, tempers flared one last time over a seemingly minor point – the question of what to call the agreement. For David Fischer the case was clear: this was a 'Safeguards Agreement' between Euratom and IAEA. This title was unacceptable for his opposite number, Helmut Sigrist. He argued that because Euratom safeguards were acknowledged in the agreement and merely had to be verified by the IAEA, it should be called a Verification Agreement. In the end, it was decided to adopt the neutral wording 'Agreement ... in Implementation of Article III ...', but in the Federal Republic of Germany the document was and still is called the Verification Agreement. 'Apart from the Germans, nobody calls this agreement a Verification Agreement', a government official from Bonn later emphasised to representatives of Germany's nuclear industry. 'There are good reasons for that, as you know', he continued (Treitschke, 1975, p. 185). This semantic difference was reflected in the first attempt to fix the details of specific facilities. The clashes over who was to be responsible for what in practice lay at the heart of the 'rearguard action' in the safeguards controversy from 1973 to 1980.

The Tug-of-War Continues

In April 1973 the IAEA, Euratom and the non-nuclear member states of the Community signed the Verification Agreement. There was no longer anything to prevent the ratification of the NPT. After parliamentary procedures were concluded, the Euratom countries' instruments of ratification were deposited in May 1975. It took another two years, filled with lengthy negotiations, before the new EC Regulation no. 3227/76 was concluded, a regulation that was binding on all Euratom member states and which provided for the adaptation of the European safeguards system to the Verification Agreement. 'The change to the new Regulation means a considerable alteration in the procedures for the Commission and for the operators' (Schleicher and Sharpe, 1977, p. 266). This Regulation took effect in January 1977. Provisions had to be made before March 1977 IAEA inspectors were allowed to travel to the Federal Republic. Thus the German government arranged for certain technical changes in its nuclear facilities, 'because the locking up of certain sensitive operational areas which the IAEA inspectors were not to enter might necessitate, among other things, certain constructional changes in the buildings' (cf. report by MPs Dr Bangemann, Dr Birrenbach, Dr Mertes, Herr Pawelczyk, dated 14 February 1974, in DS 7/1694, p. 6).

The controversy on inspection-free zones remained on the agenda. At what point were facility operators allowed to say 'stop'? When were they obliged to permit inspectors entry to installations? Settling such questions was the task of the Implementing Statute of the Verification Agreement, which the Bundestag passed in 1979. The restrictive character of this statute is quite clear in Article 1, Paragraph 2, which states that the inspections are not permitted to include measures that 'would interfere more than necessary with the nuclear activities of the facility operators ... , affect the protection of ... confidential information, ... or disturb or slow down the operation of the facility in an unacceptable way'. The reasoning was that the Verification Agreement was based on the principle 'that confidential information may be completely or only partially withheld from the IAEA inspectors'. In such cases, operators of a nuclear facility could 'prevent the IAEA inspector from carrying out the prescribed inspections' (DS 8/2779, p. 10).

A special proviso of Article 10 is worth particular attention as this also touches on the question of security policy. 'In the event of a nuclear incident, or any other extraordinary circumstance', the proviso stipulates, the operator responsible for the facility must take 'the necessary steps' to limit the IAEA's area of control. The underlying reason for this was that 'this proviso can be made use of to protect important security interests [of the federal government]'.

In the context of such restrictions, is it any wonder that the wrangle over competency within a specially established commission linking Euratom and IAEA dragged on endlessly? Even some twelve years after the signing of the Verification Agreement, the IAEA found it necessary in 1985 to complain publicly about the continuing 'difficulties and disputes' with Euratom, adding that 'To some extent these meetings can be considered as a continuation of negotiations which began in 1971' (IAEA, 1985, p. 27).

As David Fischer asked in 1985, would it not have made much more sense, and have been cheaper, for Euratom, after it had accepted the IAEA safeguards system, to leave the main part of the work to the IAEA? 'They have not done so,' Fischer added. 'Euratom ... has instead focused most of its safeguards concern on keeping to a minimum the role of the IAEA' (Fischer and Szasz, 1985, p. 73).

In December 1978 Fischer's question was discussed during meetings of the confidential DGAP 'Peaceful Use of Nuclear Energy and Non-Proliferation' project group. The list of members of that group reads like a Who's Who of Germany's nuclear community. The nuclear industry's elite (Stoll/ALKEM, Hildebrandt/KWU, Salander/DWK, Beckurts/KFA) was represented as well as the think-tank of Germany's atomic weapons policy: Uwe Nerlich, Admiral of the Fleet Herbert Trebesch, the CDU MP Kurt Birrenbach. But opinions on the future role of Euratom differed in these circles. Were Euratom inspections on top of those of IAEA not 'onerous, expensive and superfluous?', asked the participants at this round of meetings. The confidential protocol continued: 'If the community cannot even find a mutual standpoint in negotiations with the uranium supplier countries, what is Euratom good for anyway? Should the Federal Republic not rather opt for the IAEA at an international level?'

In his response to these questions, the chairman of the project group, Professor Karl Kaiser, referred not so much to the interests of the Community as to the interests of Bonn. According to the protocol, the Federal Republic in particular could

> not afford ... to let Euratom go down the drain. Euratom had proven its worth in the past and would be indispensable outwardly as a *protective shield for German interests*. The German government must at all costs avoid being jockeyed into an isolated position in the international nuclear debate. (Protocol of a meeting of the project group 'Peaceful Use of Nuclear Energy and Non-Proliferation' on 7 December 1978, p. 21; original emphasis)

Now it seems that our circle is complete. Was not this last argument for maintaining Euratom almost identical to that adduced by Adenauer in 1956 when he issued directives to his government to support the European Atomic Energy Community? At that time the chancellor declared that in the opinion of the public throughout the world, the peaceful use of the atom could not be separated from its military use. 'Germany's attempt to arrive at a purely national atomic regulation would therefore be viewed with great mistrust by other countries' (Adenauer, vol. III, p. 255).

Had not this mistrust long vanished some 22 years later? Was that 'protective shield' still necessary in 1978 even after accession to the NPT? We will return to these questions later, but before that we need to finish the analysis of Germany's controversy over the NPT with an analysis of the debate on its ratification.

Ratification of the NPT and the European Option

After the signing of the Euratom/IAEA agreement, it was possible for ratification of the NPT by the non-nuclear states of the European Community to get under way. In September 1973 the German government initiated legislation in the Bundestag on the ratification statutes for the NPT and the Verification Agreement. On 20 February 1974, after a closing debate, the Non-Proliferation Treaty was ratified and the safeguards agreement was passed by majority vote in the

Bundestag. The vision of becoming a European atomic power had played an important role in this debate too.

Disputes over Ratification

In 1973 the last round of the NPT controversy began in Bonn. It now appeared in its purest form: the dispute over the future nuclear status of the Federal Republic of Germany. It was finally stripped of all those side issues which had up to then dominated, and partly concealed, the true nature of the controversy: worries about the Soviet Union's unilateral interpretation of the treaty were refuted; the enemy state clauses were swept aside; the Soviet Union had normalised relations with Bonn; both German states were members of the United Nations. On the question of safeguards, the Federal Republic had managed to achieve everything it had aimed for. The civilian use of nuclear energy was guaranteed. Rejection of the NPT would have been damaging for the atomic industry; non-accession would have broken up the Common Market; the United States would have had to cancel delivery of fissionable material to the Federal Republic; preferential access to nuclear know-how would have disappeared.

Those who nevertheless still wanted to refuse to sign the treaty would have to bring their criticism to bear on the very purpose of the treaty – non-proliferation. It was the ratification debate which made clear the German standpoint regarding the nuclear option.

In August 1973 the chairman of the CSU in the Bavarian Landtag, Alfred Seidl, quite abruptly opened a new round of controversy on the NPT. The treaty had to be rejected because it would prevent the atomic armament of the Bundeswehr. On 11 August 1973 Seidl wrote in the *Bayernkurier*:

> If it is not possible to establish, within a suitable period of time, a European Military Force equipped with nuclear weapons, including the armed forces of the Federal Republic of Germany, then the German government will be forced to consider the possibility of arming the Bundeswehr itself with nuclear weapons. At any rate, this final resort should not be ruled out by the ratification of the NPT.

Franz Josef Strauss too, in a letter to parliamentarians CDU/CSU, warned against ratification of the NPT. Because of his efforts, the CDU/CSU's parliamentary group rejected NPT ratification by a slight majority in December 1973. During the closing vote on the NPT in the Bundestag on 20 February 1974, Bavarian MPs, including Dollinger, Höcherl, Kiechle, Schneider, Warncke and Zimmermann (who were later ministers), and the CSU politicians Biehle, Jaeger, Probst, Spranger, Stücklen and Waigel, voted en bloc against the NPT. Bavaria was the only German Land that again tried to prevent, via the Bundesrat, the ratification of the treaty in the Bundestag. The reason given was that the treaty had divided 'the peoples of the world into nuclear-weapons states and non-nuclear-weapons states' and had resulted in the 'degradation of the rights of the latter for all time. That is why several countries have not yet ratified the treaty; and the Federal Republic should follow suit' (BR-DS 145/1/74 of 7 March 1974).

None of the CSU politicians dissociated themselves from Alfred Seidl's position – although this was demanded many times. This Bavarian offshoot of the CDU maintained its position as a party which was in favour of atomic weapons for Germany.

The 'rejection wing' of the CDU was led by the later minister of state, Alois Mertes; the later defence minister and secretary-general of NATO, Manfred Wörner; and the later chairman of the parliamentary CDU, Alfred Dregger. On 20 February 1974 Mertes, as spokesman for this group, introduced into the discussion the possibility

> that our allies, especially those in Europe, might at a later date ... release the Federal Republic partly or totally from the renunciation of 1954 ... or even, as in the case of the MLF, on their own initiative grant access to nuclear weapons.

These possibilities would all be prevented by the ratification of the NPT. The main point in Mertes's line of reasoning, however, was the special relationship between Moscow and Bonn. According to Mertes, it made political sense to maintain the renunciation position of 1954. It was unacceptable, however, to enter into 'an unrestricted bilateral nuclear renunciation on the part of the Federal Republic of Germany vis-à-vis the Soviet Union' (DBT, 20 February 1984, p. 5,262).

In the Foreign Affairs Committee of the Bundestag, eight out of 15 MPs from the CDU/CSU supported Mertes's position. In the Defence Committee, the leader of the opponents to the treaty was Manfred Wörner. In December 1973 Wörner declared that even according to the American interpretation, the proliferation of nuclear weapons within non-federal European states would violate the treaty. For this reason, the security of the FRG was lessened by the NPT. Wörner told the Committee that a rejection of the treaty would neither lead the Federal Republic into an internationally isolated position nor endanger the NATO Alliance. In January 1974 those

CDU/CSU MPs in the Defence Committee agreed en bloc to this statement (*Deutscher Bundestag*, no. 14/15, 1974b). In the final roll-call vote in the Bundestag, 90 of the 201 CDU/CSU MPs voted against the treaty, including, from the rows of the CDU, Windelen and Wörner (who were later to become ministers), and Alfred Dregger, Herbert Hupka, Christian Lenzer, Erich Mende, Karl Miltner, Karl-Heinz Narjes and Walter Wallmann.

The principal criticism of the NPT was also supported by CDU MP Karl Carstens, although he acted as spokesman for the majority of MPs within his parliamentary group (Fraktion) who had agreed to accede to the treaty. In his function as the speaker for the whole 'Fraktion', Carstens listed the grave misgivings concerning the treaty: First of all, it was 'the classic example of an unbalanced treaty'; second, 'this treaty had failed to achieve its most important aim, namely universal validity'; third, it included 'a totally one-sided obligation ... towards the Soviet Union'; and fourth, February 1974 was, with respect to the poor state of the Alliance and of European integration, 'the worst possible moment one could possibly imagine to reach a final decision about the treaty' (DBT, 20 February 1974, p. 5,280).

One very substantial reason why a majority of CDU MPs had agreed to accession to the treaty in spite of these worries was the fact that the German government was prepared to impose an additional interpretative proviso to the European option in the event of ratification. Carstens said that this proviso was 'an important element in the opinion-making process of the CDU/CSU members in parliament who agreed to the treaty' (DBT, 20 April 1974, p. 5,283). Indeed, the question of the European option lay at the heart of the general discussions, and the Foreign Affairs Committee had arranged for two day-long special hearings for it. After the majority vote in favour of ratification by the Bundestag and Bundesrat, the NPT formally came into effect for the non-nuclear Euratom member states on 2 May 1975, with the joint deposition of the instruments of ratification.

Walking on Tiptoe
In spite of the differences within the CDU/CSU, it was not the quarrel between the parties which dominated the tenor of the ratification debate but the overriding question of common interest. As had been the case back in November 1969, the German government was once more endeavouring to come to as far-reaching an agreement as possible with the CDU/CSU. There was a corresponding feeling of trust and confidence within the committees. Here, the German

government was confronted with a list of more than 100 confidential questions on the NPT from MPs Birrenbach (CDU), Mertes (CDU) and Pawelczyk (SPD) (*Deutscher Bundestag*, DS 31, no. 23, 1974).

All the parties still had many doubts on the treaty. None of them wanted to limit its scope as far as the nuclear option was concerned. And there was unanimous agreement that the right to withdraw from the treaty should be guaranteed. During consultations within the committees, the German government had also stressed the importance of the *clausula rebus sic stantibus* for the future maintenance of German interests (DS, 7/1694, p. 5). There was unanimity too on the fact that in the twilight zones of civil and military nuclear research, that room to manoeuvre which had already been established during the NPT controversy had to be secured. In a report signed by MPs Bangemann (FDP), Birrenbach (CDU), Mertes (CDU) and Pawelczyk (SPD), the German government was called upon, vis-à-vis the nuclear-weapon states, to insist on Phrase 7 of the NPT preamble which guaranteed participation 'in the technological "spin-offs" relevant for civilian use which come from the development of nuclear explosive devices' (DS 7/1693, p. 8).

And, finally, there was unanimity on the desire not only to keep open the European option but to extend it within the narrow framework which the NPT permitted on that question. Therefore Willy Brandt and the chairman of the Foreign Affairs Committee, Gerhard Schröder, began to develop a new formula for the European option. The talks, which lasted for some weeks, resulted in an additional statement by the German government with respect to the depositing of the instruments of ratification. In this statement it was declared that the FRG was prepared to accede to the NPT only on condition that 'no regulation of the treaty be interpreted in such a way that it would hamper the further development of European integration, especially in the establishing of a European Union with its corresponding areas of competency' (*Bulletin*, 5 May 1975, p. 542). In contrast to the American interpretation of the NPT, which permitted the transfer of nuclear weapons only after the establishment of a European federal state and which had already been criticised in November 1969 by both the government and the opposition as being unnecessarily restrictive; according to Germany's interpretation, all the intermediate stages on the road to becoming a European nuclear power were defined as being in conformity with the NPT.

The agreement on a new European formula corresponded to a proposal by Uwe Nerlich, a leading member of the SWP think-tank in Ebenhausen. In an unpublished study, Nerlich had taken a close look at the ratification dilemma of the CDU/CSU, and recommended a method for dealing with the nuclear problem which was generally accepted, and which is still authoritative up to the present day. Nerlich gave a warning about confirming the European option too graphically and forcefully, for example in the form of a Bundestag resolution, as this would not only provoke the Soviet Union to take some counteraction but would also push allied governments into making statements dissociating themselves from it. In the current situation, proceeding in such a way would be more likely to close the nuclear option than to keep it open. Instead of making an attack on the legal limitations of the NPT, he advised a more pragmatic procedure which would take into consideration, and use, the real room to manoeuvre on the enhancement of nuclear status which had been left open within the framework of the NPT. Of more practical importance for the foreseeable future, were such 'looser forms of nuclear cooperation which do not include transfer [and] which are not covered by the NPT' (Nerlich, 1973, p. 65). Instead of interpreting the connection between the NPT and the European option as

> simply a latent conflict … it could be politically more useful to try to do the opposite, i.e. to take for granted the fact that the NPT, as interpreted by both the United States and the Western European governments, provides the framework for future developments in the field of military–nuclear cooperation: it makes clear what is not allowed and so reduces the possibilities of opposition in this area to cases of proven infringements of the treaty. (Nerlich, 1973, p. 67)

In order not to hamper the European option unnecessarily, the ratification debate on the NPT ought therefore to be held without political squabbling and with the silent agreement of all parties that 'the NPT is to be seen as a positive framework for future military cooperation throughout Western Europe'.

Indeed, the European option was discussed in the Bundestag only in cryptic terms. According to Karl Carstens (CDU): 'By this statement [which the German government will give during ratification] it shall be made certain that the non-proliferation treaty will not hamper the development of a European political union at any stage or phase of development' (DBT, 20 February 1974, p. 5,282). In the words of Martin Bangemann (FDP):

> The purpose of the non-proliferation treaty is not to permit any future increase in the number of controlling countries; as we already have two member states in the European Community

which are nuclear-weapon states, this kind of European integration ... cannot be contradicted by the treaty; it stands much more in accord with it.

At the same time, Bangemann issued a warning 'that every unnecessary discussion over such difficulties of interpretation could curtail our own position, and so we should be very careful about making such statements'. The approval of all governing parties was noted in the minutes of that session (DBT, 20 April 1974, p. 5,266). Alfons Pawelczyk (SPD) added: 'The treaty keeps the European option open. Therefore, we will agree to the treaty' (DBT, 20 April 1974, p. 5,274).

The German NPT controversy had begun during discussions on the MLF, centring on the arming of Western Europe with nuclear weapons. It ended with exactly the same issue. During debates in Germany, the European option had become the rallying point for opponents of the treaty; after the decline of the MLF, it took on the character of a substitute solution, a solution 'that seemed to keep open the way to nuclear participation for the Federal Republic' and that at the same time 'was a kind of insurance in case the Atlantic Alliance should break up, or lose its credibility some day' (Haftendorn, 1974, p. 180). Maintaining this position was the alpha and omega of the Federal Republic's NPT policy.

But both phraseology and tactics had changed between 1963 and 1973. Whereas the MLF had been pushed vociferously into the foreground by Bonn as a material or juridical option, proceedings now became a great deal smoother. While the confrontational assertions that were made on nuclear options in practice gambled them away, now counterreactions from the West and the East were anticipated, and Bonn tried to tiptoe towards achieving the maximum of what seemed to be reasonable without arousing international protest. And instead of claiming from the NPT what political reality was unable to provide, an attempt was made to upgrade and make the most of the room to manoeuvre that had been secured during the long years of controversy over the NPT. What sort of freedoms were safeguarded for the Federal Republic of Germany by the Non-Proliferation Treaty? Let us take stock.

6

Loopholes within Loopholes

Earlier chapters have dealt with how the Non-Proliferation Treaty finally came into being. Without Germany's signature, this treaty would have been worthless to both superpowers. This key position was fully exploited by the German government. None of the 150 signatory states had resisted accession to the treaty at the beginning as stubbornly as the Federal Republic of Germany had. No other non-nuclear-weapons state had nearly as much influence on the wording and interpretation of the treaty during the period of negotiations as did the FRG. As a potential seller of nuclear technology, Bonn had made a contribution towards maximising the liberalisation of such exports and minimising the possibilities that the military use of such technology would come to light. At the same time, the range of the FRG's renunciation of atomic weapons, and thus the legal room to manoeuvre within West Germany's nuclear option, had been marked by specific NATO and FRG interpretations of the treaty. It should be noted at this point that all these interpretations now, after the unification of East Germany and West Germany, are valid for Germany as a whole.

Which options did the treaty keep open? The evaluation of this question will concentrate on four points: security policy (Articles I and II), the validity and withdrawal clause (Art. X), the safeguards question (Art. III) and the fostering of atomic energy (Art. IV).

Nuclear Participation

Article I is binding on the atomic powers in two respects. First, they are not allowed 'to transfer to any recipient whatsoever nuclear weapons or other nuclear explosive devices or control over such weapons or explosive devices directly, or indirectly'. The phrase 'to any recipient whatsoever' means that the United States or Great Britain would not be allowed to pass on atomic weapons to France or any other European nuclear power. Second, nuclear-weapons states are not allowed to support or encourage or induce any non-nuclear-weapons state to produce, purchase or control nuclear weapons. Among themselves, the nuclear-weapons states are permitted to help each other out with nuclear armaments as long as this does not result in a transfer of atomic warheads. Article I, therefore, corresponds exactly with the regulations of the US Atomic Energy Act (*DoD*, 1969, p. 49).

Not defined, and therefore open to interpretation, are the terms 'nuclear weapons', 'directly or indirectly' and 'control over'. The NATO interpretation, which had been noted by the Soviet Union without contradiction but also without acknowledgement or agreement, defines these terms as follows.

'Nuclear weapons'. In the NPT this term is a synonym for 'bombs and warheads'. According to the NATO interpretation, the treaty 'does not deal with, and therefore does not prohibit, transfer of nuclear delivery vehicles or delivery systems, or control over them to any recipient, so long as such transfer does not involve bombs or warheads' (United States Senate, 1968, p. 5). This definition revised the 1954 WEU provisions which stated that every weapon is a nuclear weapon if it contains nuclear fuel or if it is expressly able to accommodate such fuel, as well as any device, group of components or substance essential for such purposes.

'Directly or indirectly'. The prohibition of indirect control over atomic weapons was regarded with especial suspicion by Bonn. Within NATO, soldiers from the Bundeswehr were trained in the use of atomic weapons with the expectation that in the event of war 'the weapons given to Germans would be released by the country possessing them' (*FAZ*, 2 April 1968). Indeed, even the United States said that the term 'directly or indirectly' used with respect to the Federal Republic was an 'artifice intended to calm the Soviets psychologically' (AA-Doc. I, attachment 2). Washington added that this term was not related to nuclear participation but only to proliferation by third parties: it was intended to prevent cases where, for example, someone might deposit nuclear weapons in an empty building for someone else to pick up later (AA-Doc. I, attachment 2).

'Control over'. The interpretation of this term was very important as it touched upon the very heart of nuclear participation. The NATO interpretation made it clear that the prohibition of nuclear controls does not affect 'Allied consultations and planning on nuclear defence', as long as through this 'no transfer of nuclear weapons or control over them results' (AA-Doc. I, attachment 2). In accordance with this, it was not permitted to delegate decisions on nuclear deployment to a nuclear planning group or similar organisation if, within this group, the non-nuclear states formed a majority to vote down an atomic power (Willrich, 1968, p. 1,471).

Moreover, the NATO interpretation expressly exempted all

arrangements for deployment of nuclear weapons within Allied territory as these do not involve any transfer of nuclear weapons or control over them unless and until a decision were made to go to war, at which time the treaty would no longer be controlling. (United States Senate, 1968, p. 5)

This complicated phrasing hints at a tricky problem. The NPT regulations are regarded as being met only as long as, within the framework of nuclear participation, control over atomic weapons clearly remains in American hands. But what role does the NPT play in the event of a crisis or a war? 'We had a terrible dilemma on that', Charles van Doren (one of the American authors of the NATO interpretation) explained to me later. Indeed, the latent contradiction between nuclear participation in NATO and membership of the NPT becomes especially clear at this point. The NPT is meant to prevent the establishment of additional nuclear powers, whereas nuclear participation is meant to enable Allied states, after clearance by the president of the United States, to act like nuclear powers. The consequence is that in that event of a decision to go to war, the NPT would no longer be valid from the viewpoint of NATO. As George H. Quester later said:

We thus have an interpretation that the ban on proliferation could be lifted as soon as a major war with the Soviet Union had broken out in Europe, an interpretation giving Bonn at least some of the psychological weight it had been seeking. (Quester, 1973, p. 176)

This question received high priority in Defence Ministry circles. In a 'top-secret' NPT analysis by the German Defence Ministry, dated 4 November 1961, it is stated:

From the German point of view, it is necessary that, in case of war, control over atomic warheads be given in part to the tactical officer in command without any consideration of his nationality. The realisation of this German opinion would be contrary to the planned treaty if it did not lose validity in the event of war. (NHP VII, pp. 1–3)

On 10 July 1968 the NATO interpretation, including the above condition, was made public by the American secretary of state, Dean Rusk. The German daily *Die Welt* thought it was remarkable that the Secretary of State emphatically stressed the invalidity of the NPT in the event of war. It is noteworthy that, with respect to this, he spoke about the 'decision to begin war' and not about a declaration of war. This nuance is interesting as it holds open the possibility of nullifying the treaty even without a declaration of war. (*Die Welt*, 11 July 1968)

Indeed, the NATO interpretation on its own could even give rise to the impression of arbitrariness: it is not only unclear who would be responsible for the decision to go to war, it is also unclear who would be responsible for answering the question of whether or not such a decision had been made by whoever had made it. Are not NATO's allies here offered the opportunity of nullifying the NPT even without the agreement of the United States?

It was precisely this question that was being discussed in the US Senate in February 1969. These debates introduced the new term 'general war,' a prerequisite for which is the involvement of the superpowers; and it was in precisely such an event that the invalidity of the NPT vis-à-vis the NATO Allies was anticipated. But such a stipulation was not to be applied to a limited local conflict, namely one which would be fought without atomic weapons and without involving the superpowers. This viewpoint, however, was not part of the 'classic' NATO interpretations; it was merely added to the minutes as an American interpretation within the scope of the debates in Congress on the ratification of the NPT (DoD, 10969, p. 44).

It was by no means to be regarded as a matter of course that nuclear participation would be combined with the NPT. Not only those states within the sphere of influence of the Soviet Union, but also several of the non-aligned states viewed these two issues as incompatible (Shaker, 1976, p. 241). Even the US Senate refused to consider a resolution on an agreement on these interpretations, mentioning the discriminating effect this would have on third parties (US Senate, Congressional Records, 13 March 1969, p. 6,338). In official German government publications on the NPT, these interpretations are not even mentioned once.

Such discretion was in inverse proportion to the importance that Bonn accorded those interpretations. In order to maximise their binding character, the German government had issued orders for the following: to inform the Soviets formally about these interpretations; to put the interpretations at the disposal of the hearings of the US Senate; to confirm the interpretations by an exchange of notes between the US secretary of state and the German foreign minister; to make public the interpretations within NATO and vis-à-vis Japan;

and to make public similar interpretations by Great Britain and Italy (Doc. XVI, p. 51).

The Grand Coalition government had placed special emphasis on the maintaining of the nuclear option in the event of war, and on receiving corresponding assurance on this from Washington and London. Within the Auswärtige Amt, criticism was aimed at the fact that the NPT would be nullified only at the beginning of a war 'and not during periods of tension or in case of a crisis, i.e. when such a deterrent could be a decisive factor in preventing a war' (AA-Doc. I, Appendix 2). Apart from the published NATO interpretations, special attention was paid to an additional NATO-American interpretation of the term 'control over'. The wording of that interpretation is unfortunately unknown, but it is plausible to view it in such a way that, in the event of war, nuclear warheads would be activated by American soldiers and, after that, left in the hands of Allied military personnel to use as they saw fit.

Support for the Atomic Powers

Article II of the NPT deals with the duties of the non-nuclear powers. They are not allowed 'to manufacture or otherwise acquire nuclear weapons or other nuclear explosive devices', or 'to accept ... from anyone ... control over such weapons or explosive devices directly, or indirectly'. Up to this point, this is a mirror-image inversion of the obligations laid on the atomic powers in Article I. But in Article II nothing is said which expressly prohibits a non-nuclear-weapons state from aiding any nuclear-weapons state or any non-nuclear-weapons state that is not a party to the NPT in the production of an atomic bomb.

One might assume that this latter loophole was closed by the fact that, according to Article III of the treaty, all nuclear exports are subject to IAEA controls. This is not the case, however, because these controls are expressly applied to materials and equipment used for 'peaceful purposes'. The conclusion drawn by Mason Willrich, former ACDA legal expert and participant in NPT diplomacy, seems to be cogent: 'Under the Treaty as it stands, there would seem to be no legal obstacle to a non-nuclear-weapon party furnishing material assistance to another non-nuclear-weapon state not a party to the Treaty for a nuclear weapons program' (Willrich, 1968, p. 1,478). Another NPT analyst has said: 'The loophole in Article II was not a theoretical one of no particular significance' (Shaker, 1976, p. 263).

This loophole was not woven into the wording of the treaty by coincidence but was quite deliberate. In the American draft of Article

II in 1965, this loophole was still closed (*EA* 20/65, D 513). It was precisely this point which Franz Josef Strauss regarded as the main 'catch' in the West's proposal. According to Strauss, the practical path to Europe's nuclear power status was hampered

> by the clause where the non-nuclear-weapons states shall undertake not to support the manufacturing of nuclear weapons. But I do not see any way of Europe's becoming, step by step, an atomic power other than by enabling the nuclear have-nots to participate financially and technologically in the development of Europe's nuclear armament. (*Rheinischer Merkur*, 27 August 1965)

In August 1967 the superpowers presented a new version of Article II – this time without the 'catch'. But it was fiercely criticised, especially by the United Arab Republic (UAR) and Sweden. The UAR wanted Article II to be a mirror image of Article I, whereas Sweden made a proposal aimed at disarmament : nuclear exports to nuclear-weapons states should either be submitted to obligatory IAEA controls to prove their peaceful use, or they should be prohibited.

Nobody knows why these protests were rejected by both Washington and Moscow. It is likely that both countries wanted to prevent limitations on their own options so that they could, for example, continue to have free disposal over uranium obtained from non-nuclear-weapons states. An initiative by the superpowers to obstruct any support for non-nuclear-weapons states who were not signatories of the treaty seemed risky under such circumstances, according to Mason Willrich, who said: 'Such an amendment might well have resulted in pressure from other nations to have the Treaty bar assistance by non-nuclear-weapon states not only to other non-nuclear-weapon states, but also to the nuclear-weapon states themselves' (Willrich, 1968, p. 1478).

The reticence of the superpowers at that time has had consequences right down to the present. In 1985 the German government answered a parliamentary question posed by the 'Greens' as to whether or not a militarily motivated transfer of nuclear goods to a nuclear-weapons state would contravene the wording or the spirit of the NPT as follows:

> According to the NPT, the transfer of nuclear goods or nuclear technology to nuclear-weapons states is in no way limited. There could be a contravention of 'the spirit of the NPT' only if someone violated the aims of the treaty by exploiting an unintentional loophole in the treaty. The fact that the transfer of nuclear goods

to nuclear-weapons states is not limited by the NPT was not only indicative of such a loophole, this fact was absolutely clear to those states involved in the negotiations on the wording of the treaty. (DS 10/4502, p. 10)

That Bonn could do little more than this is demonstrated by NATO's interpretation of the European option. There it is clearly stated that, within the framework of the NPT, a European Union of states could take on the status of a nuclear-weapons state should such a state join that union. Such a new state would, however, 'have to control *all* of its external security functions, including defence and *all* foreign policy matters relating to external security, but would not have to be so centralized as to assume all governmental functions' (United States Senate, 1968, p. 6; emphasis added).

In the final sentence of that sixth NATO interpretation, what was to remain prohibited was actually emphasised, namely the 'transfer of nuclear weapons (including their possession) or their control to any receiver, including a multilateral unit'. Up to the very last minute, the Federal Republic and Italy had tried in bilateral and NATO negotiations to get both the first and the second *all*, as well as the final sentence, removed from the interpretation – but their efforts were in vain (AA-Doc. XVII, pp. 26 ff.). Little wonder that the German government did not accept NATO's interpretation of the European option, but said, openly and in public, that it was unnecessarily restrictive and that during the ratification process it had been accentuated anew by an additional statement (DS VI/50, p. 6).

The holding open or supporting of the European nuclear option is a clear contradiction of the spirit and wording of Article VI of the treaty. That article on disarmament places an obligation not only on nuclear-weapons states but also on

each of the Parties to the Treaty ... to pursue negotiations in good faith on effective measures relating to cessation of the nuclear arms race at an early date and to nuclear disarmament, and on a treaty on general and complete disarmament under strict and effective international controls.

Although the German Government had supported the inclusion of this article, Bonn was not prepared to make it stronger or more concrete. The director of the SWP, Klaus Ritter, declared in a lecture in 1967 which was not open to the public that 'he was, in fact, sceptical of forcing the demand for a quid pro quo, especially from the nuclear superpowers, and in particular in the form of a limitation of top-ranking developments' (Forschungsinstitut, 1967, p. 53).

Thus, during NPT negotiations, Bonn was aligned among the opponents of the Swedish proposal who wanted to make sure that all nuclear imports into nuclear-weapons states would be used exclusively for peaceful use. This standpoint was a flagrant contradiction of Bonn's usual demand not to accept any differing treatment of nuclear-weapons and non-nuclear-weapons states as far as safeguards were concerned. It also differed from the position taken by the other Western Allies: not just Canada (Willrich, 1968, p. 1489) but also Italy had declared that, in future, it wanted to subject all their nuclear exports, without exception, to the NPT conditions (DAS VI, p. 198). Support for the Swedish proposal had been discussed briefly in the Inter-ministerial Working Staff of the German government, but it was soon dropped in order not to prejudice future Franco-German options. (AA-Docs. VII and VIII).

The Right to Withdraw

Paragraph 1 of Article X of the NPT stresses the right of each party to the treaty to withdraw from it when it decides 'that extraordinary events, related to the subject matter of this Treaty, have jeopardised the supreme interests of its country'. The United Nations Security Council has to be given notice of the withdrawal three months in advance and it has to be substantiated. It is not only quite unusual that such a right is made explicit in the NPT, it is remarkable that each signatory to the treaty could decide on its own whether or not any 'extraordinary events, related to the subject matter of this Treaty', might or might not necessitate withdrawal. Such a general clause could do harm to the credibility of the NPT, and the participants of the ENDC Conference in Geneva complained about this (Shaker, 1976, p. 803).

But the introduction of the right of withdrawal seemed to be necessary in order to increase the acceptance of the treaty with the threshold nations. The Federal Republic had reserved the right to make use of Article X, especially in the event of the break-up of NATO. At the instigation of Bonn, in July 1968 Secretary of State Dean Rusk had confirmed in a US Senate hearing

that if NATO were to dissolve, this might well be interpreted by some countries as one of those events affecting their vital interests which could raise the question of the withdrawal clause under the treaty, if their judgement at that time was that their own national security required it. (United States Senate, 1968, p. 43)

We have already seen the second considerable limitation to the treaty with respect to the 'classic' NATO interpretations. According to these, at the outbreak of a war the Federal Republic would immediately be given the status of a nuclear-weapons power without having to observe the three-month waiting period. In the agreements which were valid at that time it was established that, in the event of war, the president of the United States would decide if and when American atomic warheads would have to be transferred to the Bundeswehr's air force. Under the NATO interpretations of the NPT this process was expressed in a general way – not by an order given by the US president would the NPT be nullified, but on the basis of a certain situation which was described in a very vague manner. Although the political and military significance of this difference should not be overestimated, it could have played a role as far as status and prestige were concerned. If the treaty was to lose validity when war was in the offing, the giving up of status by signing the treaty did not seem half so bad. In 1989 the president of the German Clausewitz Society, retired Lieutenant-General Lothar Domröse, put this idea into words: 'Every thought about a policy of defence and security, and every strategy as well, has to take into account the existence of nuclear weapons or the possibility of producing nuclear weapons at the outbreak of a war' (*EWK* 2/89, p. 80).

Paragraph 2 of Article X of the NPT deals with the duration of the treaty:

Twenty-five years after the entry into force of the Treaty, a conference shall be convened to decide whether the Treaty shall continue in force indefinitely, or shall be extended for an additional fixed period or periods. This decision shall be taken by a majority of the Parties to the Treaty.

On 5 March 1970 the treaty came into force after the three depository states and 40 other states had ratified it. In the spring of 1995 an international conference will decide on the extension of the treaty.

The introduction of the conditional limitation to the treaty was the work of Italy, and especially the Federal Republic of Germany (Bunn and van Doren, 1991). It was feared that it would be impossible for the Federal Republic, for historical reasons, to make use of a right of withdrawal. Only if the treaty were to expire at a certain point in the future did it seem possible to withdraw without automatically being blamed for it.

Here the Federal Republic achieved partial success: the option of expiry after 25 years (plus an additional unspecified period) was part and parcel of the treaty; but before that the hurdle of a majority vote by all parties to the treaty had to be overcome.

Minimising the Controls

In Article III of the NPT, dealing with safeguards, the influence of the Federal Republic can be seen quite clearly. The basic American draft was fully revised. According to that draft, the NPT controls were to be carried out only by the IAEA; they were to be applied to both materials and facilities, and it was their aim, according to IAEA regulations, to prevent any military use of those materials and facilities. (The United States draft of 31 January 1967 is printed in full in the German edition of this book.) It was at this point, however, that the problem began. The purpose of the NPT is not identical to that of the IAEA. Whereas IAEA regulations prohibit any kind of military use of atomic energy, this is permitted by the NPT as long as it does not result in the production of finished nuclear weapons. The NPT safeguards serve 'solely' the goal of ensuring that the obligations set down in the treaty are observed. According to the American under-secretary of defense, Paul Nitze, before the US Senate, 'This means that military nuclear activities that are not directly related to the production of warheads or missiles are exempt from safeguards' (United States Senate, 1968, p. 64). This limitation covers, for example, the production of nuclear propulsion systems for submarines, or other weapons carriers, as well as the production of non-explosive nuclear devices or parts of weapons. Article 14 of the verification agreement ('no application of the safeguards to nuclear material that is intended to be used in non-peaceful actions') confirms this fact (DS 7/995, p. 11).

The special success of the German government's negotiations was that inspections were limited to fissionable material and that inspections of the facilities were prevented. In order to export a nuclear reprocessing plant, the IAEA did not have to be consulted as long as no significant amount of fissionable material was contained within it. A further limitation dealt with the fact that the controls were to be applied only to nuclear activities that were carried on 'within the territory of such a [member] State, under its jurisdiction, or carried out under its control anywhere' (Article III of the NPT). Thus those facilities in France in which the FRG had a 49 per cent share could be exempt from the controls.

Moreover, it is especially remarkable that the controls have to be implemented 'in accordance with ... the provision of this Article and the principle of safeguarding set forth in the Preamble of the Treaty'. This reference was aimed at the so-called Karlsruhe Doctrine in Clause 6 of the preamble which had been introduced into the operational part of the treaty. According to this, the application within the framework of the IAEA safeguards system, of the principle of safeguarding effectively the flows of source and special fissionable materials by use of instruments and other techniques at certain strategic points was to be furthered. In its interpretative statement of 1969, the German government had declared that this principle was a precondition for accession to the treaty.

The Federal Republic can claim a copyright on the pasage of Euratom too. Agreements were to be entered into with the IAEA 'either individually or together with other states' – the euphemism for Euratom. That inconspicuous phrase in Article III was of great significance with regard to both European policy and industrial policy: it not only strengthened and extended the position of Euratom internally, it did so outwardly as well. While other threshold powers were also interested in having the least rigid controls possible, Bonn can still lay claim to authorship of the following points: dispensing with facility inspections, anchoring the principle of safeguards on fissionable materials flows at strategic points, and the acknowledgement of the Euratom safeguards system.

In Support of Atomic Energy

The most significant result of Germany's NPT diplomacy is probably the inclusion of Article IV in the treaty. No other conditions in the treaty were so obviously the result of Bonn's activities, and with no other initiative did the Federal Republic so greatly influence the NPT and thus the further development of non-proliferation policies in general. At the beginning of 1967 Bonn began to exacerbate the controversy over the disarmament agreement by adding an important industrial dimension to it. The first public sign of this came from Willy Brandt. On 1 February 1967 he raised 'the decisive question for the German government ... as to how the negative effects of the NPT on the civilian use of nuclear energy can be prevented'. Such a danger was viewed from two different angles: first, the prohibition of nuclear explosions for peaceful purposes, according to Brandt, introduced 'considerable interference with and impairment of civilian nuclear industries in the non-nuclear-weapons states, especially if this prohibition is also extended to related technologies'; second, there were worries about spin-off. Countries such as the Federal Republic, said Brandt, should 'participate under reasonable conditions in the experience and knowledge gained by nuclear-weapons states from their military employment of nuclear energy used for peaceful purposes'. The use of atomic energy in the non-nuclear-weapons states should not only not be hampered by the treaty, it should be extended in order to 'prevent the existing technological gap between nuclear-weapons states and non-nuclear-weapons states from getting even bigger' (DBT, 1 February 1967, p. 4,165).

In the same month the United States, in an additional interpretation addressed to Bonn, suggested that the content of what was later to become Article IV should be integrated into the NPT. But more changes were to come. The German government responded to a non-public inquiry by the parliamentary SPD as follows:

> After German-American consultations, a section on protection for the peaceful [nuclear-use] sectors was added to the Western draft of the Article on controls. During further negotiations, the original goal was reached, namely that the safeguarding of nuclear energy would be laid down as a separate article (Article IV) in the operative part of the treaty. (AA-Doc. XVI, p. 69)

The significance of this political course becomes clear if we confront it with the alternatives that were still in existence when the controversy over the NPT began. One of the best-known non-proliferation experts of those years, Leonard Beaton from Great Britain, had in 1966 presented a plan for nuclear non-proliferation that was seemingly naive in its effort to freeze the nuclear status quo; at the same time, however, he represented a non-proliferation philosophy that was far ahead of its time by focusing on the non-nuclear production of energy. In 1966 Beaton argued in his book *Must the Bomb Spread?* that the handling of fissionable material suitable for the production of weapons must be regulated with the same care as is the case when dealing legally with drugs. His proposal for a non-proliferation strategy included the following items:

1. Agreement on an NPT in which non-proliferation aspects should be defined progressively in both directions: 'Restricting the publication of information and transfer of important technology by the great powers and controlling the acquisition of plutonium by the small powers.'

2. The introduction of a comprehensive test ban treaty and an end to the production of fissionable material by the superpowers. Uranium enrichment and reprocessing should be only permitted in multinational facilities.
3. Strengthening, as far as possible, the defence measures of the NATO Allies to cope with nuclear attack. Establishing a general guarantee system of the nuclear powers and an organisation for the leading threshold powers to maintain their interests within this guarantee system.
4. An agreement by the nuclear powers to abolish any status advantage based on the possession of atomic weapons (for example, membership of international institutions and participation in conferences).
5. Continuing activities to minimise the use of nuclear explosives as instruments of war.
6. A binding agreement by the leading producers of uranium not to sell any material without controls; permanent activities to limit the sale of atomic power plants which had not been submitted to controls.
7. Reorganisation of the Atomic Energy Commissions and the IAEA with the goal of ending 'proliferation of knowledge, training and technology for its own sake and to encourage wherever possible non-nuclear ways of achieving power for civil purposes. (Beaton, 1966, pp. 126–128)

The considerable concern linked to Article IV also points up something else: that the nuclear status quo should not be frozen but equalised in technological terms. In particular, the secret knowledge of the nuclear powers should be made available to the non-nuclear signatories of the treaty. The fact that this considerably increased the danger of nuclear proliferation was a good argument for preparing oneself for all contingencies by securing a 'stand-by' programme. Viewed in this way, the NPT indeed 'had a proliferating effect insofar as a number of states saw themselves confronted with the problem of ensuring a future option; and that this helped push the opinion-forming process in this direction' (Botzian, 1967c, p. 2).

Let us now take a look at the wording of Article IV and its German and American interpretations. Paragraph 1 of Article describes the research, production and use of atomic energy as an 'inalienable right'. In this respect the word 'production' is remarkable as it expressly includes the obtaining and enriching of fissionable material; but this right can be utilised only 'in conformity with Articles I and II' – a proviso that was not very popular in Bonn. After all, the manufacture of atomic weapons was, up to a certain point, identical to the processes that were used in the civil programmes too. So just how far could 'peaceful uses' go? At what point did the forbidden production of nuclear weapons begin? A high-ranking official of the then ACDA, Charles van Doren, explained it thus:

> There was a much discussion on that in the treaty negotiation. The Australians asked us to negotiate this. How far up the line can we go? And we said you can go fairly far, but cannot cross the line of actually testing a weapon and putting one together or getting components for doing this that are exclusively dedicated to weapons manufacture. (Interview with Charles van Doren, 11 October 1986, ACD)

During the Congressional hearings too, the Americans were not able to define clearly the phrase 'manufacture of nuclear weapons'. Director Foster of the ACDA could only offer the American Senate a rough guideline. According to this, activities that were clearly aimed at the purchase of an atomic explosive device were forbidden: for example, the production of a prototype of an explosive device, or the production of atomic weapons components which could be used only in atomic warheads.

> Neither uranium enrichment nor the stockpiling of fissionable material in connection with a peaceful programme would violate Article II so long as these activities were safeguarded under Article III. Also clearly permitted would be the development, under safeguards, of plutonium fueled reactors, including research on the properties of metallic plutonium. (United States Senate, 1968, p. 39).

The second paragraph of Article IV is open in its wording: 'All the Parties to the Treaty undertake to facilitate, and have the right to participate in, the fullest possible exchange of equipment, materials and scientific and technological information for the peaceful uses of nuclear energy.' This formulation was supplemented by the NATO interpretation, according to which the treaty 'only [deals] with what is prohibited, and not with what is permitted'. In other words, everything that is not expressly forbidden can be regarded as being permitted. All that is expressly forbidden is the transfer of and control over nuclear weapons, 'where bombs and warheads are meant'.

Further promises were made in the 18 April 1967 confidential letter from Dean Rusk to Willy Brandt, and in another confidential letter from Johnson to Kiesinger dated 11 December 1967. The contents of these letters are not known. The German government again emphasised its interpretation of Article IV in its note concerning accession to the NPT. According to this, the FRG's agreement to sign was based on the precondition that freedom of nuclear research and development would be guaranteed without any limitations and that nothing more than the production of complete explosive devices would be prohibited by the treaty. This unlimited freedom in nuclear research is supported by the safeguards regulations too. Doing away with the inspecting of facilities had the effect that all research centres working with minimal amounts of nuclear material were exempt from IAEA controls (Van Cleave, 1968, p. 1,056).

It should be noted that, according to the NPT, the research, development, production or purchase of components which could also be used in nuclear weapons was in no way limited or prohibited. This 'significant loophole' makes it possible, in an extreme case, legally to 'acquire a complete, and relatively quickly operational, potential nuclear weapon system' (Keller et al., 1968, pp. 31–3). But purposeful development activities in the field of atomic weapons also were not ruled out by the treaty, either in the wide field of so-called peaceful nuclear fission explosions or in the borderline areas of development in nuclear fusion necessary for the production of a hydrogen bomb.

Where peaceful nuclear explosions are concerned, it is not just from today's point of view that it seems an absurd idea to use nuclear explosions within Germany's densely populated territory in order to mine mineral resources or to remove mountain barriers. Nevertheless, such questions did play an important role in the Federal Republic's NPT diplomacy.

After the Japanese government had, in May 1968, reserved the right for Japan to have 'freedom of research with respect to the peaceful use of nuclear explosives' within the framework of the NPT (DAS VI, p. 160), Willy Brandt also tried to make the demands for such research work seem plausible. Although peaceful nuclear explosions are not a burning issue in the Federal Republic, the foreign minister briefed the press in July 1968 that 'technical developments will lead us within a very few years to a point where even in a densely populated country, such peaceful explosions could have a role to play' (DAS, VI, p. 270).

Suspicion could have been aroused by the opinion of the German government 'that the NPT should not hamper progress in the development and application of technologies in the peaceful use of nuclear explosives' (German government note of 28 November 1969). With these words, the Federal Republic had not only 'expressly reserved the right to develop nuclear warheads for peaceful purposes' (Lauk, 1979, p. 93), but at the same time the 'use' of technologies in testing nuclear explosives appeared to be made compatible with the NPT. As the peaceful atomic explosive device is technically identical to the military one, either use was prohibited by the NPT. To a great extent, however, Germany's interpretation of the NPT tried to counteract this prohibition.

With regard to laser fusion, the NPT does not try to block every road to nuclear status, just the traditional one. It prohibits the transfer of nuclear weapons and the diversion of fissionable material from facilities that have been important for the production of fissionable material – uranium enrichment and reprocessing facilities. Other technical scenarios which may lead to the bomb, such as the production of fissionable material by particle accelerators, are not considered. This is also true of the theoretical type of hydrogen bomb which can be detonated without nuclear fission. This leads to a further loophole with respect to Article IV of the treaty, the exploitation of which has been taken for granted in the West German NPT controversy. Only a few weeks after Germany signed the NPT, a working paper of the SWP Foundation in Ebenhausen emphasised that it was precisely those research activities that should be closely scrutinised which

> aim at starting nuclear fusion processes with a laser beam. Should it become possible to use lasers to detonate nuclear fusion bombs (H-bombs), the NPT could be circumvented because an igniting device based on nuclear fission, and therefore forbidden, would no longer be necessary. (Feigl, 1970b, p. 6)

It is true that up to now no method has been found to detonate an H-bomb other than through nuclear fission. But in principle, certain alternative mechanisms are possible, for example using magnetic fields or laser beams. During negotiations on the NPT such technological options were discussed in public, but they were not taken into consideration with respect to the wording of the treaty because of a reluctance to jeopardise the conclusion of the treaty, as agreement was difficult enough as it was (Quester, 1967, pp. 35–7).

This made all the more obvious the discretion with which that loophole was discussed during Germany's deliberations on the ratification of the NPT. In December 1973, CDU MP Kurt Birrenbach, in a confidential query on the NPT to the government, wanted to know 'if an apparatus using laser-beam induced fusion could not be classified as being a nuclear explosive device'. Another question from Birrenbach, expressed quite clearly the effort that was being made not to give up such a loophole:

Has an attempt been made in this question [laser development and the NPT] to clear up the matter with our allies, or does it seem to be more opportune politically not to broach this subject and thus perhaps avoid giving rise to treaties between the United States and the Soviet Union which could block the whole thing? (Deutscher Bundestag 1974, Doc. 23:7)

The government's answers to these questions were classified as 'confidential' and are still unknown. Mention must be made, however, of the fact that even where the NPT clearly attempted to prevent a path to proliferation, a whole series of loopholes remained. This points to the fact that there is one thing the NPT is unable to do: that is, to hinder the making of preparations to achieve nuclear status by all those nations which want to do so, even though they have signed the treaty.

All of these weaknesses and loopholes in the NPT were obvious to the superpowers in 1968. That they still approved of the NPT was ascribed to the fact that they were well aware that a treaty on the non-proliferation of nuclear weapons would never be achieved unless it contained such loopholes. By signing the treaty, was not the bonus for the threshold powers precisely that complete liberalisation of nuclear technology, and the fact that a country's decision on its nuclear status was entirely a matter of its own political will?

This was the logic behind the origin of the NPT. Whereas at the beginning of the controvery, the 'Irish resolution' of 1961 had appealed to the nations of the world not just to reject the proliferation of nuclear weapons but also 'not to place the information needed for their manufacture at the disposal of' the non-nuclear states (DAS II p. 155), in the end the one aim was achieved at the cost of the other. The Federal Republic of Germany had contributed greatly to this and had profited greatly as well: when the Treaty took effect in 1970, the German government signed an Agreement on the construction of uranium enrichment facilities, and in the same year put into operation its first national reprocessing plant at Karlsruhe. Bonn's policies were motivated by national considerations, but inevitably changed the policies of non-proliferation on a global scale. Since then, the proliferation of nuclear-weapons technologies has changed the face of the world.

Our closing chapter is directed towards the future. Are there lessons to be learned from Germany's policies of the 1960s which can be applied, or even which *must* be applied, to the 1990s?

7

Germany and the Bomb – What Next?

The story of Bonn's diplomacy over the NPT has been told. What remains is to distill and examine the essence of that controversy with regard to its relevance today. Can we generalise on the history of Germany's atomic weapons policy? Can we draw conclusions for the present and future of international non-proliferation? Does a retrospective survey give us a preview of what the nuclear-weapons policy of a united Germany might be?

Nuclear Ambitions versus Renunciation

The discussions about the wording of the NPT and its interpretations lasted for eight years. At that time, the direct opponents of the Federal Republic were not to be found in Moscow but in Washington and London. It was a quarrel between friends which, nevertheless, was conducted with great stubbornness and sharpness. What seems to have been a paradox in fact appears logical if we look at the context of the debate.

The NPT controversy provides an exemple of a line of conflict threading through the history of NATO up until the present day. On the one hand, it traces the endeavours of the victorious Second World War powers to prevent Germany from attaining an equal (i.e. nuclear) status and, on the other, it makes clear Germany's endeavours to balance out nuclear differences with respect to France and Great Britain. This quarrel did not turn on any understanding of safety, freedom or wealth, but on national freedom of action – in short, it concerned the balance of power. This sovereignty-related contradiction has proved to be a factor of instability and a motivating force for controversies within all the areas of NATO's nuclear policy: within the Nuclear Planning Group, with regard to the interpretation of flexible response, with respect to armament controls, and in the context of stand-by options.

In terms of the NPT controversy, this collision of interests was both the trigger and the dominating element of the debate. It has been proved that the Federal government's nuclear ambitions during the period when the treaty was being set up were a real force that dominated foreign policy and influenced Bonn's international environment; and it has been shown to what extent this ambition was opposed, repressed and circumscribed by Western nuclear powers – in part openly, in part covertly, sometimes successfully and sometimes not.

This jumbling of interests explains the interrelationship between nuclear ambitions and the renunciation of nuclear weapons. It makes no difference whether or not we look at the EDC treaty of 1952, the Adenauer renunciation of 1954, or the NPT accession of 1969: in all these cases renunciation was not a voluntary concession on the part of the Federal Republic but the expression of a temporary compromise that highlighted the nuclear contradictions between the winners and losers of the Second World War.

In relation to the international community of nations, Germany's nuclear renunciation was always accompanied by the proviso – though mostly it was not too outspoken – that the basic maintenance of the German nuclear option had not changed. In none of the cases mentioned did the renunciation of nuclear *weapons* equate with renunciation of the nuclear *option*. In national terms, it was precisely the persistence in maintaining this option which was the driving force behind Germany's nuclear policy, while the modalities of renunciation established the external limits to which the methods for maintaining the option had to be adjusted.

The Federal Republic always looked after its own best interests during the NPT controversy. Bonn had forced through optimal results in two respects: the strengthening of nuclear trade options and the weakening of nuclear safeguards. The government's policy also took on a global dimension as it contributed greatly to standardisation within the climate of international non-proliferation. The criteria that Bonn set for accession to the treaty became a yardstick for the conditions that had to be offered to all future signatory nations.

How should the final treaty be rated? Positively speaking, with its more than 150 member states the NPT is the most widely acknowledged treaty on arms controls in history. It is the only agreement that has obliged the nuclear powers and all other signatory states to enter into serious negotiations 'on effective measures relating ... to nuclear disarmament, and on a treaty on general and complete disarmament'. Psychologically speaking, the very existence of this treaty supports a climate in global policy that places a stigma on the establishment of new nuclear-weapons states and, to a great extent, isolates those nations that break the treaty. In practice, however, the treaty is fairly weak: neither the treaty itself nor the IAEA inspections are able to ensure the good behaviour of a signatory state in terms of its proliferation policies. On the contrary: as proved by Iraq, for example, member states can use the image of confidence which the treaty inspires to develop their nuclear weapons with even less interference from outside.

All this means that the treaty is not a real barrier to nuclear proliferation but is basically a mutual expression of confidence and good will. It is this function of establishing confidence which has made possible the worldwide proliferation of nuclear technology in recent decades. Today, Iraq is not the only state to provide proof of the fact that this confidence was deceitful and has supported fatal misjudgments about the consequences of the proliferation of atomic energy. The existence of the NPT implies that there is a clear borderline between the military and non-military use of nuclear energy which, in reality, does not exist. With regard to technology, every nuclear energy programme can become a nuclear weapons programme if the facility exists to enrich uranium or to reprocess spent fuel. We are wholly dependent on the intentions of individual governments as to whether or not a country excludes its facilities from IAEA inspections by making the simple declaration that they serve military purposes only. The NPT's intention to control arms is counterbalanced by the treaty's pretension to have commercial and technological value: by stressing a nation's inalienable right to develop atomic energy, the treaty creates conditions that may not be revoked as easily as a country's signature to the treaty may be.

This study has shown that the Federal Republic has to account for establishing this course of action. Would it have been possible for the German NPT diplomacy of the 1960s to have followed to an alternative course? If so, why was this alternative not pursued?

The Drive for Prestige

An alternative approach for Germany's NPT policy was presented in May 1966 by Thomas C. Schelling. A Harvard professor and director of the Center for International Affairs in Cambridge, Massachusetts, he explained that West Germany could have played a major role

> if it had been prepared to put itself at the forefront of the fight for the non-proliferation of nuclear weapons instead of hampering it. Germany is the only country in the world that could prove that a state can be big, prosperous and powerful without the atomic bomb, the only country that could take away the status of wielding the sceptre of power from the atomic weapons by voluntarily renouncing such weapons – the only country that could take over

the initiative of disarmament from the United States and the Soviet Union. (Schelling, 1966, p. 471)

Is it not self-evident that a country which has caused two world wars in Europe in this century should 'put itself at the forefront of the fight for non-proliferation of nuclear weapons'? It seems a plausible assumption that the NPT and the current state of nuclear proliferation would be different in 1967 if the Federal Republic – adapting the nuclear image of its NATO ally, Denmark, and the peace policy commitment of neutral Sweden – had thrown all its weight on the scales in favour of creating as effective an NPT as possible. The fact that this scenario appears quite irrational only confirms how diametrically opposed to this possibility Germany's approaches to foreign policy were. The alternative approach outlined by Schelling was never even discussed in the Federal Republic, and this is not a mere coincidence: a public debate on the appropriateness of maintaining the nuclear weapons option never took place in the Federal Republic. The FRG's nuclear policy stirred up entire battalions of diplomats, kept NATO committees on the go day and night, and was expressed in mountains of papers printed in *English*. In public discussions in the Federal Republic, however, the policy of maintaining a nuclear option was always placed under the taboo of nuclear secrecy and left to be handled by a discreet circle of experts. Robert Held of the *Frankfurter Allgemeine Zeitung* has called this phenomenon a 'discreet democracy by delegation'. His judgement of that circle of the 'knowing and informed' is supported by this study. Held wrote that there was

> behind the obvious and superficial wrangling in Germany's domestic policy, far-reaching national consensus about certain nuclear industrial aims of which the government *and* the opposition, union leaders, intellectuals, technicians, industrialists and bank directors declared themselves to be in favour, in rare unity. This phenomenon is not transparent and, therefore, democratically not completely in order. But it is a sort of discreet democracy by delegation and finds an apology mainly through one argument: The terms of nuclear development stretch over such long periods of time ... that the lifetime of a democratic government seems to be short in comparison. What will be necessary for the nation in 1990 can already be anticipated today. But as these decisions are not popular, a government could be tempted, bearing in mind its own brief fate, to avoid going along with them. If it responsibly renounces such opportunism, then it needs – in order to gain

courage behind the scenes – the silent consent of its major political parties, and the support of knowledgeable and informed persons. (*FAZ*, 28 June 1977)

But why was Schelling's approach, i.e. self-imposed nuclear limitation, not even risked by the 'knowledgeable and informed'? The answer to this question points to the conditions behind the founding of the Federal Republic of Germany. Here we can present only a few clues to the answer.

The policy which aimed at maximising power and status was a key element of German foreign policy from the beginning. After 1960 this was never again questioned domestically by any relevant political force. The desire for lost greatness is based on the refusal to tackle openly, and to continue to tackle, the singularity of the crimes of the Third Reich. It is based on a self-deceptive German view of history, according to which the soldiers of the Wehrmacht and the Waffen-SS were no different from any other soldiers. It is based on the surrender of 8 May 1945 which is considered by the political establishment of the FRG up to the present time not as a 'day of liberation' but as 'day zero'. In post-war times there has never been a really new beginning nor the reparation of wrongs for the sake of reparation. Instead, in 1949 the new political leadership immediately began to demand and to organise 'reparation' for the wrongs done to Germans after their defeat (the division of Germany, the limitations on arms, Germany's own displaced persons, etc.). From the very beginning, any attempt to fence in the new German power was considered a discriminatory provocation. This lent support to Germany's incapacity to accept self-imposed limitations, and it prolonged the inability simply to accept a diminished world status without feelings of resentment and the desire to strive to overcome it.

The renaissance of these patterns of thought was bolstered by the external circumstances surrounding the founding of West Germany. The anti-Soviet attitude of the West promoted Germany's position of intransigence toward the East; the Korean War lent support to the policy of re-militarisation. A foreign policy that would have given priority to the interests of the international community and self-imposed military limitation was out of the question. Only an unsparing confrontation with Germany's past could have opened up the path to a basic change in priorities. To begin anew in this fashion had been urged by certain circles of historians and by some fringe groups, but not by the centres of policymaking power or their social bases of support. Germany's nuclear policy and the mechanisms that were the driving force behind it have, since 1989, become an increasingly significant issue of global policy.

A United Germany and the Nuclear Option

In the summer of 1987 the Disarmament Conference met in Geneva to conclude a treaty – the INF treaty. But there was a stumbling block: during that summer, Chancellor Kohl had firmly insisted that the Pershing IA missiles of the Bundeswehr were to be classified as 'third country systems' and were to be kept out of the INF treaty, and therefore out of the disarmament negotiations in Geneva.

It was not only the SPD and the Greens who considered that the 'third country thesis' of the federal government was an indication that Bonn 'is pushing to attain an atomic power status just like that of France and Great Britain' (*FAZ*, 2 May 1987); in Paris and in London too, astonishment at this position was expressed. And Soviet Foreign Minister Shevardnadzy said:

> If ... the notorious Pershing IAs are regarded as a third-party weapon, the question arises again about how and with what justification this third party, i.e. the Federal Republic of Germany, is to own nuclear weapons. ... We think it appropriate to put the question directly to the representative of the Federal Republic of Germany at this conference: are there any nuclear weapons included among the arms of his country? ... Who actually has disposal over the nuclear warheads for the Pershing IA missiles? A great deal depends on the answers to these questions: the fate of the agreement about intermediate-range missiles and operative tactical missiles; the future of the nuclear Non-Proliferation Treaty. (*FAZ*, 8 August 1987)

Before the Disarmament Conference in Geneva in 1987, the disposition of 1965/6 was repeated. While in those days the NPT appeared to fail because of the German position on the MLF, in 1987 it was the Pershing IA question which threatened the INF treaty. In both cases the German-American missile alliance begun to be overshadowed by the harmony between the Soviets and the Americans. In both cases, Bonn had made its position clear and, accepting the risk of diplomatic isolation, thereby reminded the world of its demands for equal nuclear treatment.

When in 1987 Helmut Kohl finally gave in and promised to disassemble the Pershing IA missiles under certain conditions, this brought an annoyed CSU to the fore once again. F. J. Strauss later wrote that this action would cause the Germans to be 'reduced to the status of a colonial army ..., to the role of a military flea circus' (Strauss, 1989, p. 435). This episode was symptomatic of the situation: many of the problems related to the NPT in the 1960s seemed to be still on the agenda in the 1990s. This is made clear in a study by Erwin Häckel which deals with the future of the German NPT policy. It was published in 1989 by the Research Institute of the German Society for Foreign Affairs (the German counterpart of the Council on Foreign Relations in New York and the Royal Institute of International Affairs in London). He wrote:

> The adherence to the 'European option' that the Federal Republic had made a condition for its accession to the NPT remains a seemingly not very realistic but nonetheless significant model of German security policy in the search for a supranational identity. (Häckel, 1989, pp. 57–9)

Although at present the continuation of the NPT seems to be necessary and sensible, it has to be considered that an extension to the treaty would provide 'a perspective for the development of German foreign policy that is advantageous but not without contradictions when considering the long-term and most important living interests of the West German state'. Häckel thinks it unlikely that the NPT 'can exist in a changing world far longer than the turn of the millennium'. Indeed, 'the treaty was originally drawn up as a temporary status quo regulation' (Häckel, 1989, p. 63).

The other side of the NATO conflict also remains a forceful argument: the NATO allies's interest in maintaining and strengthening the non-nuclear status of the Federal Republic. That this interest may increase as a result of Germany's unification is clear. The four-power status of Berlin, the weak geographical position of West Berlin and the division of Germany – all these have been, over the past few decades, the cornerstones that constantly limited the FRG's range of action with respect to nuclear policy and were reminders of Germany's dependence on its Western allies. Under such conditions it was totally out of the question for the Federal Republic to risk, even temporarily, the sort of isolation that France accepted in terms of its nuclear weapons development. This dependence on the Western allies has vanished with German unification. Thus it is no wonder that the nuclear question played a most important role during the two-plus-four negotiations on the final conditions of Germany's unification.

Up till now only a few details on the lines of conflict in the two-plus-four diplomacy have become public. This much is certain: the question of a new renunciation of nuclear weapons gave rise to many controversies during those negotiations, as they did in relation to internal relations between the two German states.

- At first, the concern to fix Germany's ABC renunciation met with scepticism in both German foreign ministries. Wolfgang Kötter, an East German expert on non-proliferation, had this to say in a paper on non-proliferation:

  > On the Western side, scepticism was even stronger ... the question was raised whether such reconfirmation was really necessary since both states are parties to the NPT and, after all, the Federal Republic of Germany had declared its renunciation of ABC weapons in 1954. (Kötter, 1990, p. 5)

  In spite of such reservations, Germany's renunciation of ABC weapons was confirmed on 22 August 1990 at the NPT Review Conference by the then foreign minister, Hans-Dietrich Genscher.
- The inclusion of the ABC renunciation in the two-plus-four treaty (Treaty on the Final Settlement with Respect to Germany) was disputed. Instead, it was proposed that the confirmation of the renunciation be presented at some other place and that the treaty should state only that such a confirmation had been noted by the four victorious powers (interview, 16 September 1990 in Bonn, with Dr Domke, former under-secretary of the Foreign Ministry of the GDR). But Bonn did not manage to carry this proposal. The ABC renunciation was enshrined in Article III of the two-plus-four treaty, although not in the form of a new renunciation but as a 'confirmation' of the renunciation of 1954 and the NPT accession of 1975.
- Whereas in the first drafts of Article III of the two-plus-four treaty the German ABC weapons renunciation had been given a timeless quality by using the adjective 'everlasting', this important addition was eliminated in the final version of the treaty (*SZ*, 11 October 1990).
- In the West–East German pre-negotiations, the GDR delegation had insisted in vain on making the ABC renunciation a fixed part of Germany's Basic Law. The demand for 'nuclear weapons renunciation in the Basic Law' had been raised for the first time in the Pershing IA controversy by the Greens in 1987; in 1990 it had been taken up by the SPD but it failed to be carried in the

Bundestag, where it was rejected by the CDU and CSU because 'this would place a burden upon cooperation in questions of defence within NATO and Europe' (DS 12/6000, p. 105). Other unsuccessful proposals made by the GDR during the pre-negotiations were aimed at the prohibition of nuclear weapons research, at greater restrictions on the handling of nuclear exports, at a verification rule that the carrier systems suitable for atomic weapons and stationed on the territory of the former GDR should not be transformed into nuclear systems, and at a nuclear-weapons-free status for the whole of Germany (Interview with Dr Domke).

The last-mentioned proposal would have put an end to nuclear participation. There had been some opportunities to do this at the end of the Cold War. In 1989 senior officials from the Netherlands and Belgium had implied that a total de-nuclearisation of their countries might be possible if Germany decided to follow suit (Institut für Internationale Politik, 1990, p. 13). But a renunciation of nuclear participation would have been a fundamental contradiction of the federal government's nuclear orientation. At best, Bonn was prepared to confirm previously pledged renunciations during the two-plus-four talks, but not to accept any further limitations on remaining options. Unification created new opportunities with respect to Germany's nuclear policy. However, the weaknesses in the country's renunciation of nuclear weapons remained.

Maintaining the Nuclear Weapons Option?

As we have seen, all indications point to a forward drive in Germany's nuclear policy, so it seems quite evident that this topic will remain on the agenda of global policymaking for some time to come. Up to the present, however, few people within Germany have openly expressed their desire for 'a German atomic deterrent force ... in order to stabilise a democratic Europe' (Arnulf Baring, *FAZ*, 16 March 1990). In 1991 Baring once more publicly called for a 'broad national debate' on nuclear weapons for Germany: 'Regardless of what was agreed upon in 1954 and later, and regardless of what the NPT has said since 1968, this is one of the problems which we have to tackle in the future' (Baring, 1991, p. 209). The national option may play an increasingly important role as a silent diplomatic threat, especially when London and Paris reject, on a long-term basis, Germany's participation in Western European nuclear weapons policymaking. Over the next few years, however, the main emphasis will be on collective structures. As far back as 1988, the CDU demanded that London and Paris bring their nuclear potential to a 'joint European Security Union'. 'In the long term, the European Security Union has to have a European Defence Council as a decision-making body' (Christdemokratische Union, 1988, p. 13). This formulation at the conclusion of a CDU party conference closely approaches the idea of a European nuclear force. That such a nuclear force would have to be placed on the agenda some day was also stressed in October 1991 by the inspector-general of the Bundeswehr, Klaus Naumann (*Der Spiegel*, 42/91).

Greater nuclear influence within the European Union would, at least in the early stages, correspond to NATO's interpretations of the NPT. But if this were the case, nuclear renunciation would increasingly become a mere formality because Germany's real status would change 'on the quiet', although the facade would remain the same. Developments would be set in motion which an extension of the NPT could not stop. Erwin Häckel of the DGAP sees a problem in the fact that

> in the circle of the great powers ... probably in the foreseeable future some actors (Japan, India, the European Community ...) might come onto the stage who have neither the privileges of being permanent members of the UN Security Council nor enjoy being acknowledged as established nuclear-weapons states. ... How to overcome this difference in status is not yet clear ... but one should not put off considering the idea that some of these new great powers might contemplate making a legitimate claim to nuclear weapons. The NPT would be forced to face a terrible dilemma, a dilemma with apparently no way out.

Häckel's considerations lead us to what seems a rhetorical question, namely whether or not the forthcoming extension of the NPT could, under the circumstances, be tolerated by the have-nots (Häckel, 1990, p. 101). He has left unanswered the question as to *why* and *for whom* a 'terrible dilemma' would be created by the fact that great economic powers like Japan and the Federal Republic are not, at the same time, nuclear powers. For those who fought against the former Axis powers, as well as for their victims, that difference in status is certainly not a major problem. The same holds true at present for the vast majority of Germans or Japanese. But Germany's history provides proof enough of what might happen should the flames of resentment over national status some day be fanned to the point of conflagaration.

In contrast to all this, there are some convincing arguments in favour of rejecting the keeping open of Germany's nuclear options. Among these arguments, it is the historical one which again is probably the most important. From the point of view alone of respect for the victims of two global wars into which the world was precipitated by Germany, a conscious break with such foreign policy principles is called for.

In the 1960s, nuclear option policies led to latent proliferation under cover of the NPT. Today the international picture has changed: during the past 30 years nuclear deterrence has led to nuclear infection and has accelerated the spread of nuclear weapons. About 35 or 40 non-nuclear-weapons states which signed the NPT now have the technical means to go nuclear. Other non-nuclear-weapons states such as Israel which did not sign the treaty already have the atomic bomb; others, like India and South Africa, have clearly demonstrated that they can make one, or, like Brazil and Pakistan, have embarked on a military nuclear programme.

Risks of proliferation are escalating in Europe too, because of the breakdown of the old bipolar power structure which has set free old, deeply rooted nationalist aspirations. The demand of the former Polish presidential candidate Stanislaw Tyminski that his country be armed with 100 medium-range nuclear missiles 'so that we can work in peace and feel ourselves fully independent and equal to other free nations' (*Newsweek*, 10 December 1990) has so far been unique in Eastern Europe. But nevertheless, even before the breaking up of the Soviet Union, ambitions for nuclear independence in this part of the world were judged by an American analyst as risky enough to propose the 'lesser evil' strategy of arming Germany with nuclear weapons:

> The United States should encourage the limited and carefully managed proliferation of nuclear weapons in Europe. The best hope for avoiding war in post-Cold War Europe is nuclear deterrence; hence some nuclear proliferation is necessary, to compensate for the withdrawal of the Soviet and American nuclear arsenals from Central Europe. Ideally ... nuclear weapons would spread to Germany but to no other states. (Mearsheimer, 1990, p. 50)

There is no foreseeable end to the conditions which lend support to proliferation – on the contrary, the fourth NPT Review Conference in autumn 1990 was not able to come to a final conclusion because of American-British intransigence over the question of a nuclear test ban. The disintegration of the former Soviet Union has considerably accelerated the drive for proliferation, while the time for a turning point to be reached is running out.

Thus the future nuclear policy decisions of a united Germany are of great significance. Sometimes it does not take much to tip the scales one way or the other. Any upgrading of the nuclear option, any support for nuclear armaments in a Western European context, any further inching towards the bomb not only means a threat for others but will provide a reason to accelerate similar efforts. Therefore a position which declares that an end to nuclear proliferation, chiefly in unstable parts of the world, is a principal objective of international policy (Nerlich and Rentorff, 1989, p. 856) is contradictory if, at the same time, it praises the 'ethics of nuclear deterrence' as the formula to abolish war (Nerlich and Rentorff, 1989, p. 47).

Throughout the atomic age, status rather than security has been the driving force behind the creation of new nuclear-weapons powers: the British, the French and the Chinese bombs were not so much aimed at enemies as at the attempt to end dependence upon an allied superpower. If the nuclear stimulus is chiefly based on thoughts of national status, it can be satisfied only by achieving equality with the most powerful nuclear arsenal in the world. The lack of perspective in such logic was demonstrated in 1990 by the then French defence minister and socialist Jean-Pierre Chevènement. He answered the question about when France would be prepared to participate in nuclear disarmament as follows: 'As soon as the Soviets and the Americans have reduced their nuclear arsenals to a status comparable to ours – equal rights for everyone – then we can speak about nuclear disarmament' (*Der Spiegel*, 11/90).

Equal rights for everyone! How could one deny an Islamic country the right to try to reach nuclear equality with a former colonial power? Who could deny the right of equality between Pakistan and India, when Germany is striving for nuclear equality with Great Britain and France? Who could with credibility condemn nuclear weapons for a Muslim Union and at the same time support nuclear weapons for a European Union?

Experience tells us we get as much as we give – the belief that a different yardstick can be used can only perpetuate a vicious circle: the great powers point at the dangers of proliferation in the southern hemisphere in order to justify their nuclear arms, and vice versa. A policy that tries to counter nuclear non-proliferation through military actions, such as was the case in the 1991 war with Iraq, will be successful in the short term only because war as a policymaking tool acquires a new reputation, and thereby intensifies the incentive for proliferation. This conclusion was drawn years ago after an evaluation of the Israelis' preventive attack on Iraq's Osirak reactor on 7 June 1981. The analysis of Shai Feldman, of Tel Aviv University's Center for Strategic Studies, states:

> The June 7 operation is likely to induce the Arab states to accelerate their pursuit of nuclear capabilities. ... This is particularly true for Iraq. Rather than causing that country to forgo nuclear capabilities, the June 7 operation may merely propel Iraqi planners to improve the security measures surrounding their nuclear facilities. (Feldman, 1982, p. 139)

It seems unlikely that any basically different reaction will follow in the wake of the Desert Storm bomb attacks on Iraq's nuclear facilities. During the destruction of those facilities by the anti-Iraq Alliance, the American media began to point to Teheran as the next potential candidate for the bomb (*IHT*, 28 January 1991).

A position that is consistent will either defend nuclear deterrence, and with it the right for independent nuclear-weapons programmes for everyone, or it will abolish nuclear weapons without exception. This is the inherent contradiction of nuclear deterrence. Those who want nuclear weapons or who strive for nuclear participation, whether or not they want to, trigger the behaviour of others who, marching in step as if being pulled along by invisible strings, do exactly the same. This will only increase the likelihood of a nuclear war. Apparent security produces insecurity, whereas apparent insecurity, namely opting out unilaterally from the nuclear policy of deterrence, could bring about global protection against any nuclear threat. The competition to acquire the nuclear option can maximise one thing only: the risk of nuclear war.

It is quite realistic to assume that nuclear proliferation will spread in the next few years and that it will develop into breeding ground for permanent crises around the world. But a multinational solution to the nuclear-weapons problem is not in sight because of the overlapping contradictions between different areas: the North/South conflict on the question of sources of energy; the policy of disarmament and its lines of conflict within and between countries; and the primacy of international law over the reality of power politics. There is no instruction manual on how to untie this Gordian knot.

What can be seen are the few conditions which Germany would have to fulfil in order to make future solutions easier, as well as to draw lessons from its own past history. Instead of maintaining its nuclear option or even extending it, Germany of all countries could close the door to this route, firmly and unilaterally.

- Against vertical proliferation, a course of commitment can be credible and effective only if every German ambition for the enhancement of its nuclear status is clearly denied.
- Against horizontal proliferation, a course of commitment can be credible and effective only if within one's own country a stand-by policy is relinquished, and efforts are made to do without nuclear power.
- Against the race for an increasingly perfect military potential, a policy can become effective only when 'national interests' are consciously kept subordinate to global interests, and thus other nations are encouraged to act in the same way.

This approach seems unrealistic because it contradicts the traditional patterns of foreign policy. In the field of international relations today it is not the renunciation of sovereignty which counts, but superiority in weapons, high-tech prestige and global competition. Bearing this in mind, self-imposed limitation as a basis for policymaking on an international level may appear quixotic. This approach, however, is justified if you take into account the irrationality of a policy which has proved unable, in spite of the catastrophes of nuclear proliferation in the past, to achieve anything other than the making of preparations which can only lead to even greater catastrophes.

Sources and Bibliography

Persons Interviewed

Note: the time and place of each interview are given in brackets. Two-thirds of the material was recorded on tape. Interviews which were so recorded, as well as copies of documents which were not available for public view, are marked ACD (author's collection of documents).

Michael Amory (February 1989 in Brussels) was a lawyer for the European Atomic Community and was directly involved in the NPT negotiations.

Richard Balken (May 1990 in Bonn) was one of the founders of the Study Group for Arms Control, Disarmament and International Security. From 1959 to 1962 he headed the Disarmament and Security Department of the Auswärtige Amt. Between 1962 and 1967 he was head of the Parliament and Cabinet Section in the same ministry.

H.N. Boon (December 1988 in The Hague) was the Netherlands's Ambassador to NATO between 1961 and 1970; in this capacity he was concerned with the MLF, the NPT and the creation of the Nuclear Planning Group.

Rudolf Botzian (November 1989 in Ebenhausen) is a physicist. He has worked at the SWP since 1966, and is the author of a great number of SWP studies on questions relating to the NPT.

Jan Herman Burgers (February 1989 in The Hague) was the head of the Disarmament and Peace Section in the Foreign Ministry of the Netherlands in 1965 and later he was deeply involved in the NPT negotiations.

Günther Diehl (July 1990 in Bonn) was head of the Planning Staff in the Auswärtige Amt from 1960 to 1966; for some years from autumn 1967 he was head of the Press and Information Office of the federal government.

Helmut Domke (September 1990 in Bonn) was in 1990 the state secretary of the Ministry of Foreign Affairs in the GDR. He was deeply involved in the preparations for 'the Treaty on the Final Settlement with Respect to Germany' of 1990.

Charles van Doren (October 1986 in Washington, DC) was deputy head of the Legal Department of the US Arms Control and Disarmament Agency (ACDA); he formulated parts of the NPT and its interpretations, and he followed the negotiations very closely. In 1967 he participated in the German-American NPT consultations in Washington.

David Fischer (December 1988 in London) was the deputy director-general of the IAEA from 1957 to 1984 and headed the Department for International Affairs. During the safeguards talks between IAEA and EURATOM (1972/3) he headed the Vienna delegation.

Vladimir Fortakov (February 1988 in Moscow) was head of the International Organisation Department in the State Committee for the Use of Atomic Energy in Moscow in 1988, and since 1969 has been concerned with IAEA issues. In 1971/2 he participated in negotiations on INFCIRC 153.

Oleg Grinewski (February 1988 in Moscow) was ambassador-at-large and deputy foreign minister of the Soviet Union in 1988. From 1965 to 1968 he was the deputy head of the Soviet NPT negotiations delegation and participated in the NPT negotiations in Geneva.

Wolf Häfele (May 1989 in Jülich) headed the 'fast-breeder' project in 1960 and following years, and from 1967 headed the 'Control of Fissionable Materials' project at the Centre for Nuclear Research in Karlsruhe. Between 1967 and 1969 he was a member of the Interministerial Staff for the NPT and participated in the German-American NPT negotiations in Washington.

Helga Haftendorn (January 1989 in Berlin) was, from 1965, secretary of the Studiengruppe and thus directly concerned with the controversies surrounding the NPT.

Ronald Hope-Jones (December 1988 in London) was head of the Department for Arms Control and Disarmament in the British Foreign Office from 1967 to 1970.

Ben Huberman (October 1986 in Washington, DC) from 1966 to 1969, as a technical expert in the US Arms Controls and Disarmament Agency, was involved with the NPT negotiations and was especially concerned with Euratom and safeguards questions.

Nikolaj S. Kischilov (February 1988 and September 1989 in Moscow) was, in 1988, head of the Department for Disarmament and Security in the Institute for World Economy and International Security (IMEMO) in Moscow. From 1965 to 1968 he was a member of the Soviet NPT negotiating delegation in Geneva.

Franz Krapf (April 1989 in Bonn) was head of Political Department II (dealing with questions relating to Germany, East–West relations and NATO) in the Auswärtige Amt from 1961 to 1965.

Myron Kratzer (November 1986 in Washington, DC) as head of the Department for International Relations of the US Atomic Energy Commission (AEC), was involved in NPT negotiations from 1966 onwards. In 1970/1 he was head of the American delegation to the IAEA Safeguards Committee in Vienna.

Lothar Lahn (January 1989 in Bonn) was, from 1962 to 1966, head of the Disarmament and Security Section of the Political Department of the Auswärtige Amt in Bonn.

Carl Lahusen (August 1989 in Garmisch-Partenkirchen) was, from 1966 to 1968, head of the 'Global Disarmament' section of a sub-department dealing with disarmament and arms controls within the Auswärtige Amt; in this position, he was mainly concerned with the NPT. He was also one of Swidbert Schnippenkoetter's deputies and thus directly involved in German-American NPT negotiations.

C.E. Larson (October 1986 in Washington, DC) was, at the time of the NPT controversy, a member of the American Atomic Energy Commission.

Ben Loeb (November 1986 in Washington) is a former member of both the AEC and IAEA, and has worked closely on several publications with the former AEC chairman, Glenn Seaborg.

Dieter Mahncke (January 1989 in Bonn) was an official of the German Society for Foreign Affairs from 1965 onwards and was secretary of the Studiengruppe after 1968.

Uwe Nerlich (August 1989 in Ebenhausen) is study director of the Research Institute for International Policy and Security of the SWP. In his scientific work in the DGAP and the SWP, he followed the debate about the NPT from the very beginning and wrote a number of commentaries and expert reports on the subject.

Horst Osterfeld (July 1990 in Bonn) was head of the Bureau for Foreign Affairs in the Office of the Federal Chancellor from 1960 to 1969, under Chancellors Adenauer, Erhard and Kiesinger.

Wiegand Papsch (January 1989 in Bonn) was, in 1989, under-secretary in the Auswärtige Amt, and in 1972/3 he took part in the Euratom/IAEA negotiations as an envoy from Bonn.

André Petit (February 1989 in Paris) a former member of the French Atomic Energy Commission, was France's delegate to Euratom for some time after 1966. In 1970/1 he was a French delegate in the *Blue Book* negotiations in Vienna.

Rolf Ramisch (August 1989 in Munich) was in 1966 head of the section on Securing the Peaceful Use of Nuclear Energy, Safeguards, Research and Studies in the Auswärtige Amt's Department for Disarmament and Arms Control. Together with Carl Lahusen, he was one of Schnippenkoetter's closest colleagues. From 1967 to 1969 he was deputy head of the Inter-ministerial Staff for the NPT.

Ulrich Sahm (November 1989 and March 1990 in Ebenhausen and Bodenwerder) was from 1966 to 1968 head of Sub-department II A (concerned with Germany and Berlin, NATO and East Europe) in the Auswärtige Amt.

Ben Sanders (October 1986 in New York) is the founder and chairman of the Programme for Promoting Nuclear Non-Proliferation and until 1987 he was a leading member of the Disarmament Department of the United Nations. From the end of the 1950s he was a safeguards expert with the IAEA and in 1972/3 a participant in the IAEA/Euratom negotiations.

Terwisscha van Scheltinga (February 1989 in The Hague) was, from 1965, head of the Department for Political and International Security Questions in the Netherlands Foreign Ministry, and in this position was closely involved with the NPT.

Fritz-Rudolf Schultz (July 1990 in Mainz) was an FDP MP from 1965 to 1969, and headed the FDP Working Group for Foreign Policy and Defence.

M.I. Shaker (December 1988 in London) was, in 1988, Egypt's ambassador to Great Britain. During the NPT negotiations he was a member of the Egyptian ENDC delegation and in 1985 he served as president of the third NPT Review Conference.

Helmut Sigrist (January 1989 in Bonn) was, in 1964 and following years, director-general of Euratom, and was responsible for external relations with other countries. In 1971/2 he headed the Euratom delegation in the negotiations with the IAEA.

Berndt von Staden (July 1990 in Bonn) was, up to 1963, the chief of cabinet for Walter Hallstein, and from 1963 to 1968 a senior council official at the German Embassy in Washington. He was concerned with the German-American negotiations on details of the NPT.

Werner Ungerer (February 1989 in Brussels) was, in 1965 and following years, responsible for Euratom in the Auswärtige Amt. For several years after 1967 he headed the section on International Technical Cooperation and was a member of the Inter-ministerial Staff for the NPT. In 1970/1 he was head of the German delegation in the IAEA Safeguards Committee.

Lawrence Weiler (October 1986 in Washington, DC) was, from 1966 onwards, one of the closest colleagues of Adrian Fisher, deputy director of ACDA. He was a member of the American NPT negotiations delegation in Washington and Geneva.

Documents of the Auswärtige AMT

AA-Doc.I: AA-Vorlage für den Bundesverteidigungsrat vom 20.1.1967 (AA II B1-81.01/80/67 Geheim, 40 Ausfertigungen) mit Anlagen:

- Anlage 1: Aktueller Wortlaut des NPT-Entwurfs;
- Anlage 2: Interpretationen des Artikel I und II;
- Anlage 3: Fernschreiben Nr.144 vom 18.1.67 aus Washington betreffs NPT-Erkundungsgespräch;
- Anlage 4: Vermerk über die Auswirkungen eines NPT auf den Abstand zwischen den Atom- und Nichtatommächten im wissenschaftlichen, technischen und industriellen Bereich;
- Anlage 5: NPT-Memorandum der japanischen Regierung an die US vom 28.12.1966.

AA-Doc.II: AA-Vorlage für Bundesverteidigungsrat/Nachgang (AA, II B1-81.01/80II/67 Geheim, 63 Ausfertigungen: Wortlaut und Übersetzung eines Aide-Memoire der US vom 24.1.1967.

AA-Doc.III: Aide-Memoire der US vom 31.1.1967 betreffs Art. III (AA II B3-81.00/2-170/67 Geheim, 40 Ausfertigungen).

AA-Doc.IV: Protokoll der 2. Sitzung des Interministeriellen Arbeitsstabes 'Nichtverbreitungsvertrag' vom 17.2.67 (II B-NV-258I/67 Verschlus-ssache-Vertraulich).

AA-Doc.V: Gegenüberstellung der Entwürfe US und UdSSR für den NV-Vertrag vom 24.5.1967 (AA II B1-81.01-1023/67 Geheim).

AA-Doc.VI: Gemeinsamer NV-Entwurf der KO-Präsidenten vom 12.6.67 (AA II B1-81.01-1132/67 Geheim).

AA-Doc.VII: Niederschrift über Sitzung NV-Arbeitsstab vom 10.10.67 (IIB3-81.00/3/1773/67 Geheim).

AA-Doc.VIII: Entwurf für Artikel III auf Grundlage des Ergebnisses der Beratungen des Arbeitsstabs NV-Vertrag vom 10.10.67 (IIB3-81.00/2/1771/67 Geheim).

AA-Doc.IX: Sowjetischer Entwurf für Kontrollartikel III (vermut. Nov. 1967; AA II B1-81.01-1023/67 Geheim).

AA-Doc.X: Niederschrift über Sitzung NV-Arbeitsstab vom 14.11.67 (IIB3-81.00/3/2014/67 Verschluss-sache-Vertraulich).

AA-Doc.XI: Übersetzung eines Aide-Memoire über den Stand der Verhandlungen über Art.III mit der Sowjetunion vom 13.11.67 (ZA5-80.00-35/67 Geheim).

AA-Doc.XII: Schreiben Ramisch an SWP, z.Hd. Ritter vom 5.12.67 (AA II B 3-81.00/32144/67 Verschluss-sache-Vertraulich).

AA-Doc.XIII: Niederschrift über Sitzung NV-Arbeitsstab vom 29.3.68 (I B3-81.00/3/50768 Verschluss-sache-Vertraulich).

AA-Doc.XIV: Aufzeichnung vom 4.2.69 über Wortlaut der Ausführung von von Guttenberg auf der VI.Wehrkunde-Tagung 1969 in München (II B1-81.00/69).

AA-Doc.XV: Kabinettsvorlage NV Juni 1969: Vortrag des Bundesministers des Auswärtigen vor dem Kabinett am 23.4.69: 'Der Vertrag über die Nichtverbreitung von Kernwaffen' (32 pages).

AA-Doc.XVI: Vertrauliche Anworten des AA auf Anfragen der SPD-Bundestagsfraktion von März 1969 zum NV-Vertrag (99 pages).

AA-Doc.XVII:Vertrauliche Antworten des AA auf Anfragen der CDU/CSU-Bundestagsfraktion von November 1968 und Februar 1968 zum NV-Vertrag (114 pages).

Documents of the 'Nuclear History Programme'

NHP I Abschrift der Zeitzeugenbefragung zum 'ABC-Verzicht' am 1./2.Juli 1988 in Ebenhausen.

NHP II Abschrift der Zeitzeugenbefragung 'Die Nuklearpolitik der Bundesrepublik Deutschland' vom 13.Juli 1987 in Bonn.

NHP III NHP-Aktenmaterial, Fü B III, Rohübers.-Ausf. vom US-Memorandum über Rüstungskontrolle und Berlin-Verhandlungen, undated, Tgb.Nr. 4737/61, Geheim.

NHP IV NHP-Aktenmaterial, S III 3: Sprechzettel des Herrn General Inspekteurs für den Vortrag bei Herrn Minister, Bonn den 24.08.1965, Tgb.Nr. 261/1965, Geheim.

NHP V NHP-Aktenmaterial, Aufzeichnung von Herrn Staatssekretär Carstens vom 25.8. 1966, St.S. – 1917/66 Geheim.

NHP VI NHP-Aktenmaterial, S III 3, Besprechungsmappe für Reise Bundeskanzler – Minister von Hassel, 20.9.1966, Tgb. 236/66 Geheim.

NHP VII NHP-Aktenmaterial, Fü B III 8 an Fü B III, Betr.: Europäische Sicherheit, 4. November 19161, Tgb.Nr. 579/61 streng Geheim.

IV. Periodika, Archive, Nachlässe.

Documents of the National Security Council Archives

DoS I: Bill Moyers, Memorandum for the President, Subject: Non-Proliferation Treaty, 17 July 1966.

DoS II: William C. Foster, Memorandum for the Secretary, Subject: Steps to Achieve a Non-Proliferation Agreement, 15 September 1966 (secret – four copies).

DoS III: Soviet adjustments in working group draft to meet U.S. objections (secret).

DoS IV: Outgoing telegram, Department of State, 26 October 1966, (secret).

DoS V: Dean Rusk, Memorandum for the President, Subject: Suggested Language for the Non-Proliferation Treaty: Relationship to Existing and Possible Allied Nuclear Arrangements (secret – four copies), end of October to beginning of November 1966.

Periodicals, Personal Papers and Archives

For this book, the following were consulted or referred to:

Unedited verbatim minutes of federal German press conferences, 1965–69.

Bulletin des Presse- und Informationsamtes der Bundesregierung, 1965–69.

Bundestag: minutes of meetings and printed matter.

Bundesrat: minutes of meetings.

European Parliament: minutes of meetings.

Congressional Records of the US-Senate from January 1966 to March 1969.

Keesing's Contemporary Archives 1965–75.

Dokumentation zur Abrüstung und Sicherheit, vols. I–X (1943–72).

Europa-Archiv, 1952–75.

Documents on Disarmament, 1965–9.

Press archives of the Bundestag.

Press archives of the Hamburger Weltwirtschaftsarchivs.

New York Times, 1965–9.

Der Spiegel, 1965–9.

Wehrkunde, 1965–75.

Wehrtechnische Monatshefte, 1965–8.

atomwirtschaft, 1965–75.

Atom & Strom, 1965–75.

Bulletin of the Atomic Scientists, 1965–75.

Aussenpolitik, 1965–75.

Deutsche Aussenpolitik, 1965–75.

Blätter für deutsche und internationale Politik, 1965–75.

Foreign Affairs, 1965–75.

International Affairs, 1965–75.

Files of the 'Nuclear History Programme' (Source: Seminar für politische Wissenschaft der Rheinischen Friedrich-Wilhelmsuniversität Bonn,

Lehrstuhl für Wissenschaft von der Politik und Zeitgeschichte, Prof. Dr Hans-Peter Schwarz).

Minutes of meetings of the Studiengruppe für Rüstungskontrolle, Rüstungsbeschränkung und internationale Sicherheit der Deutschen Gesellschaft für Auswärtige Politik (Source: 1967: Nachlass von Fritz Erler, Archiv der Sozialen Demokratie, Friedrich Ebert Stiftung, Bonn).

Nachlass von Fritz Erler (ibid.).

Documents from the Archivs des Deutschen Liberalismus in der Friedrich-Naumann-Stiftung, Gummersbach.

Documents from the Ludwig Erhard-Stiftung, Bonn.

Documents from the Hanns-Seidel-Stiftung (Archiv für Christlich-Soziale Politik), Munich.

Bibliography

Adenauer, Konrad (1965–8), *Erinnerungen*, vols I–IV, Stuttgart.

Advisory Commission on Problems of Disarmament and International Security and Peace (1966), *The Problem of Non-proliferation of Nuclear Weapons and Nuclear Cooperation within NATO* (unofficial translation), Amsterdam, (ACD).

Advisory Committee on Disarmament and International Peace and Security (1967), *The Problem of the Non-proliferation of Nuclear Weapons and the Control of the Peaceful Uses of Nuclear Energy*, The Hague, (ACD).

Albright, David (1986), 'Safeguards at Alkem', FAS/NUC Report no.1, Washington, DC.

Arbeitskreis Atomwaffenverzicht ins Grundgesetz (1989), *Atomforschung in Geesthacht – Schleichwege zur Atombombe?*, Hamburg.

Arms Control and Disarmament Agency (1967–9), *6th–8th Annual Reports to Congress*, Washington, DC.

Arms Control and Disarmament Agency (1969a), *International Negotiations on the Treaty on the Non-proliferation of Nuclear Weapons*, Washington, DC.

Auswärtiges Amt (ed.) (1972), *Die Auswärtige Politik der Bundesrepublik Deutschland*, Cologne.

Bader, William B. (1968), *The United States and the Spread of Nuclear Weapons*, New York.

Bagge, Erich (1972), 'Aus Kernphysik und Ultrastrahlung', *Atomkernenergie*, no. 3.

Bandulet, Bruno (1970), *Adenauer zwischen Ost und West*, Munich.

Baring, Arnulf (1969), *Aussenpolitik in Adenauers Kanzlerdemokratie*, Munich.

Baring, Arnulf (1991), *Deutschland, was nun?*, Berlin.

Baring, Arnulf and Sase, Masamori (1977), *Zwei zaghafte Riesen? Deutschland und Japan seit 1945*, Stuttgart.

Barnes, Harley Hassinger Jr. (1976) 'The Nuclear Non-proliferation Treaty: Participants, Interests and Processes in American Foreign Policy Formulation', dissertation, Rutgers University, New Brunswick, NJ.

Beaton, Leonard (1966), *Must the Bomb Spread?*, Harmondsworth.

Beaton, Leonard and Maddox, John (1962), *The Spread of Nuclear Weapons*, London.

Beaton, Leonard and Maddox, John (1962a), 'Die Bundesrepublik und die Frage der Atomrüstung', *Europa-Archiv*, no. 21.

Besson, Waldemar (1970), *Die Aussenpolitik der Bundesrepublik*, Munich.

Birrenbach, Kurt (1967), 'Der neue gemeinsame Entwurf der Vereinigten Staaten und der Sowjetunion für einen Nichtverbreit-ungsvertrag am 24. August 1967', Stellungnahme vom 27.9.1967 für die CDU/CSU-Fraktion (ACD).

Birrenbach, Kurt (1984), 'Als Beauftragter des Bundeskanzlers in Washington', in D. Oberndörfer (ed.), *Begegnungen mit Kurt Georg Kiesinger*, Stuttgart.

Birrenbach, Kurt (1984), *Meine Sondermissionen*, Düsseldorf.

Börner, Bodo (1968), *Rechtsfolgen des Atomsperrvertrages für die Bundesrepublik Deutschland*, Düsseldorf.

Botzian, Rudolf (1967b), 'Hinweise auf mögliche Regelungen der künftigen Kontrollkompetenzen von Euratom', SWP-AZ 114, 31.5.1967, n.z.p.U., Ebenhausen (ACD).

Botzian, Rudolf (1967c), 'Aufzeichnungen zur Frage der Kontroll-Regelungen im Rahmen eines NV-Vertrages', SWP-AZ 117, 11.9.1967, Ebenhausen (ACD).

Botzian, Rudolf (1967d), 'Vorüberlegungen zu einem NV-Kontroll-statut', SWP-AZ 119, 7.11.1967, Ebenhausen (ACD).

Botzian, Rudolf (1967e), 'Hinweise zu den in einem Verifikations-abkommen zwischen IAEO und EURATOM zu regelnden technischen Punkten', SWP-AZ 120, 7.11.1967, Ebenhausen (ACD).

Botzian, Rudolf (1967f), 'Bemerkungen zur militärischen Nutzung kon-trollierter Kernreaktoren im Rahmen des NV-Vertrages', SWP-AZ 121, 20.12.1967, Ebenhausen (ACD).

Botzian, Rudolf (1969), 'Atomwaffensperrvertrag und Lieferabkom-men Euratom-US', in *atomwirtschaft* 2.

Botzian, Rudolf (1974), 'Kernexplosionen zu friedlichen Zwecken im Zusammenhang des Nichtverbreitungs-Vertrages', SWP-Arbeitspa-pier 2058, Ebenhausen (ACD).

Botzian, Rudolf and Nerlich, Uwe (1967a), 'Auswirkungen eines Vertrages über die Nichtverbreitung von Atomwaffen auf den zivilen Sektor technisch-industrieller Entwicklungen', SWP-AZ 107, 23.1.1967 n.z.p.U., Ebenhausen (ACD).

Boulanger, W. (1972), 'Das Verifikationsabkommen IAEO-Euratom', in *atomwirtschaft* 9/10.

Brandstetter, Karl J. (1989), *Allianz des Misstrauens*, Cologne.

Brandt, Willy (1969), *Zum Atomsperrvertrag*, Berlin.

Brandt, Willy (1989), *Erinnerungen*, Frankfurt am Main.

Buchan, Alastair (1964), *The Multilateral Force: An Historical Perspective*, Adelphi-Paper 13, London.

Buchan, Alastair and Windsor, Philip (1963), *Arms and Stability in Europe*, London.

Bundesminister der Verteidigung (ed.) (1971), *Einwirkung gepulster Kernstrahlung auf Baugruppen in Kampfpanzern*, Bonn.

Bunn, George (1989), 'The Debate over Banning Transfer of Nuclear Weapons', (draft, 21 April, 50 pp.; *AdV*).

Bunn, George and Van Doren, Charles N. (1991), 'Options for Extension of the NPT: The Intention of the Drafters of Article X.2', in George Bunn, Charles N. Van Doren, David A.V. Fischer, *Options & Opportunities: The NPT Extension Conference of 1995*, Southampton.

Buteux, Paul (1984), *The Politics of Nuclear Consultation in NATO 1965–1980*, New York.

Calamo, Luisa (1967), 'Non-Proliferation in Italy', in *lo spettatore internazionale* 3.

Calogero, Francesco (1967), 'The Non-Prolifaration Treaty', in *lo spettatore internazionale* 3.

Carstens, Karl and Mahnke, Dieter (1972), *Westeuropäische Verteidigungskooperation*, Munich.

Chassin, L.M. (1957), 'Bemannte Flugzeuge oder Raketen?', in *Wehrkunde* 9.

Christdemokratische Union (1988), *Unsere Verantwortung in der Welt*, Bonn.

Clausen, Peter Anthony (1973), 'Superpower-Ally Tensions in American Foreign Policy: The Non-proliferation Treaty and the Atlantic Alliance', dissertation, University of California, Los Angeles.

Clemens, Walter C. (1968), *The Arms Race and Sino-Soviet Relations*, Stanford, Calif.

Cleveland, Harlan (1970), *NATO: The Transatlantic Bargain*, New York.

Czempiel, Ernst-Otto and Schweitzer, Carl-Christoph (1984), *Weltpolitik der USA nach 1945*, Bonn.

Dalma, Alfons (1965), 'Die Allianz und die Proliferation von Kernwaffen', in *Wehrkunde* 1.

Department of State (1959), *Treaties and Other International Acts*, Series 4276, Washington, DC.

Department of State (1983), *Foreign Relations of the United States: Western Europe Security* (vol. V.), Washington, DC.

Department of State (1986), *Foreign Relations of the United States 1955–1957* vol. IV: *Western European Security and Integration*, Washington, DC.

Deubner, Christian (1977), *Die Atompolitik der westdeutschen Industrie und die Gründung von Euratom*, Frankfurt am Main.

Deutscher Bundestag (ed.) (1957), *Materialien zum Gesetz zu den Verträgen vom 25. März 1957 zur Gründung der Europäischen Wirtschaftsgemeinschaft und der Europäischen Atomgemeinschaft*, Bonn (ACD).

Deutscher Bundestag (ed.) (1960), *Materialien zum Gesetz über die friedliche Verwendung der Kernenergie und den Schutz gegen ihre Gefahren (Atomgesetz) vom 23. Dezember 1959*, Bonn (ACD).

Deutscher Bundestag (ed.) (1974a), *Gesetzesmaterialien, erstellt unter Mitarbeit des Bundesrates, über das Gesetz zu dem Übereinkommen vom 5. April 1973 zwischen dem Königreich Belgien, dem Königreich Dänemark, der Bundesrepublik Deutschland, Irland, der Italienischen Republik, dem Grossherzogtum Luxemburg, dem Königreich der Niederlande, der Europäischen Atomgemeinschaft und der Internationalen Atomenergie-Organisation in Ausführung von Artikel III Absätze 1 und 4 des Vertrages vom 1. Juli 1968 über die Nichtverbreitung von Kernwaffen (Verifikationsabkommen)*, Bonn (ACD).

Deutscher Bundestag (ed.) (1974b), *Gesetzesmaterialien, erstellt unter Mitarbeit des Bundesrates, über das Gesetz zu dem Vertrag vom 1. Juli 1968 über die Nichtverbreitung von Kernwaffen*, Bonn (ACD).

Donnelly, Warren H. (1972), *Commercial Nuclear Power in Europe: The Interaction of American Diplomacy with a New Technology*, Washington, DC.

Donnelly, Warren H. (1976), *Nuclear Weapons Proliferation and the International Atomic Energy Agency*, Washington, DC.

Epstein, William (1976), *The Last Chance*, New York.

Etzioni, Amitai (1964), 'Germany's Finger on the Atom', in *Nation*, 12 October.

Euratom – Die Kommission (1958), *Abkommen über Zusammenarbeit zwischen der Europäischen Atomgemeinschaft (Euratom) und der Regierung der Vereinigten Staaten von Amerika mit Anlagen und Arbeitsdokumenten*, 8 November (ACD).

Feigl, Hubert (1970a), 'Radiologische Kampfstoffe und ihre Kontrollprobleme', SPW-AP 1027, Ebenhausen (ACD).

Feigl, Hubert (1970b), 'Möglichkeiten der militärischen Anwendung der Laser-Technik und Aspekte einer vertraglichen Begrenzung oder Sperrung', SWP-AP 1026, Ebenhausen (ACD).

Feldman, Shai (1982), 'The Bombing of Osiraq-Revisited', in *International Security*, 2.

Fischer, David A.V.(1984), 'The Role of the IAEA', in J. Simpson and A.G. McGrew (eds), *The International Nuclear Non-Proliferation System*, Southampton.

Fischer, David A.V. (1990), 'Der Vertrag über die Nichtverbreitung von Kernwaffen: Ziele und Erfolge', in Eisenbart and von Ehrenstein (eds), *Nichtverbreitung von Nuklearwaffen*, Heidelberg.

Fischer, David A.V. (1991), 'Article X.2 of the Nuclear Non-Proliferation Treaty and the Nature of its 1995 Extension Conference', in George Bunn, Charles N. Van Doren and David A.V. Fischer, *Options & Opportunities: The NPT Extension Conference of 1995*, Southampton.

Fischer, David and Szasz, Paul (1985), *Safeguarding the Atom: A Critical Appraisal*, London.

Fisher, Adrian S. (1967), 'Issues Involved in a Non-Proliferation Agreement, in S. D. Kertesz (ed.), *Nuclear Proliferation*, London.

Forschungsinstitut der Deutschen Gesellschaft für Auswärtige Politik (1965), *Internationale Rüstungslage und Bündnispolitik 1965*, Bonn (ACD).

Forschungsinstitut der Deutschen Gesellschaft für Auswärtige Politik (1967), *Die Wandlungen der westlichen Sicherheitspolitik und ihre Auswirkungen auf die Deutschland-Frage*, Bonn (ACD).

Foster, William C. (1965), 'New Directions in Arms Control and Disarmament', in *Foreign Affairs* no. 4, July.

Gerstenmaier, Eugen Streit und Frieden hat seine Zeit (korrigierte gebundene Satzfahne', no date or place of publication given (ACD).

Gijssels, Jan (1978), 'L'Accord entre Euratom et l'AIEA en application eu traite sur la non-proliferation des armes nucleaires', in *L'Annuaire français de droit international* (cited in the text under the English translation for the EC: 'The Agreement between Euratom and the IAEA on the Implementation of the treaty on the non-proliferation of nuclear weapons' – EG-Doc. XII/132/78-EN) (ACD).

Gilinsky, Victor (1985), 'Restraining the Spread of Nuclear Weapons: A Walk on the Supply Side', in J. Snyder and S. Wells (eds), *Nuclear Proliferation*, New York.

Goldschmidt, Bertrand (1974), 'International Nuclear Collaboration and Article IV of the NPT', in SIPRI (ed.), *Nuclear Proliferation Problems*, Stockholm.

Goldschmidt, Bertrand and Kratzer, Mycle (1978), 'Peaceful Nuclear Relations: A Study of the Creation and Erosion of Confidence', working paper for the International Consultative Group on Nuclear Energy, London/New York (ACD).

Gordon, Philip H. (1994), 'The Normalization of German Foreign Policy', in *Orbis*, Spring.

Greiner, Christian (1986), 'Zwischen Integration und Nation. Die militärische Eingliederung der BRD in die NATO, 1954 bis 1957', in L. Herbst (ed.), *Westdeutschland 1945–1955*, Munich.

Grewe, Wilhelm G. (1960), *Deutsche Aussenpolitik in der Nachkriegszeit*, Stuttgart.

Grewe, Wilhelm G. (1967), 'Über den Einfluss der Kernwaffen auf die Politik', in *Europa-Archiv*, no. 3.

Grewe, Wilhelm G. (1979), *Rückblenden 1976–1951*, Frankfurt am Main.

Die Grünen (ed.) (1988), *Atomwaffenverzicht ins Grundgesetz*, Bonn.

Häckel, Erwin (1989), *Die Bundesrepublik Deutschland und der Atomwaffensperrvertrag*, Bonn.

Häckel, Erwin (1990), 'Zukunftsprobleme der Internationalen Nuklearpolitik', in Eisenbart and von Ehrenstein (eds), *Nichtverbreitung von Nuklearwaffen*, Heidelberg.

Häfele, Wolf (1966), *Politische Probleme der Kernenergieentwicklung im heutigen Deutschland*, October *(AdV)*.

Haftendorn, Helga (1974), *Abrüstungs- und Entspannungspolitik zwischen Sicherheitsbefriedung und Friedenssicherung*, Düsseldorf.

Haginoya, T. (1985), 'The National System of Safeguards: Experience in Japan', in *IAEA-Bulletin*, Summer.

Handzik, H. (1967), *Die Genesis der Nonproliferations-Politik der USA gegenüber den späteren Nuklearmächten*, Part I: *1943–1954*, SWP-Aufzeichnung no. 111, May, Ebenhausen (ACD).

Handzik, H. (1968), *Die Genesis der Nonproliferations-Politik der USA gegenüber den späteren Nuklearmächten*, Part II: *1955–1963*, SWP-Studie no. 124, January 1968, Ebenhausen (ACD).

Hanrieder, Wolfram F. (1970), *Die stabile Krise*, Düsseldorf.

Heiden, Horst (1967), 'Was stört Bonn am Sperrvertrag?', in *Blätter für deutsche und internationale Politik* 3.

Hepp, Marcel (1968), *Der Atomsperrvertrag*, Stuttgart.

Hibbs, Mark (1993), 'Euratom Tries to Enlist U.S. Industry Help in Securing Presidential Waiver', *Nuclear Fuel*, 11 October.

Horlacher, Wolfgang (1969), 'Die Aussenpolitik – Geburtshelfer der Grossen Koalition', in A. Rummel (ed.), *Die grosse Koalition 1966–1969*, Freudenstadt.

Houck, Frank S. (1985), 'The Voluntary Safeguards Offer of the United States', in *IAEA-Bulletin*, Summer.

Huyn, Hans Graf (1966), *Die Sackgasse*, Stuttgart.

Institut für Internationale Politik (1990), *Die atomare Planung der Nato nach dem Ende des Kalten Krieges*, Wuppertal.

International Atomic Energy Agency (1985), *Safeguards in Europe*, Vienna.

Johnson, Brian (1977), 'Nuclear Power Proliferation', in *Energy Policy*, September.

Johnson, Lyndon B. (1971), *The Vantage Point*, New York.

Kaiser, Karl (1989), 'Wozu Atomwaffen in Zeiten der Abrüstung?', in *Europa-Archiv 9*.

Kelleher, Catherine M. (1967), 'German Nuclear Dilemmas 1955–1965', dissertation, Boston.

Kelleher, Catherine M. (1975), *Germany & the Politics of Nuclear Weapons*, New York.

Keller, Anton; Bollinger, Heinz et. al. (1968), 'On the Economic Implications of the Proposed Non-proliferation Treaty', in *Revue de Droit International* 1.

Kelly, Peter (1971), 'Safeguards – Five Views', *IAEA-Bulletin* no. 2.

Kissinger, Henry A. (1965), *Was wird aus der westlichen Allianz?*, Düsseldorf.

Klejdzinski, Karl-Heinz (1984), 'Mitsprache – aber kein Veto-Recht', in *Loyal* 4.

Koch, Peter (1985), *Konrad Adenauer*, Reinbek.

Kohl, Wilfried L. (1971), *French Nuclear Diplomacy*, Princeton, NJ.

Kohler, Beate (1972), *Der Vertrag über die Nichtverbreitung von Kernwaffen und das Problem der Sicherheitsgarantien*, Frankfurt am Main.

Koller, Roland (1984), '"Pax sovietica" oder nukleare Macht?', in *Europäische Wehrkunde* 1.

Kötter, Wolfgang (1990), 'German Non-Proliferation Policy', Charlottesville (working paper; AdV).

Kramer, H. (1976), *Nuklearpolitik in Westeuropa und die Forschungspolitik der Euratom*, Cologne.

Kramish, Arnold (1968), 'Der Vertrag über die Nichtverbreitung von Kernwaffen am Scheideweg', in *Europa-Archiv*, 24.

Kramish, Arnold (1970), *Die Zukunft der Nichtatomaren*, Opladen.

Kratzer, Myron B. (1971), 'Safeguards: Five Views', in *IAEA-Bulletin*, vol.13, no. 2.

Kratzer, Myron B. (1983), 'Historical Overview of International Safeguards', in Congressional Research Service, *Nuclear Safeguards*, Washington, DC.

Krone, Heinrich (1974), 'Aufzeichnungen zur Deutschland- und Ostpolitik 1954–1969', in R. Morsey and K. Repgen (eds), *Untersuchungen und Dokumente zur Ostpolitik und Biographie*, Mainz.

Kuan, Hsin-Chi (1973), *Der Vertrag über die Nichtverbreitung von Kernwaffen und die Bundesrepublik Deutschland*, Frankfurt am Main.

Küntzel, Matthias (1985), 'Atomwaffensperrvertrag und nukleare Optionen der Bundesrepublik', in *Blätter für deutsche und internationale Politik* 8.

Küntzel, Matthias (ed.) (1986), *Atombomben – Made in Germany?*, Cologne.

Küntzel, Matthias (1987), 'Auf leisen Sohlen zur Bombe? Bonner Begehrlichkeiten und der Atomwaffenverzicht', in Schelb (ed.), *Reaktoren und Raketen*, Cologne.

Küntzel, Matthias (1988), 'Die schwedische Atombombe', in *Mediatus* 11.

Küntzel, Matthias (1991), 'Die Bundesrepublik Deutschland zwischen Nuklearambition und Atomwaffenverzicht. Eine Untersuchung der Kontroverse um den Beitritt zum Atomwaffen-Sperrvertrag', dissertation, Hamburg.

Küntzel, Matthias (1992), *Bonn und die Bombe*, Frankfurt am Main.

Lambeth, Benjamin S. (1970), 'Nuclear Proliferation and Soviet Arms Control Policy', in *Orbis* 2.

Lauk, Kurt J. (1979), *Die nuklearen Optionen der Bundesrepublik Deutschland*, Berlin.

Leuthäuser, K. D. (1975), *Möglichkeiten und Grenzen der Implosion und Kompression von Kernspaltungsmaterial*, Stohl bei Kiel.

Lider, Julian (1986), *Origins and Development of West German Military Thought*, vol. I: 1949–1966, Aldershot.

Lovins, Amory, Lovins, Hunter et. al. (1980), 'Nuclear Power and Nuclear Bombs', in *Foreign Affairs*, summer.

McCloy, John J. (1962), 'Balance Sheet on Disarmanent', in *Foreign Affairs* no. 3, April.

McNamara, Robert (1962), 'Rede vor der Universität Michigan in Ann Arbor am 16.6.1962', in *Europa-Archiv* 14.

Mahncke, Dieter (1972), *Nukleare Mitwirkung*, Berlin.

Mandelbaum, Michael (1979), *The Nuclear Question: The U.S. and Nuclear Weapons 1946–1976*, London.

Mearsheimer, John J. (1990), 'Why We Will Soon Miss the Cold War', in *Atlantic Monthly*, August.

Murphy, Patrick W. (1974), 'The Response of the Federal Republic of Germany to the Challenge of the Nuclear Non-Proliferation Treaty', dissertation, Columbia University.

Neher, Kurt (1959), 'Besuch im deutsch-französischen Forschungsinstitut', in *Der deutsche Soldat* Jg.23, Heft 1.

Nerlich, Uwe (1965), 'Die nuklearen Dilemmas der Bundesrepublik Deutschland', in *EA* 17.

Nerlich, Uwe (1968), 'Aufzeichnung zur bevorstehenden Konferenz der Nichtnuklearwaffenstaaten in Genf vom 29.8.–29.9.1968', SWP-AZ 149, 24.July (ACD).

Nerlich, Uwe (1973), *Der NV-Vertrag in der Politik der BRD*, Ebenhausen.

Nerlich, Uwe and Rendtorff, Trutz (1989), 'Die Zukunft der nuklearen Abschreckung', in Nerlich and Rendtorff, *Nukleare Abschreckung*, Baden-Baden.

Nerlich, Uwe and Thiel, Elke (1967), 'Hinweise zur Beurteilung des Verhältnisses von Kernwaffenverzicht und allgemeiner technologischer Entwicklung ("Spin-off"-Effekt und "technologische Lücke")', SWP-AZ 108, 1.March n.z.p.U. (ACD).

Neustadt, Richard E. (1970), *Alliance Politics*, New York.

Newhouse, John (1970), *De Gaulle and the Anglo-Saxons*, London.

Nieburg, Harold L. (1964), *Nuclear Secrecy and Foreign Policy*, Washington, DC.

Osgood, Robert E. (1962), *NATO – The Entangling Alliance*, Chicago.

Osterheld, Horst (1986), *'Ich gehe nicht leichten Herzens ...'*, *Adenauers letzte Kanzlerjahre*, Mainz.

Otto, Karl A. (1977), *Vom Ostermarsch zur APO*, Frankfurt.

Peil, Eckehart (1965), *Die Sicherheitsüberwachung deutscher Kernenergieunternehmen*, Göttingen.

Pendley, Robert and Scheinman, Lawrence (1975), 'International Safeguarding as Institutionalized Collective Behavior', in *International Organization* 3.

Petri, Alexander (1970), 'Die Entstehung des NV-Vertrages – Die Rolle der Bundesrepublik Deutschland', dissertation, Tübingen.

Presse- und Informationsamt der Bundesregierung, 'Vertrag über die Gründung der Europäischen Verteidigungsgemeinschaft', Bonn.

Presse- und Informationsamt der Bundesregierung (1969), 'Vertrag über die Nichtverbreitung von Kernwaffen – Dokumentation zur deutschen Haltung und über den deutschen Beitrag', Bonn.

Pretsch, J. (1968), 'Das 3. deutsche Atomprogramm 1968–1972', in *atw* 1.

Pringle, Peter and Spigelman, James (1981), *The Nuclear Barons*, New York.

Quester, George H. (1967), 'Is the Nuclear Non-proliferation Treaty Enough?', in *Bulletin of the Atomic Scientists*, 11.

Quester, George H. (1973), *The Politics of Nuclear Proliferation*, Baltimore, Md.

Radkau, Joachim (1983), *Aufstieg und Krise der deutschen Atomwirtschaft 1945–1975*, Reinbek.

Randermann, Philipp-Heiner (1975), 'Probleme im Zusammenhang mit den Verhandlungen über das Verifikationsabkommen', in Institut für Völkerrecht der Universität Göttingen (ed.), *Drittes Deutsches Atomrechts- Symposium*, Cologne.

Richardson, James L. (1966), *Germany and the Atlantic Alliance*, Cambridge, Mass.

Ridder, Helmut (1986), 'Betreibt die Bundesrepublik eine militärische Atomenergiepolitik?', in M. Küntzel (ed.), *Atombomben – Made in Germany?*, Cologne.

Sanders, Benjamin (1975), *Safeguards against Nuclear Proliferation*, Stockholm.

Sanders, Benjamin and Rainer, R.H. (1977), *Safeguards Agreements – Their Legal and Conceptual Basis*, Salzburg (IAEA-Doc. CN-36/452).

Scheinman, Lawrence (1970), 'Euratom and the IAEA', in B. Boskey and M. Willrich (eds), *Nuclear Proliferation: Prospects for Control*, New York.

Scheinman, Lawrence (1987), *The International Atomic Energy Agency and World Nuclear Order*, Washington, DC.

Schelb, Udo (ed.) (1987), *Reaktoren und Raketen*, Cologne.

Schelling, Thomas C. (1966), 'Kontinuität und Neubeginn in der NATO', in *Europa-Archiv* 13.

Schleicher, Hans and Sharpe, Bernhard (1977b), 'The Euratom Programme', in American Nuclear Society, *Executive Conference on Safeguards*, Hyannis, Mass.

Schlesinger, Arthur M. (1965), *A Thousand Days*, London.

Schmidt, Helmut (1961), *Verteidigung oder Vergeltung*, Stuttgart.

Schoenbaum, David (1968), '"Ein Abgrund von Landesverrat" – Die Affäre um den Spiegel', Munich.

Schöfbänker, Georg (1991), *Proliferation Problems and Bomb Making Capacity - The Case of the Federal Republic of Germany*, Senatsinstitut für Politikwissenschaft der Universität Salzburg, Salzburg.

Schütze, Walter (ed.) (1983), 'Frankreichs Verteidigungspolitik 1958–1983', in *Militärpolitik Dokumentation*, Heft 32/33, Frankfurt am Main.

Schwartz, David N. (1983), *NATO's Nuclear Dilemmas*, Washington.

Schwarz, Hans-Peter (1985), *Adenauer und Frankreich*, Bonn.

Schwarz, Hans-Peter (1991), *Adenauer – Der Staatsmann: 1952–1967*, Stuttgart.

Seaborg, Glenn and Loeb, Benjamin (1987), *Stemming the Tide*, Lexington, Mass.

Shaker, Mohamed L. (1976), *The Treaty on the Non-Proliferation of Nuclear Weapons*, Genf.

Shub, Anatole (1967), 'Non-Proliferation for Non-Scientists', *Encounter* 5, p. 85.

Simonitsch, Pierre (1970), 'Die internationale Überwachung des Atomsperrvertrags: eine schwere Geburt', in *Gewerkschaftliche Monatshefte* 11.

Smith, Jean Edward (1963), *The Defense of Berlin*, Baltimore, Md.

Soell, Hartmut (1976), *Fritz Erler – Eine politische Biographie*, Berlin.

Sommer, Theo (1967), 'Deutsche Nuklearpolitik', in *Österreichische Zeitschrift für Aussenpolitik* 1.

Soutou, Georges-Henri (1989), 'Die Nuklearpolitik der Vierten Republik', in *Vierteljahreshefte für Zeitgeschichte* 4.

Sozialdemokratische Partei – Vorstand (ed.) (1957), *Hintergründe der Atomdebatte im Bundestag*, Bonn.

Spector, Leonard (1984), *Nuclear Proliferation Today*, Washington, DC.

Stanley, Timothy W. (1965), *Nato in Transition: The Future of the Atlantic Alliance*, New York.

Steinbruner, John D. (1974), *The Cybernetic Theory of Decision*, Princeton, NJ.

Stikker, Dirk U. (1965), *Men of Responsibility*, London.

Stockholm International Peace Research Institute (1972), *The Near-Nuclear Countries and the NPT*, Stockholm.

Stoltenberg, Gerhard (1967), 'Kernforschung und Atomenergie', in *Wehr und Wirtschaft* 4.

Strauss, Franz Josef (1965), 'An Alliance of Continents', in *International Affairs* 4.

Strauss, Franz Josef (1989), *Die Erinnerungen*, Berlin.

Stützle, Walther (1973), *Kennedy und Adenauer in der Berlin-Krise 1961–1962*, Bad Godesberg.

Takagi, Jinzaburo (1993), *Civil Plutonium Surplus and Proliferation*, Tokyo.

Thomas, John R. (1962), 'Soviet Behavior in the Quemoy Crisis of 1958', in *Orbis* 1.

Treitschke, Wolfgang (1975), 'Vom NV-Vertrag für EURATOM aufgeworfene wesentliche Probleme und deren Lösung im Verifikationsabkommen', in Institut für Völkerrecht der Universität Göttingen (ed.), *Drittes Atomrechts-Symposium*, Cologne.

Ullman, Richard H. (1989), 'The Covert French Connection', in *Foreign Policy* 75, summer.

Ungerer, Werner (1973), 'Das Verifikationsabkommen Euratom/IAEA', in *Aussenpolitik* 2.

Ungerer, Werner (1975), 'Die Rolle internationaler Organisationen bei der Behinderung missbräuchlicher Verwendung der Kernenergie', in Kaiser and Lindemann (eds), *Kernenergie und internationale Politik*, Munich.

United States Senate (1968), 'Hearings before the Committee on Foreign Relations', 91. Congress, 2. 'Session on the Treaty on the Non-proliferation of Nuclear Weapons, July 10, 11., 12 and 17, 1968, Washington, DC.

United States Senate (1969), 'Hearings before the Committee on Foreign Relations', 91. Congress, 2. 'Session on the Treaty on the Non-proliferation of Nuclear Weapons', February 27 and 28, 1969', Washington, DC.

United States Senate (1969), 'Hearings before the Committee on Armed Services', 91. Congress, 1. 'Session on Military Implications of the Treaty on the Non-Proliferation of Nuclear Weapons', February 27 and 28, 1969, Washington. DC.

Van Cleave, William R. (1968), 'The Non-proliferation Treaty And Fission-Free Explosive Research', in *Orbis* 4.

Van der Mey, L.M. (1989), 'Non-Proliferation of Nuclear Weapons', in Philip Everts and Guido Walraven (eds), *The Politics of Persuasion: Implementation of Foreign Policy by the Netherlands*, Aldershot.

Weilemann, Peter (1983), *Die Anfänge der Europäischen Atomgemeinschaft*, Baden-Baden.

Williams, Shelton L. (1971), *Nuclear Non-proliferation in International Politics: The Japanese Case*, Denver, Colo.

Willrich, Mason (1968), 'The Treaty on Non-Proliferation of Nuclear Weapons: Nuclear Technology Confronts World Politics', in *Yale Law Journal* 8.

Winnacker, Karl and Wirtz, Karl: (1975), *Das unverstandene Wunder*, Düsseldorf.

Wohlstetter, Albert (1961), 'Über die Teilnahme an der nuklearen Rüstung', in *EA* 11 and *EA* 12.

Zieger, Gottfried (1975), 'Die rechtliche Problematik des NV-Vertrages und des Verifikationsabkommens der Europäischen Atomgemeinschaft mit der IAEO, in Institut für Völkerrecht der Universität Göttingen (ed.), *Drittes Deutsches Atomrechts-Symposium*, Cologne.

Index